Markets and Moral Regulation
Cultural Change in the European Union

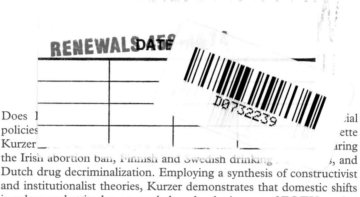

Does ̤ ̤ ̤ ̤ ̤ .ial
policies ̤ ̤ ̤ ̤ ̤ ette
Kurzer ̤ ̤ ̤ ̤ ̤ ring
the Irish abortion ban, Finnish and Swedish drinking ̤, and
Dutch drug decriminalization. Employing a synthesis of constructivist
and institutionalist theories, Kurzer demonstrates that domestic shifts
in values and attitudes, spurred along by the impact of EC/EU market
integration, are in fact bringing about a convergence in European
morality norms. Alcohol control policies are being liberalized, the Irish
abortion proscription is being redefined, and Dutch drug toleration is
pushed into a more punitive direction. *Markets and Moral Regulation*
argues that a crucial agency is European law and its role as a market
regulator: as market forces invade these cultural and moral spheres,
protective barriers disintegrate. The result is that cultural and social
domains are increasingly exposed to the influence of market
competition.

PAULETTE KURZER is Associate Professor of Political Science at the
University of Arizona. Her recent publications include *Business and
Banking: Political Change and European Integration in Western Europe*
(1993).

Themes in European Governance

The evolving European systems of governance, in particular the European Union, challenge and transform the state, the most important locus of governance and political identity and loyalty over the last 200 years. The series *Themes in European Governance* aims to publish the best theoretical and analytical scholarship on the impact of European governance on the core institutions, policies and identities of nation-states. It focuses upon the implications on issues such as citizenship, welfare, political decision-making, and economic, monetary and fiscal policies. An initiative of Cambridge University Press and the Programme on Advanced Research on the Europeanisation of the Nation-State (ARENA), Norway, the series includes contributions in the social sciences, humanities and law. The series aims to provide theoretically-oriented, empirically-informed studies analysing key issues both at the European level and within European states. Volumes in the series will be of interest to scholars and students of Europe within Europe and worldwide. It will be of particular relevance to those interested in the development of sovereignty and governance of European states and in the issues raised by multi-level governance and multi-national integration throughout the world.

Markets and Moral Regulation

Cultural Change in the European Union

Paulette Kurzer

CAMBRIDGE
UNIVERSITY PRESS

PUBLISHED BY THE PRESS SYNDICATE OF THE UNIVERSITY OF CAMBRIDGE
The Pitt Building, Trumpington Street, Cambridge, United Kingdom

CAMBRIDGE UNIVERSITY PRESS
The Edinburgh Building, Cambridge CB2 2RU, UK
40 West 20th Street, New York NY 10011–4211, USA
10 Stamford Road, Oakleigh, VIC 3166, Australia
Ruiz de Alarcón 13, 28014 Madrid, Spain
Dock House, The Waterfront, Cape Town 8001, South Africa

http://www.cambridge.org

First published 2001

Printed in the United Kingdom at the University Press, Cambridge

Typeface Plantin 10/12 pt   *System* 3b2   [CE]

A catalogue record for this book is available from the British Library

Library of Congress Cataloguing in Publication data
Kurzer, Paulette, 1957–
Markets and moral regulation: cultural change in the
European Union / Paulette Kurzer.
    p.   cm. – (Themes in European governance)
Includes bibliographical references and index.
ISBN 0 521 80289 X – ISBN 0 521 00395 4 (pb.)
1. Markets – European Union countries – Moral and ethical aspects.
2. European Union countries – Social policy.
3. Europe – Economic integration.
I. Title.   II. Series.
HF5474.A2   K87   2001
306.48′2–dc21   00–052928

ISBN 0 521 80289 X hardback
ISBN 0 521 00395 4 paperback

Contents

Tables

Preface

This book is about the impact of market integration and supranational institution-building on Europe's cultural diversity. Europe is known for its rich mélange of cultures and this diversity, many observers agree, impedes the task of building a genuine political union. I ask in this study whether cultural diversity is diminishing and, if so, how this process unfolds, and what the actual consequences will be for Europe. My findings indicate that member governments are experiencing a loss of national sovereignty in the cultural sphere and that external pressures result in an ever so slight convergence of different styles of thought and actions. But I also show that the actual pace of adaptation is extremely gradual and that the immediate effect on the European Union is modest. My case studies are alcohol control policy in Finland and Sweden, drug policy in the Netherlands, and abortion in Ireland. I selected these issue areas because each sheds light on the conviction and collective rules of the national polity and thus opens a window on to Dutch, Irish, Finnish, and Swedish culture. At their most basic, drug and alcohol policies are public measures to regulate the circulation of mind-altering substances in society. But the way in which governments define the challenge and the kinds of measures they pursue communicates how a national community assesses the risks of intoxication for the individual and society. In turn, that assessment is colored by specific legal, historical, social, and institutional factors and is embedded in a public discourse and narrative. Likewise, the Irish constitutional ban on abortion encapsulates the centrality of Catholic teaching in Irish politics, culture, and institutional structures.

In the 1990s, the national leadership in each country faced serious obstacles in trying to preserve current arrangements. Dutch drug policy has been pushed into a more punitive direction, Nordic alcohol control policy has liberalized, and Irish views on abortion have been softening. The timing and direction of change leave little doubt that regional integration carries some responsibility for the loss of autonomy to pursue a different kind of approach to drugs, alcohol, or abortion. None the less, the idea that regional integration accounts for cultural homogenization is counter-intuitive because the European Union is extremely respectful of the cultural idiosyncrasies of its member states.

Collective rules and mass opinion are subject to Europeanization, but not because the European Union expects conformity and pursues a program of cultural homogenization. Rather, I contend that market integration diminishes cultural disparity. The four freedoms of the single market, which obviously constrain macro-economic autonomy, also limit the ability of central government to adhere to a set of moral choices and policy programs at odds with the rest of the European Union. Again, the reason for this is not because the European Union itself insists on broader conformity. Instead, the greatest constraint is the movement of people. The removal of borders produces negative externalities that make it costly to continue to insist on tackling universal predicaments such as substance abuse in a unique fashion. Consider how hard it is to take a tolerant approach to drug use when surrounding countries are still wedded to the idea of suppressing all drug use. Or, to take another example, how do Nordic authorities curb access to alcohol when Swedes and Finns can take a short ferry ride and stock up on cheap liquor? This book examines the dilemmas of wanting to be different in a globalizing or Europeanizing world.

The introductory chapter lays out the basic structure of the argument, followed by empirical analysis of the formation, operation, and adjustment to post-Maastricht Europe of national arrangements to govern socially sensitive activities. Reading the chapters may give the impression that I consider alcohol control policies, drug decriminalization, and abortion ban objectionable. The analysis in each chapter takes a critical tone in part to explore the underlying tensions and contradictions in the formulation and implementation of the policies or constitutional arrangements. Personally, however, I am of the opinion that in a multicultural world with multiple moralities and multiple lifestyles no size fits all. In fact, we can learn from the Nordic governance of drinking because it helps raise awareness of the potential risks of alcohol consumption. The Dutch harm reduction approach to drug usage is not the promised land, but it seems infinitely superior to the zero-tolerance policies pursued by the US federal government. And I have no opinion on the constitutional ban on abortion in Ireland. I do not feel it is appropriate to question the decisions of the Irish legislature.

This book turned out to be a far more massive project than I had anticipated. It would not have been possible to complete it without the generous material and moral support provided by people and institutions too numerous to list. I would nevertheless like publicly to thank at least some friends, colleagues, and organizations for their time, goodwill, and expertise.

The library and documentation centers at the National Research and Development Center for Welfare and Health in Helsinki (STAKES), the National Institute for Consumer Research in Oslo (SIFA), the Swedish Council for Information on Alcohol and other Drugs in Stockholm (CAN), and the Center for Drug Research at the University of Amsterdam (CEDRO) were indispensable and provided me with a congenial setting to gather the required materials for this project.

In addition, I am appreciative of the feedback and assistance of Caroline Sutton and Trygve Ugland in Norway. In Finland, while a guest at STAKES, I had the good fortune to meet Esa Österberg, Jussi Simpura, and Christoffer Tigerstedt. Thomas Rosenberg, editor of *Nordisk alkohol- & narkotikatidskrift*, faithfully sent me the latest issues of this journal without complaint. Officials at the Dutch Ministry of Public Health, Wellbeing, and Sport provided substantial background information. Many officials and academics, moreover, made time available to discuss the smaller details and larger picture of this research project. I am grateful for having had the opportunity to speak to them.

An early version of this argument was presented at the workshop on "Globalization, Europeanization, and Political Economy in Europe" organized by Steven Weber at the University of California, Berkeley. I thank all the participants at the workshop for their comments, especially Vanna Gonzales.

The interviews and research would not have been possible without the generous support of the American-Scandinavian Foundation and the Social and Behavioral Sciences Research Institute at the University of Arizona.

People who read drafts of chapters, sharing their knowledge and offering much support and editorial advice, are Jeffrey Anderson, David Andrews, Alice Cooper, Peter Katzenstein, Ron Roizen, and Nicholas Ziegler. I owe a special thanks to Vivien Schmidt for her friendship and her tremendous faith in the end result of this project, to Steven Weber for having read several chapters more than once, and to Christine Ingebritsen for sharing her enthusiasm of everything Nordic.

Academic work is not easily separable from one's life. I am extremely fortunate to have a loving and supportive family. David Spiro, my husband, took care of the family during my trips abroad, and continues to be my closest partner. Finally, without the constant love and attention of Ezra and Katya, the book would have been completed a great deal sooner.

PAULETTE KURZER
Tucson, AZ

1 Markets versus morality

Charles Mackay (1814–89), a Scottish poet, journalist, song-writer, and author of *Memoirs of Extraordinary Popular Delusions*, once wrote that nations, like individuals, have their whims and their peculiarities, their seasons of excitement and recklessness. If nations have indeed such things as national personalities and habits, then the past ten years offer an intriguing glimpse of how they have adapted to post-Maastricht Europe. This book examines the fate of national cultures, defined here in anthropological terms as everyday socialization, beliefs, norms, institutions, and common behavior in light of the challenges brought by European institution- and market-building. To be sure, numerous studies explore the challenges faced by national governments as they attempt to preserve or redefine national identities or cultures.[1] My contribution to this debate is twofold. First, I describe the formation of national identity and institutions emblematic of the national traits of a country. I concentrate on the national governance of socially sensitive policies and will argue that variations in morality norms shed light on some of the most important aspects of state and national identity. My examples are Dutch drug policy, more liberal than the rest of Europe, Nordic alcohol control policy, more restrictive than the rest of Europe,

---

[1] For very different examples of writings which predict an end to national cultures: Mike Featherstone, *Undoing Culture: Globalization, Postmodernism, and Identity* (Thousand Oaks, CA: Sage, 1995); Ernest Gellner, *Culture, Identity, and Politics* (New York: Cambridge University Press, 1987); Anthony Giddens, *The Consequences of Modernity* (New York: Cambridge University Press, 1990); Eric Hobsbawn, *Nations and Nationalism since 1780* (New York: Cambridge University Press, 1990). A more ambiguous assessment is found in Susan Berger and Ronald Dore (eds.), *National Diversity and Global Capitalism* (Ithaca: Cornell University Press, 1996). Other examples of the literature on national cultures and European integration are: Sharon Macdonald (ed.), *Inside European Identities: Ethnography in Western Europe* (Providence, RI: Berg, 1993); Bernd Baumgartl and Adrian Favell (eds.), *New Xenophobia in Europe* (Boston: Kluwer Law International, 1995). Some scholars simply believe that attacks on national identity lead to strengthening of expression of existing identities without turning hostile to outsiders and Europe. Ole Wæver, Barry Buzan, Morten Kelstrup, and Pierre Lemaitre, *Identity, Migrant and the New Security Agenda in Europe* (London: Pinter, 1993).

and Irish policy towards sexual morality, more conservative than the rest of Europe.[2]

Second, I will discuss how constitutive rules, specifying proper behavior, cope with pressures emanating from the expansion of European governance, policies, and institutions. This book's overall conclusion is that national peculiarities are shrinking and that a modest rate of cultural convergence has occurred. Dutch drug policy is becoming more punitive, Nordic anti-drinking measures are liberalizing, and Irish attitudes towards abortion are softening. The timing and direction of these trends are highly suggestive of explanatory factors related to the widening scope of EU activities.

In my discussion of divergent morality norms, I seek to expand on the key assumptions advanced by the growing body of constructivist research[3] and sociological institutionalism.[4] Constructivist international relations scholars claim that the community of states or world culture shapes state identity and preferences. They contend that states often do not have a clear sense of where they stand on an issue, and like individuals, slowly develop perceptions of interests and understandings

---

[2] I use the term "drugs" throughout the book even though the reference is to a particular class of pharmaceuticals. Narcotics is a mislabel because cocaine and amphetamines are stimulants and have the opposite effect to that of sleep-inducing drugs. Even heroin and cannabis are not true narcotics because they do not aid sleep. Any reference to "Nordic" includes Norway, Sweden, Finland, and Iceland but excludes Denmark. Denmark is, however, a Nordic country but it does not share the same anti-alcohol tradition as the other four countries. Also note that "Irish" or "Ireland" always refers to the Republic of Ireland.

[3] Jeffrey T. Checkel, "The Constructivist Turn in International Relations Theory," *World Politics*, 50 (1998), 324–48; Martha Finnemore, *National Interests in International Society* (Ithaca: Cornell University Press, 1996); Ann Florini, "The Evolution of International Norms," *International Studies Quarterly*, 40 (1996), 363–90; Peter Katzenstein (ed.), *The Culture of National Security: Norms and Identity in World Politics* (New York: Columbia University Press, 1996); John Gerard Ruggie, "What Makes the World Hang Together? Neo-Utilitarianism and Social Constructivist Challenge," *International Organization*, 52 (1998), 855–85.

[4] John Boli and George M. Thomas (eds.), *Constructing World Culture: International Nongovernmental Organizations since 1875* (Stanford: Stanford University Press, 1999); Neil Fligstein, *The Transformation of Corporate Control* (Cambridge, MA: Harvard University Press, 1990); Martha Finnemore, "Norms, Culture and World Politics: Insights from Sociology's Institutionalism," *International Organization*, 50 (1996), 325–48; John W. Meyer, "The World Polity and the Authority of the Nation-State," in George M. Thomas, John W. Meyer, Francisco O. Ramirez, and John Boli (eds.), *Institutional Structure: Constituting State, Society, and the Individual* (Beverly Hills: Sage, 1987), 41–70; Walter W. Powell and Paul J. DiMaggio (eds.), *The New Institutionalism in Organizational Analysis* (Chicago: University of Chicago Press, 1991); W. Richard Scott and John W. Meyer (eds.), *Institutional Environments and Organizations: Structural Complexity and Individualism* (Thousand Oaks, CA: Sage, 1994); Yasemin Nohuglu Soysal, *The Limits of Citizenship: Migrants and Postnational Membership in Europe* (Chicago: University of Chicago Press, 1994).

of situations through ongoing interaction with other states or transnational organizations and institutions. States assimilate templates of international meanings, adhere to certain norms, and hold common expectations about appropriate behavior.[5] These norms are subsequently internalized and are taken for granted. Although the practitioners of constructivism present slightly different versions of this argument, all of them claim that social structures, which contain shared knowledge, material resources, and practices, construct identity and are produced and reproduced by agents/actors, who in turn are embedded in the social structures.[6]

In selecting these case studies, I draw attention to situations where countries adhere to a style of action at odds with wider structures found in the EU. International or European norms, accordingly, may or may not foster, depending on the circumstances, common patterns of behavior among dissimilar states. Although many European liberal principles have become internationalized with the expansion of the West, the countries and issues in question deviate from European or international practices and structures.[7] National officials remain faithful to old models of thinking because the new categories of cognition and action repudiate state and national identity. That is to say that international norms shape human and state behavior in some, but certainly not all, areas of political life and that some states refuse to adapt to new evolving institutional practices with the result that new European concepts fail to penetrate national consciousness, institutions, and repertoires of action.

The plan of this book is threefold: first, to chronicle how national practices have withstood the ascendance of European or Western

---

[5] For different applications, see Deborah Barrett and David John Frank, "Population Control for National Development: From World Discourse to National Policies," in Boli and Thomas (eds.), *Constructing World Culture*, 198–221; Audie Klotz, *Norms in International Relations: The Struggle against Apartheid* (Ithaca: Cornell University Press, 1995); Thomas A. Loya and John Boli, "Standardization in the World Polity: Technical Rationality over Power," in Boli and Thomas (eds.), *Constructing World Culture*, 169–97; Nina Tannenwald, "The Taboo on Nuclear Weapons," *International Organization*, 53 (1999), 433–69.

[6] Emanuel Adler, "Seizing the Middle Ground. Constructivism in World Politics," *European Journal of International Relations*, 3 (1997), 319–63; Alexander Wendt, "Anarchy is What States Make of It: The Social Construction of Power Politics," *International Organization*, 46 (1992), 391–425; Alexander Wendt, "Collective Identity Formation and the International State," *American Political Science Review*, 88 (1994), 384–96.

[7] Hedley Bull, *The Anarchical Society: A Study of Order in World Politics* (New York: Columbia University Press, 1977); Barry Buzan, "From International System to International Society: Structural Realism and Regime Theory meet the English School," *International Organization*, 47 (1993), 327–52; Gerrit Gong, *The Standard of "Civilisation" in International Society* (Oxford: Clarendon Press, 1984).

models of thinking and action, second to specify how adaptational pressures actually produce change and which agents push for change, and third to understand the future of European integration. I define Europeanization as institutional adjustment to wider European rules, structures, and styles and as the diffusion of informal understandings and meanings of EU norms. The aim is to explore the long-term effect of European agreements on national identities, values, institutions, and policies and to specify the causal mechanisms responsible for the dissemination of European-oriented values after a considerable time lag.

Cultural norms and national identity

Norms point decision-makers in the direction of solutions that are considered effective and sensible by the relevant audience. They are templates that sort out how to assess a new situation and what kind of action to take. State leaders rely on norms to diagnose a situation and design an action plan in congruence with national expectations. Normative standards are frequently institutionalized and routinized. Once they are embedded in institutions and procedures, their meaning is no longer questioned and is taken for granted. Decision-makers rely on "tool-kits" to solve problems and organize activities. The symbols, stories, rituals, and worldview in turn legitimize the selection of a particular policy course because the population holds expectations that governments take this sort of action.[8] Obviously, international norms are likely to remold domestic prescriptions of behavior if a prior cultural or institutional compatibility already exists. Policy officials do not gravitate towards a "tool-kit" that clashes with national patterns of recognized repertoires of action. Occasionally, cultural markers are ambiguous and open to different interpretations, which then creates room for the introduction and absorption of international norms. Once they are incorporated into domestic institutions and structures, they fashion behavior along a certain model.

Once in a while, a state will be strongly attached to its way of doing things and will decisively reject "mainstream" (i.e. European) approaches and conventions. This book gives three examples of normative models that prescribe standards of behavior that are relatively unusual and singular to a country. For example, the Netherlands does

---

[8] Ann Swidler, "Culture in Action: Symbols and Strategies," *American Sociological Review*, 51 (1986), 273–86. See also James G. March and Johan P. Olsen, *Rediscovering Institutions: The Organizational Basis of Politics* (New York: The Free Press, 1989).

not buy into the global prohibitionist regime on drugs.[9] It has taken the view that drug-taking is mainly a public health challenge. Since 1976, the Dutch parliament has supported drug decriminalization and harm reduction. Sweden and Finland repudiate the post-1945 liberal approach to alcohol consumption. Parliaments in the Nordic countries restrict the sale of alcohol to state-owned stores and levy high alcohol taxes. In 1983, the Republic of Ireland ratified an amendment to the constitution with the aim of creating an abortion-free zone.

The particular actions to regulate drugs, drinking, and sexuality reflect a very specific understanding of the relations between state and society, of the responsibility of the state to shield society from human passions and risky behavior, and of the self or personhood. Nordic societies mistrust the enduring appeal of mind-altering substances and suspect individuals of lacking the necessary self-discipline to desist from abuse and dependency. In turn, substance abuse constitutes a direct threat to economic prosperity and the social wellbeing of society. According to this view, the personal inconveniences of drinking restrictions pale compared with the constraints on individual freedom on account of chemical dependency.

The Irish believe that individual autonomy and definition of the good life are best served by strict adherence to the Catholic ethos. Catholic doctrine guides state policies in areas of life of special importance to the Church, namely the family, education, and health. This form of policy intervention is taken for granted because the Irish voter perceives no contradiction between one's personal needs and the leading tenets of the Church.[10] By contrast, in the Netherlands, the state shuns highly moralistic agendas and encourages individuals to discipline themselves. After recreational drug use reached epidemic proportions, the authorities decided on a nonabsolutist solution and gave permission for the sale of cannabis in specially licensed coffee shops.

Most likely, countries, like individuals, always hold certain issues or projects close to their heart. There must be numerous incidents of a mismatch between domestic and international norms. Nevertheless, these morality policies merit special attention because they go beyond formal prescriptions on how to tackle substance misuse or how to cope with the decline of tradition and religious authority. As the following

---

[9] Ed Leuw and I. Haen Marshall (eds.), *Between Prohibition and Legalization: The Dutch Experiment in Drug Policy* (New York: Kugler Publications, 1994); Marcel De Kort and Ton Cramer, "Pragmatism versus Ideology: Dutch Drug Policy Continued," *Journal of Drug Issues*, 29 (1999), 473–93.

[10] Tom Inglis, *Moral Monopoly: The Rise and Fall of the Catholic Church in Modern Ireland* (Dublin: University College Dublin Press, 1998); Joe Lee, *Ireland 1912–1985: Politics and Society* (New York: Cambridge University Press, 1985).

chapters will show, the morality standards describe what it means to be Finnish, Swedish, Dutch, and Irish respectively. They are cultural markers, which dictate how to talk about the issues, what to expect from others, and what others expect from you. Because state and collective identities grew out of particular historical experiences and are unique to a country or a group of countries they cement the bonds that unite a people and also sustain external identity.[11] State and national identity is thus partly formed in opposition to shared international norms and differentiates a country (or geographic cluster of countries) from its (their) neighbors.[12]

For example, bookshelves are filled with autobiographical accounts of what it means to grow up Irish and thus Catholic.[13] The unique devotion to Catholicism of the population of the Irish Republic is a source of both internal identification and external differentiation. Not all European Catholic nations link their national identity to strict adherence to the Catholic ethos. An Italian, although nominally Catholic, has other ways of describing his or her national identity. The history of the emancipation of the Irish people bequeathed a legacy that fused Catholicism and modern Irish identity. The Catholic ethos governs state policy and prescribes how the state and society must behave. This pattern of state action gives Ireland its distinctive character and sharply contrasts with that of, say, Britain. Along similar lines, restrictive drinking rules grew out of the early and successful efforts by popular movements to impose external forms of discipline on societies undergoing the wrenching experiences of urbanization and industrialization. The strong aversion to mind-altering substances characterizes an aspect of "Nordicness" quite distinct from the personalities of other European peoples. The Nordic uneasiness with regard to mind-altering substances is attributed to "communication anxiety" (being shy) and to the reliance on liquor to overcome social inhibitions. Long, dark winters, according to Nordic conventional wisdom, deprived Finnish and Swedish people of regular contact with strangers and stunted the growth of strong interpersonal skills.[14] When together, to ease sociability, Finns and Swedes drink heavily with terrible consequences for the

---

[11] Brian C.J. Singer, "Cultural vs. Contractual Nations: Rethinking their Opposition," *History and Theory*, 35 (1996), 309–37.

[12] Even in the international security field, states pursue preferences and objectives divorced from international structures and beliefs. Elizabeth Kier, "Culture and French Military Doctrine Before World War I," in Katzenstein (ed.), *The Culture of National Security*, 186–215.

[13] For example, Frank McCourt, *Angela's Ashes. A Memoir* (New York: Scribner, 1996); Nuala O'Faolain, *Are you Somebody? The Life and Times of Nuala O'Faolain* (Dublin: New Island Books, 1997).

[14] A classic joke about the painfully taciturn Finn is as follows. Two Finns sit at a bar.

physical and social health of the individual and society. Binge drinking (heavy drinking at one sitting), however, became a legitimate target for state intervention following the ascendance of the social democratic movement, which equated boozing with disorder and unpredictability and deployed the institutions of the welfare state to curb alcohol consumption.[15]

Dutch drug policy is also a testimony to an aspect of Dutchness. Dutch subscribe to the idea that moral decisions are private affairs and, accordingly, that private activities should not be prohibited, banned, curbed, or restrained by outside agencies. The public health focus of Dutch drug policy emerged from a tradition that permitted society to find its moral center. If Sweden and Finland prefer to raise certain collective moral principles and to hold out certain life projects as more desirable than others, the Netherlands allows its citizens to pursue life projects even if they prove to be very harmful and destructive. The state is not actively involved in structuring the lives of its citizens along a particular dimension and does not assert a hierarchy of values.[16] Citizens can form their own opinions and evaluate what is manageable or not.

In short, different countries construct different moral environments, which provide clues on how to regard and solve questionable private activities. Most norms do not last for more than a generation because each new cohort group confronts different experiences and selects different guideposts on how to organize life. Frequently, norms are contested and only gain dominance if the majority endorses the value framework. The norms described in this study continued to be recognized by the majority as valid, appropriate, and germane in spite of tremendous structural changes in the workplace, the family, career paths, and international fashions. One of the reasons for their longevity is that state and social institutions maintained and reproduced the moral environment, thereby vouching for their robustness and flexibility.[17] State policy, formulated and administered by institutions, immersed new generations of citizens in appropriate standards of behavior and

---

After hours of silence one raises a glass and says "Cheers." His friend snaps back, "We didn't come here to talk."

[15] Åke Daun, *Swedish Mentality* (University Park, PA: Pennsylvania State University Press, 1996); Jean Phillips-Martinsson. *Swedes, As Others See Them* (Stockholm: Affärsförlaget, 1981); Harry G. Levine, "Alcohol Problems in Nordic and English-speaking Cultures," in Malcolm Lader, Griffith Edwards, and D. Colin Drummond (eds.), *The Nature of Alcohol and Drug Related Problems* (New York: Oxford University Press, 1992).

[16] Bo Rothstein, *Just Institutions Matter: The Moral and Political Logic of the Universal Welfare State* (New York: Cambridge University Press, 1998).

[17] Ron Jepperson, Alex Wendt, and Peter Katzenstein, "Norms, Identity, and Culture in National Security," in Katzenstein (ed.), *The Culture of National Security*, 63–64.

devised ways to ward off demands for adjustments or change. But the cultural norms also endured because they spoke of a truth, accepted by the majority as beyond questioning. Institutions, to be effective and retain legitimacy, must formulate objectives and execute policies in congruence with fundamental beliefs of society.[18] The deep attachment of the Irish to Catholicism is both the outcome of the critical role played by the clergy during the prolonged struggle against British colonialism and the reason why the ecclesiastical hierarchy and lay Catholic movements continue to represent collective opinion and demarcate available policy options.[19]

A similar analysis explains the interaction between cultural values and reproduction of temperance ideals in Sweden and Finland. Nordic social welfare officials and public health agencies continuously raised awareness of the dangers of substance abuse and oversaw the operation of the state alcohol company, which controlled all aspects of the production, trade, retail, and distribution of alcoholic drinks.[20] Public campaigns, research reports, and parliamentary legislation kept attention focused on the country's drinking problem, a dilemma recognized by many voters as severe and urgent. Because mass opinion recognized the dangers of alcohol for society, social welfare agencies and alcohol policy officials succeeded in constituting and reconstituting the drinking problem, eventually substituting a highly moralistic discourse for scientific models on aggregate alcohol consumption and its impact on alcohol-related accidents, injuries, disease, mortality, and social dislocation.

Dutch social service agencies and public health officials articulated a vision of society in which the state was not charged with the task of enforcing a particular mode of behavior. Drugs in general were condemned but drug users were considered regular members of society who need and deserve assistance and care. Even Dutch law enforcement espoused a philosophy that precluded intrusive monitoring of private acts of more or less law-abiding individuals. The policy measures and

---

[18] The empirical chapters examine at length the creation of morality norms. I do not assume collective norms and identity and examine both their origins and the generative process of consolidation and adaptation.

[19] Tom Inglis, *Lessons in Irish Sexuality* (Dublin: University College Dublin Press, 1998); Paul Keating and Derry Desmond, *Culture and Capitalism in Contemporary Ireland* (Brookfield, VT: Ashgate, 1993); Sheelagh Drudy and Kathleen Lynch, *Schools and Society in Ireland* (Dublin: Gill & Macmillan, 1993).

[20] Jan Blomqvist, "The 'Swedish Model' of Dealing with Alcohol Problems: Historical Trends and Future Challenges," *Contemporary Drug Problems*, 25 (1998), 253–321; Harold D. Holder, Eckart Kühlhorn, Sturla Nordlund, Esa Österberg, Anders Romelsjö, and Trygve Ugland, *European Integration and Nordic Alcohol Policies: Changes in Alcohol Controls and Consequences in Finland, Norway, and Sweden* (Brookfield, VT: Ashgate, 1998).

narrative were accepted by the majority since they agreed with the central premises of this approach.

In each country, state policy and institutions provided detailed and broad scriptures of symbols, narratives, and discourse to construct cognitive categories through which politicians, officials, and individuals framed problems and solutions.[21] Because institutions forge common standards of behavior, dictate a certain course of action, and create criteria for judging what is appropriate, the likelihood of adopting new European standards is low unless a "goodness of fit" exists.[22] When basic compatibility exists, European meanings of particular activities raise few controversies. If European norms and practices run completely counter to national rules and practices, then European conventions confront many hurdles. By far the biggest obstacles are the very same institutions whose existence hinges on the survival of the moral environment. If Sweden and Finland liberalize and deregulate the liquor market and adopt a non-Nordic model of informal control mechanisms, the state monopoly company and social welfare agencies active in the alcohol field forfeit their claims on state funding to run programs, employ specialists, and gather specialized knowledge. Aside from institutions, however, the electorate also rallies against external pressures because European formulations of socially sensitive issues contradict basic ideas on how to tackle problems such as alcohol or drug dependency. Prohibitionist drug policies are not compatible with the moral permissiveness of the Dutch, Continental drinking models are irreconcilable with the Nordic desire for order and security, while post-Christian materialism and individualism negate the definition of a good Irish man or woman.

Many different arguments can be brought to bear to make the same point: this area of political and social life, in contrast to capital markets, telecommunication, monetary policy, state aid, or environment, is shielded from pressures to adjust to European structures and rules. To discover that cultural institutions, so intimately tied to the identity of the nation-state, are subject to Europeanization is extraordinary. It suggests that member states are in fact being recast along a European model

---

[21] Paul DiMaggio, "Culture and Economy," in Neil J. Smelser and Richard Swedberg (eds.), *The Handbook of Economic Sociology* (Princeton: Princeton University Press, 1994), 27–58; Mary Douglas, *How Institutions Think* (Syracuse: Syracuse University Press, 1986); March and Olsen, *Rediscovering Institutions* 22–26; Thomas R. Rochon, *Culture Moves: Ideas, Activism, and Changing Values* (Princeton: Princeton University Press, 1998), 5.

[22] Maria Green Cowles, Thomas Risse, and James Caporaso, "Europeanization and Domestic Change," in their *Transforming Europe: Europeanization and Domestic Change* (Ithaca: Cornell University Press, 2001), 1–20; David Strang and John W. Meyer, "Institutional Conditions for Diffusion," in Scott and Meyer (eds.), *Institutional Environments and Organization*, 100–13.

against their preferences and conscious desires! Much of the literature on European integration has focused on the loss of economic, fiscal, and monetary autonomy and the codification of EU rules in structuring product and capital markets, environmental regulations, employment rights, regional aid, and transportation. Relatively little attention has been paid to the possibility that cultural expressions of national sovereignty are subject to similar kinds of pressures.[23]

The European Union and morality norms

To find that morality norms, which define collective identity, are moving towards a European-wide formulation is surprising, to say the least. To be sure, EU institutions and Community law exert no direct, focused pressure on member states to shed national approaches to the regulation of socially sensitive activities. There are no transparent European measures on how member states ought to deal with substance abuse and sexual permissiveness. EU legislation does not call for new policies at the national level to regulate drug and alcohol use or abortion. The reason for this lack of direction from above is self-evident. Universal (European) norms barely exist and scarcely frame a shared understanding among like-minded states. It is of great concern to students of European integration that Europe contains a vast array of cultural legacies and normative standards. The attempt to formulate European-wide norms or advance greater harmonization repeatedly founders on the shoals of unrelenting emotional opposition which obstructs the drafting of a common policy at the supranational level. For the proponents of the European ideal, the retention of cultural diversity in post-Maastricht Europe hampers the quest for further political integration and the fulfillment of the goal of "ever closer union." The argument is therefore rather circular. Cultural differences between nations in Europe persist because of the lack of a strong central authority able to unify and homogenize the people of Europe while the lack of such a centralized authority can be largely attributed to cultural diversity and historical differences.[24]

[23] See, however, the collection of articles in Thomas Christiansen, Knud Erik Jørgensen, and Antje Wiener (eds.), "The Social Construction of Europe," *Journal of European Public Policy*, 6 (1999), 528–719.
[24] Briggid Laffan, "The Politics of Identity and Political Order in Europe," *Journal of Common Market Studies*, 34 (1996), 81–102; Anthony D. Smith, "A Europe of Nations – or the Nation of Europe?" *Journal of Peace Research*, 30 (1993), 133; see also his, "National Identity and the Idea of European Unity," *International Affairs*, 68 (1992), 55–76; Stephen Wood, *Germany, Europe, and the Persistence of Nations: Transformation, Interests, and Identity 1989–1996* (Brookfield, VT: Ashgate, 1998).

The response of the European Commisson has been to advance a strategy of "unity-in-diversity." European identity is not meant to be monolithic but to be a composite based on the compatibility of contrasting identities.[25] Government leaders are urged to place greater emphasis on cultural and educational exchanges in order to sensitize Europeans to both points of commonalties and differences.

Although the European Union consists of a mélange of cultures, European societies none the less share a basic consensus on certain broad issues. Thanks to the prominence of the discourse on rights and the triumph of science in addition to the consolidation of the social welfare state, most countries grant women reproductive rights, normalize drinking, and prohibit the recreational use of psychotropic drugs.[26] Since the 1970s, Western (European) society has placed immense value on personal freedom and on allowing individuals to shape themselves mostly through their consumption of goods, services, and pleasure or leisure activities. Free individuals are supposed to regulate themselves and live their lives in accordance with their own personal choices. Governments or political leaders supply knowledge of the consequences of different choices with the view of increasing the likelihood that people will make the right choice. Coercion is employed to aid those who are unable to choose and are considered at risk or risky.[27]

From this follows the simple principle that self-regarding activities are not the domain of state intervention unless they harm others. Abortion is a lawful medical procedure in just about every EU member state because the status of the unborn is subordinate to the right of women to determine their lives. The choice of an abortion is part of a woman's desire to seek self-fulfillment as a person and does not harm other members of society. Alcohol, although widely recognized as an intoxicant and regarded by Anglo-Saxon, Protestant societies with a certain measure of ambivalence, is a licit good and widely available in the West. Problem drinking is a matter of personal anguish and those who struggle

---

[25] Melissa Pantel, "Unity-in-Diversity: Cultural Policy and EU Legitimacy," in Thomas Banchoff and Mitchell P. Smith (eds.), *Legitimacy and the European Union* (New York: Routledge, 1999), 46–65.

[26] Scott and Meyer (eds.), *Institutional Environments and Organizations*; Powell and DiMaggio (eds.), *The New Institutionalism in Organizational Analysis*. Sociologists attribute this convergence to global cultural rules based on Weberian notions of rationality. One debate in the international relations field attributes it to the dissemination of European liberal principles. Compare Albert Bergesen (ed.), *Studies of the Modern World-System* (New York: Academic Press, 1980) and Hedley Bull and Adam Watson (eds.), *Expansion of International Society* (Oxford: Clarendon Press, 1984).

[27] Nikolas Rose, *Inventing Our Selves: Psychology, Power, and Personhood* (New York: Cambridge University Press, 1996); Mariana Valverde, *Diseases of the Will: Alcohol and the Dilemmas of Freedom* (New York: Cambridge University Press, 1998).

with alcoholism or dependency are encouraged to seek treatment through self-help movements. Most countries only limit the consumption of alcohol when it can potentially harm others, such as when driving under the influence of alcohol, for example, but otherwise rely on unwritten rules and informal control mechanisms to delineate standards for normal drinking.

Drug-taking is in a category by itself and receives a very different treatment in Western/European society. Since the 1920s, a generalized panic has infected many societies, owing to fear of the "drug fiend." Opiates, morphine, cocaine, and marijuana were thought to lead to immediate addiction and most governments banned the commercial trade of these substances. Because medical use was also limited, their consumption was restricted and law enforcement agencies assumed jurisdiction. Drugs became associated with crime and their suppression obsessed governments across the political spectrum in many different countries.[28]

Although EU member states agree in principle on how to deal with substance abuse (alcohol abuse is a private matter; drug abuse is a law and order issue) and grant women reproductive rights, it is also understood that some countries hold different opinions and beliefs with regards to universal problems. For this reason, the EU itself does not demand conformity and harmonization and there are no European guidelines for abortion legislation, anti-drug programs, and alcohol regulation. Drugs are governed by policy competencies that have remained firmly in the hands of national authorities: criminal justice and public health. Although the Amsterdam treaty added a subsection on consumer protection (which covers public health), it is mostly concerned with the dangers of contaminated food and barely mentions alcohol or drug dependency. Likewise, alcoholic beverages are not singled out for special treatment anywhere in Europe except in Sweden and Finland in the EU (and Norway and Iceland outside it). There is no European-wide alcohol control policy and the term itself is a source of confusion in the capitals of non-Nordic member states. Abortion, needless to say, is very far removed from the legislative output of the EU.

[28] The global prohibition on recreational drug use is not wholly rational. See Troy Duster, *The Legislation of Morality: Law, Drugs, and Moral Judgement* (New York: The Free Press, 1970); Erich Goode and Nachman Ben-Yehuda, *Moral Panics: The Social Construction of Deviance* (Cambridge: Blackwell, 1994); Jerome Himmelstein, *The Strange Career of Marihuana* (Westport, CT: Greenwood Press, 1983); David F. Musto, *The American Disease. Origins of Narcotic Control* (New Haven, NJ: Yale University Press, 1973); Terry M. Parssinen, *Secret Passions, Secret Remedies. Narcotic Drugs in British Society* (Philadelphia: Institute for the Study of Human Issues, 1983); Craig Reinarman and Harry Levine (eds.), *Crack in America* (Berkeley: University of California Press, 1997).

Still, there is little doubt that Dutch drug policy is turning more punitive, that Nordic alcohol control policy is being liberalized, and that Irish opinions on abortion have softened. Purely domestic factors do not fully and accurately account for the timing of the changes currently taking place. Liberalization of drinking rules began with the accession of Sweden and Finland to the EU. The renewed focus on anti-drug sanctions coincided with the launching of the intergovernmental arrangements to improve judicial and police cooperation in the 1990s. Ireland is the weakest case in that value shifts concerning attitudes towards abortion and religion mainly originated domestically. Even in Ireland, though, developments at the European level have had an impact on mass opinion and parliamentary deliberations.

Diffusion of norms and adaptation of European standards

Since institutions articulate and defend shared norms, they mediate between international norms and structures and domestic change.[29] Institutional sociologists and constructivist scholars in the international relations field identify three kinds of mechanisms that link domestic and international norms. On one side of the debate is the transnational network model. It claims that international norms trickle down to the national level as a result of the pressure tactics of non-governmental organizations and groups, which form an alliance with domestic groups. International activists and national pressure groups then shame national governments into adopting new conventions. Environmental and human rights issues illustrate this dynamic in which elite decision-makers are resistant to new multilateral action plans but are cajoled and pressed by scientists, intellectuals, and outside analysts to join the cause.[30] Elites do not necessarily internalize the new prescriptions and mainly respond to strong societal pressure for action, although they may eventually appropriate the new rules as the guiding norms in decision-making.[31]

---

[29] Jeffrey T. Checkel, "Norms, Institutions, and National Identity in Contemporary Europe," *International Studies Quarterly*, 43 (1999), 83–114.

[30] Emanuel Adler and Michael Barnett (eds.), *Security Communities* (New York: Cambridge University Press, 1998); John Boli and George M. Thomas, "INGOs and the Organization of World Culture," in Boli and Thomas (eds.), *Constructing World Culture*, 13–49; Margaret Keck and Kathryn Sikkink, *Activists beyond Borders: Transnational Advocacy Networks in International Politics* (Ithaca: Cornell University Press, 1998); Klotz, *Norms in International Relations*.

[31] Jeffrey T. Checkel, "International Norms and Domestic Politics: Bridging the Rationalist – Constructivist Divide," *European Journal of International Relations*, 3 (1997), 477.

Needless to say, the transnational network model as exemplified in the literature on epistemic communities or on Greenpeace-like organizations does not get us very far in understanding the influence of Europe on systems of moral governance. For one, the Irish ban on abortion and Dutch drug decriminalization do not constitute authentic transnational challenges that bring together diverse interests from different political systems to organize a joint campaign in favor of secular humanism or prohibitionist drug policies. It suffices to say, without much further discussion, that non-governmental transnational organizations do not figure at all in this story.

A second mechanism discussed in the literature involves elite learning. Decision-makers assimilate new values and interests due to their frequent contact with other agents who influence their intersubjective understanding of the appropriate role of the state. If, moreover, uncertainty dogs decision-making, domestic agents are even more likely to be receptive to new ideas and concepts. In the absence of relevant information, outside agents are able to supply new ways of analyzing a situation and national elites are likely to accept new categories of thinking.[32] Diffusion through learning also happens if international norms are in fact domestic norms, which have been externalized. The international environment is then a mirror image of national norms, which guide domestic action and a basic complementariness promotes diffusion.[33]

Learning may indeed be a powerful diffusion mechanism. Yet when applied to the four case studies examined in this book, the elite learning model falls apart. My investigation shows that the leadership occupies a quite different niche since they resolutely turn away from competing models with the argument that they are incompatible with national preferences. Elite officials are moral entrepreneurs and are not easily converted by outsiders who do not share their fundamental outlook.[34] This is why anti-alcohol policies, drug decriminalization, and the

---

[32] Walter W. Powell and Paul J. DiMaggio, "The Iron Cage Revisited: Institutional Isomorphism and Collective Rationality" and Walter W. Powell, "Expanding the Scope of Institutional Analysis," in Powell and DiMaggio (eds.), *The New Institutionalism*, chs. 3 and 8; Peter Haas (ed.), *Knowledge, Power, and International Policy Coordination* (Columbia, SC: University of South Carolina Press, 1996).

[33] Thomas Berger, "Norms, Identity, and National Security in Germany and Japan," in Katzenstein (ed.), *The Culture of National Security*, 317–56; Ethan Nadelmann, "Global Prohibition Regimes: The Evolution of Norms in International Society," *International Organization*, 44 (1990), 479–526; Thomas Risse-Kappen, "Collective Identity in a Democratic Community," in Katzenstein (ed.), *The Culture of National Security*, 357–99.

[34] Andrew Moravcsik, "A New Statecraft? Supranational Enterpreneurs and International Cooperation," *International Organization*, 53 (1999), 267–306.

abortion ban exist in the first place. Decision-makers stay with what they know irrespective of the availability of new information and the fashionableness of new practices in the rest of Europe.[35]

Finally, there is a third model of diffusion that complements the elite learning process. Institutional sociologists believe that diffusion happens through the homogenization of institutional structures. International culture and Weberian definitions of rationality convince elites to embrace a particular mode of organization even if the organizational structure is counter to their self-interest. Countries adopt identical organizations because they imitate others and arrange domestic structures in a similar fashion regardless of the logic of such arrangements.[36] The resulting institutional isomorphism influences cognitive action and brings about uniform cultural values.[37]

My point of departure, elaborated in the empirical chapters, is that isomorphism failed to shape the institutions of the four countries, which then led to different policy responses and regulatory regimes. Countries are characterized by different values but this difference is the outcome of different institutional characteristics.[38] There is no European equivalent of the Nordic system of alcohol sales in state-owned stores and extremely high excise taxes. Analogously, there is no European equivalent of the 1937 Constitution of the Republic of Ireland, which omits to institute the separation of Church and state.

One final transmission mechanism merits attention. Both the elite learning model and institutional isomorphism single out the community of experts as one of the main transmission belts.[39] Scientists and specialists are in contact with their peers in other member states, read the current literature, attend conferences and conventions, and are exposed to competing models of intervention. They easily acquire

[35] Christine Ingebritsen, "The Politics of Whaling in Norway and Iceland," *Scandinavian Review*, (Winter 1997/98), 9–15.

[36] Dana P. Eyre and Mark C. Suchman, "Status, Norms, and the Proliferation of Conventional Weapons: An Institutional Theory Approach," in Katzenstein (ed.), *The Culture of National Security*, 79–113

[37] Frank Dobbin, *Forging Industrial Policy* (New York: Cambridge University Press, 1994); John W. Meyer, John Boli, and George M. Thomas, "Ontology and Rationalization in the Western Cultural Account," and John W. Meyer, "Rationalized Environments," in Scott and Meyer (eds.), *Institutional Environments and Organization*, 9–28 and 32–54; Meyer, Boli and Thomas, "World Society and the Nation-State," *American Journal of Sociology*, 103 (1997), 144–81; Powell and DiMaggio, "The Iron Cage Revisited".

[38] Peter Gundelach, "National Value Differences: Modernization or Institutionalization?" *International Journal of Comparative Sociology*, 35 (1994), 37–59.

[39] Loya and Boli "Standardization in World Polity"; and Evan Schofer, "Science Associations in the International Sphere, 1875–1990," in Boli and Thomas (eds.), *Constructing World Culture*, 249–66.

knowledge of how other countries deal with more or less identical challenges and possess therefore information relevant to the decision-making process. In the Netherlands and Nordic countries, scientists and academics routinely sit on special advisory panels in recognition of their expertise. Yet diffusion of international norms only works if the new model makes compelling sense to its relevant audience. Scientists, too, must sense a "fit" between European norms and national opinions and convictions. Nordic alcohol researchers and Dutch drug specialists engage in research funded by the state, receive much of their training at home, and are frequently employed by publicly financed institutions. It is no surprise to discover that scientists are inclined to select a course of action consistent with national prescriptions. Public health or abortion is not an exact science with conclusive research findings. Drug and alcohol dependencies are associated with dozens of different treatment philosophies and receive very different diagnoses in different settings. Scientists ask different questions and obtain different answers to the extent that they may not be able to have a serious transnational or cross-cultural dialogue.[40]

If decision-makers deflect external pressures, then who or what pushes for adaptation to European templates of thinking and doing? A corollary question regards how these agents succeed in transposing new norms into actual policy reforms. After all, changed norms do not always automatically lead to new policies. The real world is full of examples of states that resolutely refuse to make the necessary adjustments to shifts in values, new thinking, new models of intervention, new conditions, and new EU rules.[41]

I argue in this book that dissociation from the established model of rules and practices had already taken place prior to any encounters with the European Union. Presumably, institutionalized collective ideas and public discourse are representative of mass opinion. In democracies, leaders supposedly articulate the cultural sensibilities of the people. It is possible, though, that leaders because of their participation in policy networks and dependence on existing institutional configurations do not keep up with mass opinion, which is drifting towards a different set of ideas, values, or agenda. Indeed, people in each country began to

---

[40] Training, education, and certification of elite creates different customs, professional judgments, and ideational predisposition. Peter Hall, "Policy Paradigms, Social Learning, and the State: The Case of Economic Policy-Making in Britain," *Comparative Politics*, 25 (1993), 275–96; J. Nicholas Ziegler, *Governing Ideas: Strategies for Innovation in France and Germany* (Ithaca: Cornell University Press, 1997).

[41] See the chapters in Cowles et al. (eds.), *Transforming Europe: Europeanization and Domestic Change*; Beate Kohler-Koch and Rainer Eising (eds.), *The Transformation of Governance in the European Union* (New York: Routledge, 1999).

embrace concepts related to the free autonomous individual prior to the latest phase in EU regulatory expansion. Of special importance is the completion of the Single Market, which endows people with new rights as European consumers. A borderless Europe accelerates the process of Europeanization because it entices people to disregard domestic restrictions on alcohol, drugs, or abortion by exercising their rights as European consumers. The Single Market results in "sin tourism," as people skip across borders to purchase goods or services not readily available at home or available only at much higher prices. In turn, this kind of tourism frays the cultural narrative and stability of institutionalized norms.

Agent of change: movement of people

National identities are sticky and unlikely to change frequently. Something out of the ordinary must occur before national identities undergo a transformation. A crisis, for example, can disturb established norms and intersubjective understandings and usher in fresh debates on collective beliefs and policy regimes. No real crisis shook up the morality regimes described here. But popular assent to drug decriminalization, blanket ban on abortion, and drinking restrictions had begun to dwindle. Each set of beliefs and policy tools had its fair share of detractors. Collective rules embedded in structures of meaning were undoubtedly taken as a given by a large majority. Yet no democratic society is without dissension.[42]

Domestic critics of the morality standards silently hoped for support and sympathy from the European Commission or Council. In reality, the EU acquiesced to the demands made by member governments for special consideration. For example, the Netherlands succeeded in inserting a short paragraph in the Schengen Convention to guarantee that increased European-wide cooperation against international drug trafficking would not spill over into forced harmonization of national drug control strategies. Ireland insisted on a separate protocol to the Treaty of European Union (Maastricht Treaty) to the effect that future European Court of Justice decisions could not void and nullify the eighth (anti-abortion) amendment of the Irish Constitution. Swedish and Finnish negotiators extracted concessions from the Commission to protect the state-owned retail monopoly from outside competition.

In retrospect, the movement of people has an effect strikingly similar

---

[42] Johan P. Olsen, "Europeanization and Nation-State Dynamics," in Sverker Gustavsson and Leif Lewin (eds.), *The Future of the Nation State* (New York: Routledge, 1996), 250–53.

to that of the free movement of capital because it reduces the autonomy of decision-makers to pursue deviant policy strategies. The same pressures that force national governments to abandon policy agendas contrary to expectations of market actors also govern state regulation of human vices. While none of the institutions belonging to the EU – the Court, Parliament, Council, and Commission – would ever dare to propose uniform moral standards, the pressures brought to bear on national cultural peculiarities resemble the way in which capital mobility punishes unorthodox macro-economic policies and thus limits the sustainable option of central governments.

Just as capital seeks the highest returns and the best investment climate globally without risking its access to national markets, individuals seek consumer goods and services at affordable prices without detaching themselves from the national polity. Individuals seek freedom by designing their own lives. The ethic of autonomous selfhood is firmly implanted in the Western mind. We are encouraged to believe that freedom lies with our daily activities of endless personal choices. Individuals, as sovereign consumers, therefore possess the kind of cultural competence to engage in physical arbitrage. They exploit national differences in tax regimes and legal arrangements and go abroad to obtain cheap liquor, unavailable medical procedures, and banned drugs. The results are abortion, alcohol tourism, and drug tourism. On the one hand, all of us are familiar with the bargain shopper syndrome since many of us are on the perennial look-out for the best deal. On the other, sin tourism differs from our daily pursuit of a bargain. A trip to Italy to purchase fine Italian clothing has no public ramifications. Possibly, it may hurt importers of Italian apparel or domestic retail stores but it does not carry weighty political consequences. Sin shopping, however, in the context of the morality regimes described in this study has tremendous unanticipated ramifications.

Irish and Nordic people engage in ordinary vices, which is the sort of conduct we all expect and is nothing spectacular or unusual. These vices are a common sight everywhere and are not limited to the Irish and Swedes and Finns. All of us display elements of dishonesty and hypocrisy at one point or another. Although ordinary vices taint both citizens and political leaders of liberal democracies, most of us realize that good citizens are not necessarily good humans. Liberal democracies emphasize freedom and individual pursuit of life choices and evince a considerable degree of tolerance for vice. This stems from the original formulation of liberalism, which postulates a trade-off between on the one hand tyranny which extracts obedience to a certain set of virtues and on the other liberty which discourages moderation and temperance.

Although liberalism promotes corruption, despotism demeans us and turns us into sly, conniving, dishonest individuals. Out of fear, we would display outwardly all appropriate virtues but without conviction and by relying on dishonesty and hypocrisy. Thus dishonesty and ordinary vices are the price of living in a functioning democracy.[43]

Deceptive practices are so common that most of us do not stop to examine the consequences of our choices. Nevertheless, the aggregate cheating of numerous individuals fundamentally distorts the original cognitive and normative meaning of the morality standards. Consider, for example, that the establishment in each country routinely dismissed as irrelevant any criticism of collective rules and policy measures. National leaders and experts accused proponents of competing ideas and practices of betrayal since they questioned "national truths."[44] The morality standards were reasonable, complemented the national character, and were beyond and above questioning, so the common refrain ran. Critics who urged alcohol liberalization were narrow-minded and self-interested, according to the official Finnish and Swedish rhetoric, since the repeal of anti-drinking measures would lead to widespread alcohol misuse and greater prevalence of assaults, suicides, homicides, accidents, child abuse, etc. Likewise, repressive sanctions to eradicate drug-taking were foolish, claimed Dutch officials, since they foster deviancy and the growth of an underclass, which lives off crime and harms society. Abortion advocates in Ireland were barely heard at all. They truly constituted a small, embattled minority of Dublin liberals.

Opponents who challenged the *status quo* ran into the twin roadblock of powerful institutions resistant to change and of apparent general assent to the cultural narrative. It is against this backdrop that the ordinary vices of law-abiding citizens assume great significance. Suddenly, marginalized voices point to the flow of sin tourism to argue that "the majority" no longer recognizes the morality standards as legitimate. Sin tourism removes the veil of silence that suppressed open and critical discussion of the morality standards. It prompts fresh scrutiny of widely held beliefs and attitudes and inures people to the idea that a debate on these topics is no longer taboo.

Cracks in the morality frameworks

In all four countries, the authorities employed similar tactics to mute criticism and silence opponents. Policy officials routinely waved off any foreign or outside criticism by mentioning the cultural specificity of the

---

[43] Judith N. Shklar, *Ordinary Vices* (Cambridge, MA: Harvard University Press, 1984).
[44] Douglas, *How Institutions Think*, 112.

morality framework. Thus, the Dutch cited their approach to the regulation of abortion, euthanasia, homosexuality, and pornography to illustrate the country's commitment to nonabsolutism. Finnish and Swedish authorities diffused criticism by claiming that their country struggled with a drinking problem and that many citizens entertained a troubled relationship with alcohol. And the Irish sidestepped negative commentary on their efforts to create an abortion-free zone at home by citing the special Irish devotion to Catholicism. By mentioning the undeniable cultural roots of each regulatory regime, they stifled any further discussion. Furthermore, defenders of the morality framework listed the health advantages or social benefits of the arrangements to mute complaints and criticism. Restrictive drinking rules produce a healthier and better society. Drug decriminalization protects the population from crime, drug-related fatalities, and social marginalization. Ban on abortion keeps moral decay and chaos at bay. These policies are both culturally specific, and beneficial and effective.

Cheating turns such arguments on their head. As ever larger numbers of Irish women avail themselves of the "English solution" (abortion in England), this raises questions about the unique Irish attachment to the articles of the faith. Apparently, Irish women are willing to distinguish between institutionalized religion and private morality. They may still be religious but it is the kind of religion in which some rules are bent or ignored by virtue of their impracticality or unreasonableness. In that case, it can no longer be said that the Irish people desire to be governed by the teachings of the Church and that government decisions, embodying the Catholic ethos, are perfectly aligned with the Irish definition of the good life. In addition, abortion tourism defeats the whole purpose of the anti-abortion amendment, which is meant to protect the life of the unborn. How does the constitutional ban protect the life of the unborn if a growing number of pregnant Irish women seek abortions abroad?

In a similar way, the flow of Finnish and Swedish consumers who buy cheap liquor in Estonia and Denmark respectively suggests that people's attitudes to alcohol curbs have undergone a real shift. People no longer accept the trade-off inherent in individual sacrifices, in the form of restrictions on private consumer choices, made for the sake of protecting others from chemical dependency. Consumers are not willing to put the welfare of the community ahead of individual needs. They, like their counterparts elsewhere in the EU, want affordable liquor in regular private stores. Furthermore, when people drink ever larger volumes of imported or illicit liquor, how can state officials claim to protect public health by limiting the availability of alcohol?

For the Netherlands, the problem is slightly different because it is the cheating by others that is the cause of many problems. The inflow of drug tourists, however, resulted in ever louder calls to screen drug buyers (impossible to do) or to close down retail outlets that sell drugs in order to stem the flow of visitors. The call to close down coffee shops and to bar foreigners from buying drugs in the Netherlands defeats the entire aim of the harm reduction policy because it endows the police with a whole new array of repressive tasks and pushes addicts/users underground where they come into contact with the criminal underworld. The demand for more repressive sanctions to deter foreigners from purchasing cheap drugs also suggests that the permissive Dutch are really not that different from the Germans or French. And if the Dutch, to which we can add the Finns, Swedes, and Irish, *act* no differently than other Europeans, does it make sense to claim that they *are* different?

Such questions were brought up by diverse groups of oppositional forces who use the phenomenon of cheating to demand policy reforms and adjustment along European lines.[45] Support for their agenda of adaptation to European norms also came from the EU itself. Although the EU does not expect harmonization, the member states had to make a few concessions in exchange for derogation of established Community rules or political agreements. Swedish and Finnish authorities agreed to de-monopolize wholesale distribution, trade, and production in the alcoholic beverage market and to raise the limit on travelers' imports.[46] The Netherlands agreed to introduce new restrictive legislation to promote better intergovernmental cooperation on policing and drug trafficking. The Irish authorities were caught in a court case that questioned the principle of proportionality, repeatedly affirmed by the European Court of Justice (ECJ), that presupposed a rough symmetry between the exemptions from Community law and domestic objectives.

Different groups and interests mobilized on behalf of conformity with European doctrine and rules have another powerful tool available to them. They can recapitulate European Union rhetoric and symbolism to take on opinion leaders at home. Thus, in Finland and Sweden, the press, outside analysts, and the private food sector advanced the benefits of free unrestrained markets to convince decision-makers to step up further liberalization and deregulation of the alcoholic beverage market. In the Netherlands, the popular media, local residents in areas with a

---

[45] For a similar argument applied to a totally different area, see Amy Gurowitz, "Mobilizing International Norms: Domestic Actors, Immigrants, and the Japanese State," *World Politics* 51 (1999), 413–45.

[46] Holder et al. *European Integration and Nordic Alcohol Policies.*

high concentration of drug dealing, and law and order types referred to European-wide debates on the threat to internal security due to the increased activities of transnational crime organizations, many of which engage in drug trafficking, to call for stronger police actions against open drug scenes. In Ireland, liberals referred to the judgment of the ECJ, which defined abortion as a lawful medical service, to stir interest in at least an honest debate on the blanket prohibition on abortion.

The emergence of a new language paves the way for the formation of new thinking and erodes the shared understanding of appropriate standards of behavior. It divides the electorate and policy establishment because some groups will side with systemic norms such as market deregulation and liberalization and others will try to preserve the old system of mores. The fact that the rules are debatable in the first place already signifies that a real change is underway.

Europeanization of norms

Cultures dictate not what we think but how we think. The institutions, which articulated and defended a culture, remained unchanged yet attitudes and opinions shifted, so the removal of borders became a grand opportunity for sin tourism. This leads to the question of why values changed *prior* to the friction caused by the free movement of people. To be sure, the Single Market did not occasion a shift of values; rather, it enabled individuals to satisfy their new desires for cheap liquor or drugs or an abortion. It seemed obvious that liberal notions of autonomy and individuality would eventually eclipse Nordic and Irish tradition, despite the fact that this tradition had survived the Western expansion of individualism.[47] Irish sexual morality and Nordic views on drinking hark back to a different era when society relied on a single unifying moral authority to determine life choices. The morality frameworks lasted as long as they did because they spoke to certain prejudices and needs in each culture. Nothing lasts forever, however, and the rise of new generations of voters far removed from the defining moments that shaped the normative climate eroded attachment to these ideals.

The ban on abortion and anti-drinking measures reflected an earlier ethos of a pre-industrial or industrializing society. Structural transformation of society produced a generation effect in that cohorts born after the 1960s had totally different life experiences and were less wedded

---

[47] Paul Heelas, Scott Lash, and Paul Morris (eds.), *Detraditionalization: Critical Reflections on Authority and Identity* (Cambridge, MA: Blackwell, 1996). For a variation on this theme, Susan Cotts Watkins, *From Provinces into Nations: Demographic Integration in Western Europe* (Princeton: Princeton University Press, 1991).

to the temperance-influenced narrative on drinking and Catholic-dominated discourse on sexuality.[48] A key intervening variable, however, which to some extent accelerated the decline of tradition, is growing familiarity with broader Western thinking and growing aware-ness of how professional or life experiences across Europe converge in spite of divergent national or cultural roots.

Television, cinema, advertising, electronic communication, and travel have created an ubiquitous Western globalized culture. Exposure to alternative models of regulation and the worldwide spread of consumer commodities, art styles, mass media and tourism links national tastes and preferences to global markets and engenders the homogenization of lifestyles. Europeanization possesses a dual meaning. It refers to the subtle process of cultural assimilation in which middle-class ethics cross boundaries to tie people together.[49] In this context, cultural homogeni-zation is both the cause and effect of people dressing alike, buying similar products, listening to identical music, and watching the same films and television programs.[50] But Europeanization also refers to the impact of regional integration and it is the second kind of transforma-tion that eventually impels political leaders to listen to demands for adjustments.

Political agreements to create a borderless Europe encouraged rule-breaking and opened the way for a revisiting of social facts or the "truth," not by demanding institutional conformity but by supplying people with a new language to challenge the cultural meanings at home.[51] Tensions already existed in the morality regimes and support had already declined. Market integration aided critical voices that had been around for a while and could exploit the growing inconsistencies for their own purposes.

Does this mean that one of the prerequisites for successful European institution-building, namely the bridging of cultural diversity, is ful-filled?[52] Do the case studies provide a reason to predict a future of better political cooperation in the EU? Probably not, because the changes

[48] Marlis Buchmann, *The Script of Life in Modern Society* (Chicago: University of Chicago Press, 1989); Diane Crane, "Introduction," in Diane Crane (ed.), *Sociology of Culture* (New York: Routledge, 1994), 6–22.

[49] Peter Ester, Loek Halman, and Ruud de Moor (eds.), *The Individualizing Society: Value Change in Europe and North America* (Tilburg: Tilburg University Press, 1993).

[50] Wæver et al., *Identity, Migrant and the New Security Agenda in Europe*, 42.

[51] Emery Roe, *Narrative Policy Analysis: Theory and Practice* (Durham, NC: Duke University Press, 1994); Vivien Schmidt, "Politics, Values, and the Power of Discourse in the Reform of the Welfare State," in Fritz Scharpf and Vivien Schmidt (eds.), *From Vulnerability to Competitiveness: Welfare and Work in the Open Economy* (New York: Oxford University Press, 2000), 229–309.

[52] Smith , "A Europe of Nations".

sketched out in this study do not imply a total fading of collective self-identity and a decisive end to a distinctive approach to the regulation of socially sensitive activities. Swedes and Finns are still suspicious of spirits, the Dutch oppose the heavy reliance on police powers for the sake of a drug-free society, and Irish people accept abortion mainly in exceptional circumstances. The distance between national norms and those of the EU has narrowed. But a distinction remains between Dutch thinking on drugs and that of Sweden, for example, and French attitudes towards drinking and those of the Nordic countries. In the long term, however, it is safe to predict that regional integration is diminishing Europe's diversity and that the people of Europe are becoming more alike. The process may take years, if not decades, but the direction is towards more homogenization.

Looking ahead

Real-world puzzles require advanced and sophisticated methodological analysis.[53] Irrespective of which methodology – rational choice, institutionalism, constructivism – is superior, a synthesis of each school of analysis uncovers different fragments of the puzzle. This puzzle, I maintain, consists of three distinct pieces. First, norms, which govern morality standards, are unlikely to fall under the spell of European integration, international society, or global culture. Morality norms epitomize a distinct and convoluted cultural legacy and delineate the nation's traits or passions. Elite decision-makers and professional communities show little inclination to conform to conventional lines of thinking because they trust their own approach and because powerful institutions ward off claims for an alternative construction of cognitive framework and action plan. None the less, morality standards are in the process of becoming Europeanized, which is the first piece of the puzzle. Why, of all areas of political life, would the governance of moral codes of conduct encounter adaptational pressures?

A close reading of the empirical case studies lends no support for a purely institutional interpretation of change. State agencies and expert communities acquire a distinct interest in the survival of the existing regulatory regime. They defend and shield the morality norms from Europeanization; they are not the agents of change. It is in spite of their spirited defense that morality standards are undergoing modification. The second part of the puzzle, therefore, is who or what is pushing for

[53] Checkel, "International Norms and Domestic Politics"; Peter Hall and Rosemary Taylor, "Political Science and the Three New Institutionalisms," *Political Studies*, 44 (1996), 936–57.

change, and why? My answer is that people as self-interested individuals take advantage of the Single Market in ways strikingly similar to the means–end calculations of economic agents. Since a sizable number of individuals in each country were no longer fully committed to the morality standards, the removal of frontiers and the new rhetoric emanating from the EU propelled a surge in cross-border activities. These activities in and by themselves need not bury the morality regimes. Cheating was a common problem for many years. But the Single Market by lowering the barriers against cheating increases the incentives to evade domestic rules and entices large numbers of people to take advantage of this opportunity.

The third piece of the puzzle is why the cross-border activities of individuals spill over into institutional change. After all, many polities are able to thwart and escape change for years. Examples abound of procrastinating member states, which take their time to transpose new EU laws and directives. Considering that culture is one of the institutions least likely to undergo adjustment, we would expect to discover hardly any adaptation at all. The key to this riddle is that once individuals begin to engage in massive deception, opponents deprived of access to policy process and decision-making procedures exploit this strange phenomenon to contest the narrative of the morality framework and to question its overall utility for society. They use EU institutions and laws to put additional pressure on authorities to clarify their policy position and to bring the country's rules into alignment with prevailing thinking in the rest of Europe. Institutional change, which mostly describes Finland and Sweden and less so the Netherlands, follows shifts in values and orientation after organized interests have taken advantage of the tension between proclaimed morality standards and actual behavior displayed by citizens.

The following chapters are organized to elaborate these points. The first task is to examine the process of identity construction and norm building. Historical forces gave rise to particular ideas and solidified them in institutions and state policy. Over time, the norms adapted to the expansion of the welfare state and were taken for granted. The second part of the argument looks at what happens when these institutionalized norms meet the European governance of the Single Market and the formation of intergovernmental arrangements to improve policing/internal security. Nordic alcohol policy conflicts with the free movement of goods. Dutch drug policy hampers cooperation in European policing. Abortion is only peripherally related to initiatives taken by the EU in the past fifteen years but contradicts key principles upheld by functioning democracies and thus Community law and human rights conventions. In every case, opponents who push the government to consider further adjustments to yield to Community law (Ireland), to European-wide judicial coordination (the Netherlands), and to anti-trade discrimination (Finland and Sweden) exploit minor friction with the EU. In all four countries, the adjustments are modest and do not suggest a wholehearted discarding of existing norms. Nevertheless, there is little doubt that the direction of change is towards deregulation and liberalization in Ireland, Finland and Sweden and towards more restrictions in the Netherlands.

2   Binge drinking: the evolution of alcohol control policy in Finland

Drinking is a social activity and different cultures assign different meanings to alcohol. Rituals in the Nordic[1] countries centered on drinking distilled liquor outside mealtimes and the main objective was to get drunk. Social occasions were frequently accompanied by binge drinking (sporadic bouts of excessive drinking) and drunkards were a common sight in public spaces. All forms of inebriation arouse moral and political opposition and are considered legitimate terrain for government control. After the 1880s, binge drinking was considered offensive. Temperance associations, growing out of Christian evangelical movements, preached first against spirits and then against drinking, and blamed weak self-control for destructive drinking practices, incompatible with a modernizing society. For many Finns, moreover, binge drinking was indicative of the nation's underdevelopment. National officials argued that the taciturn introvert Finn metamorphosed into an aggressive drunk after drinking even modest amounts of alcohol because Finland was a primitive and insular community and did not yet possess the trappings of higher civilizations. Destructive binge drinking was both a cause and a symptom of Finland's backwardness.

In actuality, Nordic statistics on alcohol production and consumption do not validate this savage imagery of a nation filled with aggressive drunks. Many within agrarian European societies drank excessive amounts of alcohol and "boozing" is typically associated with the use of spirits, not with the level of development of the nation.[2] In both Finland and Sweden, anti-alcohol sentiments arose, not because society was teetering on the verge of permanent intoxication, but rather because social tolerance of a particular drinking style declined. Gradually, the rejection of certain drinking styles spilled over into a rejection of alcoholic beverages generally. Why Finnish and Swedish people turned against spirits and boozing is an exceedingly tangled question. But one

---

[1] Nordic refers only to Norway, Sweden, and Finland, not to Denmark.

[2] Please note that binge drinking among young adults is common in many Western societies, including the USA, and that the favorite beverage of the young is beer.

factor is the rise of Christian evangelical movements and their renunciation of activities that thwart a commitment to self-improvement and concrete change. Temperance societies grew out of revivalist Protestant-Christian cultures, which preached self-control and opposed the gratification of simple pleasures such as drinking. Temperance movements called for personal abstinence, which was impractical for most people, so that state intervention was required to enforce a more fitting code of conduct for a modern society.

What sets the Nordic countries apart, however, is not the rise of Protestant-affiliated temperance movements in the late nineteenth century. Many Western societies (the USA, the UK, and Canada) became obsessed with drinking and witnessed the rise of religious-inspired temperance movements. Yet in the Anglo-Saxon countries, the appeal of temperance waned after 1945 and drinking routines became normalized. Only the Nordic countries continued to micro-manage the entire alcohol industry through institutions that are, presently, still in existence. Four questions must therefore be examined in this chapter and the next:

1 Why were Finnish and Swedish authorities reluctant to deregulate and liberalize alcohol policy after the decline of hard drinking?
2 How did they justify the persistence of restrictions on individual consumer choice?
3 What induced voters to comply with the rules created by public officials once the moral stigma on drinking had abated?
4 How does the drinking issue relate to the construction of collective self-identity?

The first three questions must be understood against the context of the Nordic variant of the welfare state. The Nordic welfare state demands individual sacrifices since the wellbeing of the community takes precedence over individual choice and freedom. Substance abuse, according to the social welfare rhetoric, is a collective problem because everybody can acquire a dependency problem and everybody is affected by the reckless actions of misusers. Since the state cannot predict who will become a problematic drinker, collective restraints ensure that nobody is singled out and that everybody is protected from the actions of drunks. The last question, however, requires a special inquiry into Nordic perceptions of self and the definition of the good life because there is something very Finnish or Swedish about their approach to chemical substances and intoxication.

Most Western countries, even though their aggregate consumption of pure alcohol is higher than that of Sweden and Finland, do not single out alcohol abuse as a social or public health issue. They simply do not think that, of all the intractable challenges faced by modern society, drinking is one that requires special attention. Most societies would also question the trade-off inherent in universal restrictions on consumer choice for the sake of stopping a few drunks from causing damage. Everyone agrees that the activities of individuals with an excessive amount of alcohol in their bloodstream can hurt innocent people. Yet Western or European societies would hesitate to institute general curbs on drinking in order to avoid such unfortunate events. Liberal societies argue that this is the price of "freedom." They may impose stiff penalties on those who are found to be driving under the influence of alcohol, but they are unlikely to use state agencies to curb the drinking habits of the general population.

The particular Nordic formulation of substance abuse (which includes drugs) harks back to a worldview promulgated by evangelical Christian movements which hold a fatalistic and pessimistic view of a human being's ability to turn away from life's temptations yet store much faith in the ability of an individual to lead him/herself to salvation and redemption. In contrast to mainstream Christian churches, missionary movements believed that people could achieve salvation by seeking self-improvements and social change. But inebriation prevented an individual from becoming a better person. This concept of the self also drove the early Swedish and Finnish workers movements. Temperance dovetailed with the social democratic agenda of improving the lot of the disadvantaged and labor leaders urged workers to become diligent, morally enlightened, reliable, and conscientious members of society by abstaining from alcohol.

In Finland, moreover, the debate on alcohol and drinking coincided with the attempt to gain statehood and political emancipation. The assault on distilled liquor, which started in the 1880s, revealed Finland's growing aspiration for independence from Czarist Russia and the desire of the Social Democratic Party to enfold agrarian workers and urban migrants in its new organization. The political left coupled prohibition with general suffrage and social improvements, forging a political and psychological link between abstinence, thrift, and material and spiritual uplifting. The public fight to ban alcohol from daily life sought to liberate the Finnish people from a harsh and difficult agrarian existence and from oppressive Russian rule.

After 1960, the moral stigma of drinking began to disappear. Yet anti-drinking restrictions remained intact and the state retained its near complete control over alcohol production, distribution, and trade. Over time, the ideological justification for alcohol control policies moved from morality to science and to the public health benefits derived from restrictive drinking measures. Alcohol-related mortality and morbidity rates were low and taxpayers' money, which otherwise had to be spent on treating alcohol-related injuries and diseases, could be allocated to other social welfare programs. Once the temperance movement lost its bearing, many Finnish consumers were still doubtful whether a Continental (non-Nordic) alcohol regime of cheap prices and easy availability would work. The image of the hard-drinking Finn was deeply embedded in the national collective narrative and widely recognized as an accurate description of the average (male) person. Anti-drinking restrictions kept boozing in check and safeguarded public order.

This chapter examines the "hard drinking culture" and places it within a particular historical context. While there is a kernel of truth in the allegation that Finnish people embraced a particularly destructive drinking style, the "hard drinking culture" is none the less a social construction that addresses concerns about the level of development of a dependent territory in the decaying Russian Empire. The image survived the emergence of the modern state in part because it described what it meant to be Finnish. Whereas other, non-Nordic, countries abandoned all pretense of trying to restrict people's access to liquor, the Finns (and Swedes) kept anti-buyer restrictions intact mostly on the grounds that there was a need for this kind of state control. The reason why, of all people, Swedes and Finns could not be trusted with alcohol was routinely attributed to the Nordic mentality. According to conventional wisdom, Finnish and Swedish men and women are tongue-tied, inhibited, and introvert. They must rely on liberal quantities of alcohol to facilitate interpersonal communication. Excessive drinking lifted social restraints, thereby facilitating social interaction, but it also posed a threat to the well-ordered society.

Alcohol legislation, voluntary associations and prohibition

For centuries, the population of the Nordic countries drank beer until the technique of distillation spread from Russia to Finland and Sweden. Spirits displaced beer in the mid-seventeenth century because they represented an economical and effective way of transforming surplus grain into a marketable commodity and because they produced swill as a by-product that could be used as cattle fodder. The Swedish monarchy, which controlled the Finnish territory, took an immediate interest in taxing spirits or stills and excise duties became an important source of fiscal revenues. In the mid-eighteenth century, the Swedish monarchy created a system of crown distilleries to increase its state revenues and to preserve surplus grain for bread. Finnish peasants fiercely opposed this monopoly, which was abandoned in 1787. Soon every farm, peasant, and landowner could distill spirits although the distillation season was limited to October through the end of May. Taxes were raised on the size of the farm or the amount of grain used in town distilleries. After the Russian annexation of Finland in 1809, Swedish laws remained in force and Finnish farms produced considerable quantities of vodka. The Finnish administration limited the season of distillation to three months to prevent further growth in the supply of spirits and forbade the use of modern distillation equipment in 1829. After 1859, it was decreed that a town could only have one functioning distillery and urban home distilling more or less disappeared.

Until 1865, every farm, after having met its set quota of grain, used surplus grain to produce distilled spirits. The finished product was subsequently drunk by all who were part of the grain harvest: agricultural day workers, leaseholders, and freeholding peasants. Prosperous farms registered higher levels of alcohol consumption than poor farms and years of good harvests resulted in greater vodka consumption than did meager ones. The upper class as well engaged in boisterous drinking parties, which turned into more refined habits such as champagne suppers after the 1850s.[3] In 1865, the Finnish administration decided to deny farms the right to distill their own spirits in order to promote factory-produced alcohol, which would conserve precious grain by employing more efficient methods of distillation as well as improve tax revenues. The administration collected taxes on factory-produced spirits and sold licenses to the highest bidder to set up a town distillery. Local authorities licensed retail outlets and rural districts could formulate their own rules with respect to off-premise sales.[4]

The first temperance movement, Friends of Temperance, was founded in 1884, and tended to attract members of the upper class.[5] The purpose of the national organization was to guide society into a new direction with a new set of values and habits, consistent with bourgeois norms. Its activities encompassed more than a pledge to abstain from alcohol. Temperance societies urged their members to participate in clubs, field trips, reading groups, tea parties, and sports activities because their objectives went beyond the call for moderation to contain

---

[3] Matti Peltonen, "A Bourgeois Bureaucracy," in Matti Peltonen (ed.), *State, Culture, and the Bourgeoisie: Aspects of the Peculiarity of the Finnish* (Jyväskylä: University of Jyväskylä Press, 1989), 44.

[4] Esa Österberg "From Home Distillation to the State Alcohol Monopoly," *Contemporary Drug Problems*, 12 (1985), 33–40.

[5] Henrik Stenius, "The Breakthrough of the Principle of Mass Organization in Finland," *Scandinavian Journal of History*, 5 (1980), 197–217.

a political mission of edification.[6] Temperance activists held the view that alcohol abuse was pathological and harmful to society and that drunks were such a disgrace that they did not belong in a decent society.[7] The Friends of Temperance claimed that the administration had a duty to treat drunks and to fund temperance activities. After 1885, the administration provided some money for temperance activities, and many local notables who had joined the Friends of Temperance societies banned spirits from their rural districts.

During the 1890s, the temperance movement underwent a radical transformation. Already a decade earlier, when the temperance movement counted about 8,500 registered members, the bulk of its membership was found in the towns, not in the countryside. Rather than peasants, the temperance societies attracted artisans, landless peasants, agricultural laborers, and town dwellers.[8] Since the character of the temperance societies was not exactly conservative and agrarian, the leadership eventually changed hands from rural notables to political radicals aligned with the rising Social Democratic Party. Under new leadership, the temperance movement advocated, aside from statutory prohibition, electoral reforms to achieve political equality and social improvements. The new leadership of the temperance movement was more radical and openly attacked the manufacture and sale of alcohol in the towns.[9]

Supporters of the socialist cause used the temperance agenda to build up their organization. In 1898, the temperance leaders and social democratic sympathizers organized a so-called strike for temperance, which mobilized about 70,000 people. After the strike, a group of left-wing intellectuals founded the Social Democratic Party in 1899, but its connections with temperance continued to be very close. During the unrest of 1905, when the Russian Empire was buffeted by social turmoil, Finnish social democratic leaders called for the introduction of general suffrage and the legislation of statutory prohibition.[10]

Until 1905, in spite of the growing radicalization of the temperance movement, the upper or ruling class had positive attitudes towards mass

---

[6] Irma Sulkunen, *History of the Finnish Temperance Movement: Temperance as a Civic Religion*, trans. Martin Hall (Lewiston, NY: Edwin Mellen, 1990), 64–66, 105–06; Irma Sulkunen, "Temperance as a Civic Religion: The Cultural Foundation of the Finnish Working-Class Temperance Ideology," *Contemporary Drug Problems*, 12, (1985), 281.

[7] Sulkunen, *History of the Finnish Temperance Movement*, 69.

[8] Sulkunen, *History of the Finnish Temperance Movement*, 108.

[9] Ilpo Koskikallo, "The Social History of Restaurants in Sweden and Finland," *Contemporary Drug Problems*, 12 (1985), 28.

[10] Risto Alapuro, *State and Revolution in Finland* (Berkeley: University of California Press, 1988), 104.

movements in general and the temperance movement in particular. As bureaucrats in a dependent state, civil servants were tolerant towards the demands of other social groups in society. The Finnish elite sought to tie voluntary associations to the state to reinforce the state and bind civil servants, many of whom were original Swedish-speakers, closer to the people. National unity was an important precondition for preserving autonomy and for averting Russification.[11] There was also little fear that the proliferation of associational life would draw the ire of the Russian authorities. Cultural activities passed the approval of the Russian censor.[12]

The alcohol question in a broader context

One of the puzzles of the alcohol and temperance story is the simple observation that most Finns were in fact very modest drinkers and that consumption of pure alcohol per capita per annum declined from an average of 5–7.5 liters in 1850s to less than 2 liters after 1866.[13] Various statistical compilations of European trends in alcohol consumption, published at the turn of the century, placed Finland at the bottom of the chart.[14] A relatively modest per capita consumption of alcohol is to be expected in a territory located between latitudes of 60° and 70° N. Finland is saddled with poor soil, lack of mineral wealth, long cold winters, and an inhospitable climate generally through the rest of the year. Many peasants had to exist on bread made of chaff and birch-bark even during years of normal harvests. Even when cultivation techniques improved during the second half of the nineteenth century, the great majority of the farming population lived off small plots of land that did not yield a bountiful harvest during the best of times, let alone during years of cold springs and extra short summers. In certain parts of the country, peasants turned to begging in the winter to feed their families.

---

[11] William C. Martin and Karen Hopkins, "Cleavage Crystallization and Party Linkages in Finland, 1900–1918," in Kay Lawson (ed.), *Political Parties and Linkage: A Comparative Perspective* (New Haven, NJ: Yale University Press, 1980), 198–203.

[12] Martti Häikiö, *A Brief History of Modern Finland* (Helsinki: University of Helsinki Press, 1992), 12, 18. However, at home, the Russian authorities suppressed voluntary temperance societies: Stephen White, *Russia Goes Dry: Alcohol, State and Society* (New York: Cambridge University Press, 1996), 14–15.

[13] Koskikallo, "The Social History of Restaurants in Sweden and Finland," 24; Matti Peltonen, "The Problem of Being a Finn," in Marjatta Rahikainen (ed.), *Austerity and Prosperity: Perspective of Finnish Society* (Helsinki: University of Helsinki Press, 1993), 180.

[14] Sulkunen, "Temperance as a Civic Religion" 282, n. 2. She lists at least ten different sources for her estimates of per capita consumption of absolute alcohol, which is given as 2.05 liters between 1900 and 1904. The French consumed 23 liters of alcohol per capita at that time.

After the arrival of the timber-processing industry, many farmers worked in the forest during the slow months and deep poverty disappeared in many areas of the country.[15] Nevertheless, grain was a precious commodity and many households did not have sufficient surpluses to produce large quantities of vodka.

Moreover, the law of 1866, which introduced factory-made liquor, had unexpected consequences for the countryside. Many peasants and tenants did not have the extra cash to purchase factory-made spirits and the ban on home distilling led to a decline in vodka consumption. By 1900, consumption fell even further because local authorities banned the sale of alcohol from their districts under pressure from local temperance societies. Only a very small number of districts (1.2 percent) still permitted beer to be served in public spaces. Otherwise, beer was available for home consumption but distilled spirits had disappeared altogether. The Finnish countryside was basically "dry" by 1900 and most of the alcohol was consumed in the towns in specially licensed liquor stores. Although this is just an estimate, given that alcohol disappeared from the countryside, the average consumption of an urban dweller was around 5 liters of pure alcohol per year while the rural population was said to consume around 0.8 liters.[16] Most Finns, of course, lived in the countryside until 1945.

It is, therefore, a mystery why temperance societies became so popular and why prohibition carried such enormous appeal. Considering the modest consumption of alcohol in Finland, the rise and popularity of temperance must be attributed to factors other than the debilitating drinking habits of Finnish peasants. There is little compelling evidence that the Finnish nation indulged in *brännvin* (schnapps) while neglecting its families, communities, and religious duties. Some individuals may have been incurable drunks but the average Finnish man (and woman) did not consume outsized quantities of hard liquor.

Yet support for prohibition was genuine and drinking was viewed with true abhorrence. In 1885, 30,000 individuals in dozens of parishes signed a petition in favor of prohibition. At that time, the actual membership of the Friends of Temperance stood at 8,175. In 1900, no fewer than 140,000 people appealed to the government to legislate prohibition. Yet only a fraction of these people bothered to join a temperance society because membership had not risen much above the 8,000.[17] Apparently,

---

[15] D.G. Kirby, *Finland in the Twentieth Century* (London: C. Hurt, 1979), Appendix D, p. 222.

[16] Pertti Alasuutari, *Desire and Craving: A Cultural Theory of Alcoholism* (Albany: State University of New York Press, 1992), 182, n. 2.

[17] Sulkunen, *History of the Finnish Temperance Movement*, 85.

the moral climate was opposed to alcohol and fostered a public mentality sympathetic to the goals of the teetotaler movement. But temperance activism itself appealed to a narrow group of individuals for whom teetotaler societies functioned as a surrogate to meet other needs.

The administrative elite in Helsinki supported temperance activities because they helped in bridging the gap between society and the state. The Finnish elite spoke Swedish in contrast to the mass of peasants who spoke the vernacular Finnish language. Temperance mobilization was a way of bringing the mass of Finnish-speaking peasants closer to the Swedish-speaking administration.[18] Local rural notables saw temperance as a proper lifestyle because it instructed the poor to spare their meager resources by not wasting them on liquor, especially after the growth of a rural landless and uprooted population burdened local communities in charge of poor relief.[19] For others, having joined one of the new evangelical Christian churches, drinking was labeled a major sin. For poor families, factory-produced alcohol was out of reach and they turned against drinking out of convenience and bitterness. In other words, different social groups could fold their own agenda into the demand for prohibition.

Strikingly, it was mostly urban dwellers who became members of a temperance society although support for prohibition was probably higher in rural areas. Temperance societies in urban areas brought individuals together for reasons that were only partly related to the moral crusade against drinking. In the last decade of the nineteenth century, the Finnish agrarian economy experienced a major transformation. The rise of forestry and the timber industry and the increased significance of dairy farming (milk and butter) modified and transformed the system of social relations in the countryside. The decline of grain or rye and the rise of dairy farming led to capital-intensive and mechanized farming and widened the gulf between those who owned land and those who were landless. The gap broadened even further as timber became a cash source on which the freeholding peasant began to rely. Many landowning peasants moved from subsistence agriculture, based upon the model of a self-sufficient rural community, to specialization and commercialization.[20] The transfer was gradual and varied by

---

[18] See, Kirby, *Finland in the Twentieth Century*; Alapuro, *State and Revolution in Finland*.
[19] Klaus Mäkelä and Matti Viikari, "Notes on Alcohol and the State," *Acta Sociologica*, 20 (1977), 174.
[20] Frederick Bernard Singleton, *A Short History of Finland* (New York: Cambridge University Press, 1989), 90–92; Matti Peltonen, *Talolliset ja Torpparit: Vuosisadan vaihteen maatakouskysymys Suomessa* (Helsinki: SHS, 1992), 399–423. See also Dieter Senghaas, *The European Experience: A Historical Critique of Development Theory* (Dover, NH: Berg, 1985).

regions, but it hurt the crofter (leaseholder) population, who leased small plots of land and paid their rent mainly in labor.

The countryside articulated a strong hostility towards alcohol because the 1866 act destroyed an important aspect of peasant autonomy. The rise of a commercial market for spirits was at the expense of the peasant community, which distilled surplus grain to celebrate the communal act or collective effort to provide for livelihood in a harsh and unpredictable environment. The distillation of spirits served a special social role in peasant communities and signified a measure of control over the use of a precious commodity (grain) that otherwise was transferred to the wealthy and educated. Therefore, anti-alcohol opinion rose after 1866 when the state removed from the peasants the right to distill liquor and gave it to the upper classes in the towns, thereby eroding the independent status of peasants and the collective identity of peasant farms. The transformation of the rural economy only hardened the sense of loss and resentment against manufactured vodka. Yet many peasants did not join temperance societies despite their support for prohibition. Rather temperance societies appealed to the floating population of tenants, cottagers, and agricultural laborers with no firm roots anymore in the countryside nor any definite place in the urban economy because the societies offered comradeship and self-help. This group was also sympathetic to the program of the Finnish labor movement, thereby forging strong links between temperance and social democracy.[21]

One of the first legislative Acts of the new republic of Finland led to statutory prohibition in 1918. Predictably, prohibition gave an enormous boost to bootlegging and home distilling, while the educated upper classes engaged in elaborate schemes to procure alcohol. In the end, their stealthy behavior, the enormous extent of smuggling, and the popularity of home distilling delegitimized the entire experiment.[22] In December 1931, Finland held its first ever referendum and 70 percent of the voters chose to repeal statutory prohibition.[23] What clinched the decision for many was that illicit home distilling and smuggling boosted alcohol consumption to heights that had not been seen either before or after prohibition. Moreover, during the Great Depression, the state was

---

[21] Alapuro, *State and Revolution in Finland*, 118.

[22] Singleton, *A Short History of Finland*, 172–73; Esa Österberg, "Finland," in Timo Kortteinen (ed.), *State Monopolies and Alcohol Prevention* (Helsinki: Social Research Institute of Alcohol Studies, 1989), 109–11.

[23] David Arter, *Politics and Policy-Making in Finland* (New York: St. Martin's Press, 1987), 32. International economic pressures also played a role in the repeal of prohibition. France threatened to boycott Finnish timber and paper products if French wines were barred from the Finnish market: Ernest Hurst Cherrington, *Standard Encyclopedia of the Alcohol Problem*, (6 vols., Westerville, OH: American Issue Publishing, 1925–30), vol. III, 991.

asked to shoulder a greater burden to assist the unemployed yet could not squeeze more revenues out of a declining national economy. The ensuing fiscal crisis convinced many voters of the need to legalize alcohol so that the state, rather than private (and corrupt) individuals, could reap the profits of the alcohol trade.[24]

Institutions of the alcohol policy regime

After the repeal of the Prohibition Act, parliament passed the 1932 Alcohol Act. At the center of the Alcohol Act stood the Finnish State Alcohol Monopoly (Alko). Alko controlled all the manufacturing, exporting, importing, and distribution of alcohol. A tight rein was kept on the private sector, which was permitted to sell alcohol in restaurants that were licensed by Alko. A private wine/liqueur industry continued to exist to market fruit wines and specialized berry liqueurs. Beer brewing was also kept in the private sector. But Alko, which operated its own distilleries and bottling factories, none the less supervised the production and distribution costs of the private sector. The ultimate aim of the Finnish State Alcohol Monopoly was to eliminate the profit motive and private interests from the alcoholic beverage trade. To a large extent, it succeeded in excluding private profit-oriented interests from the market of alcoholic beverages, which were only available in state retail stores. Private agents could not import alcohol nor could they manufacture vodka, Finland's favorite drink.

The cabinet appointed the management board of Alko and the Ministry of Social Affairs and Health supervised Alko's operations. The law vested Alko with broad powers to set the prices of alcoholic beverages in retail and off-premise establishments. It also licensed tourist hotels to serve alcohol to overnight guests. One of the peculiarities of the 1932 Act was that it retained a quasi prohibition in the rural areas, which lasted until the late 1960s.[25] No Alko stores were opened in the countryside and very few "first class" restaurants were allowed to serve alcohol in rural areas.

The Alcohol Act also stipulated that all customers be registered in the nearest retail outlet to keep a record of their purchases. The Act approved measures to punish people who consumed excessive alcohol and each person required a certificate, after 1950, to purchase fortified wines and distilled liquor. Monopoly officials together with local police

---

[24] Jorma Kallenautio, "Finnish Prohibition as an Economic Policy Issue," *Scandinavian Economic History Review*, 29 (1981), 215.

[25] Most Finns lived in the rural areas. Less than a third of the population resided in towns in 1950. Kirby, *Finland in the Twentieth Century*, Appendix D, p. 222.

and social agencies investigated individual purchases and tens of thousands of people had their certificates revoked due to abuse. The control system was abolished in 1957 although sales coupons continued to be in use until the early 1970s.

In 1969, parliament passed the Medium Beer and Alcohol Act and removed some of the more coercive control mechanisms. Retail outlets were opened in the countryside and the sales personnel of Alko no longer needed to record individual alcohol purchases. The management of Alko was eager to experiment with a new strategy to wean Finnish drinkers from binge drinking by promoting wine and beer, which were more likely to be consumed during mealtime and less likely to be treated like a drug.[26] To accomplish this new objective, the law permitted ordinary stores and restaurants to sell medium-strength beer (alcohol content of 3.7 to 4.7 percent).[27]

Various studies had forecast a rise in alcohol consumption of 15 percent after the new liberalization rules came into effect.[28] The actual increase in alcohol consumption was closer to 46 percent while the sales of medium-strength beer increased by 240 percent. Sales of distilled liquor increased by around 10 percent.[29] The surge in drinking caught lawmakers unawares and a parliamentary Alcohol Committee was appointed in 1976, which recommended a tightening of the new rules. In 1977, a new law prohibited all public advertisements of alcoholic beverages and from 1978 Alko outlets were closed on Saturdays during the summer (opened again in 1991). Establishments that sold medium-strength beer were closely supervised to ensure their compliance with age restrictions on buyers and restaurants were denied extended opening hours.[30] Prices were increased and no more Alko outlets were opened or licensed. The authorities also paid more attention to public education to warn about the dangers of alcohol.

The new measures after 1977 did not measurably alter the thrust of the Medium Beer and Alcohol Act of 1969. Politicians had been more or less forced to liberalize the alcohol control system after rising resent-

[26] Mäkelä and Viikari, "Notes on Alcohol and the State," 172.

[27] Pekka Kuusi, *Social Policy for the Sixties; A Plan for Finland*, trans. Jaakko Railo, (Helsinki: Finnish Social Policy Association, 1964); Pekka Kuusi, *Alcohol Sales Experiment in Rural Finland*, trans. Alfred Westphalen, (Helsinki: Finnish Foundation for Alcohol Studies, 1957).

[28] Esa Österberg, "Finnish Social Alcohol Research and Alcohol Policy," *Nordic Alcohol Studies*, 11 (1994), 62.

[29] Klaus Mäkelä, Esa Österberg, and Pekka Sulkunen, "Drink in Finland: Increasing Alcohol Availability in a Monopoly State," in Patricia Morgan, Jan de Lint and Eric Single (eds.), *Alcohol, Society, and the State: The Social History of Control Policy in Seven Countries* (Toronto: Addiction Research Foundation, 1981), 52.

[30] Mäkelä et al., "Drink in Finland," 42–46.

ment against detailed intervention in social (private) matters and after pressures from the tourism and catering industries. The rapid decline of the temperance movement removed the single largest obstacle to liberalization because temperance activists, over-represented in parliament, had been able to block earlier legislation.[31] The alcohol control regime after 1969 primarily counted on restricting the physical availability of liquor and on high retail prices to guide drinking volumes and styles.[32] Excise taxes kept all prices very high. Nevertheless, consumption of alcohol rose steadily from 4.5 liters of pure alcohol per capita per annum in 1970 to 7.5 liters in 1988. Revenues from alcohol sales and taxes averaged between 7 and 10 percent of all central government revenues in the 1960s and 1970s and still comprised 6 percent of central government revenues in 1997.[33]

Ideas and rationalizing the commitment to temperance

The Finnish parliament had already passed a prohibition bill in 1907, which was vetoed by the Senate, the voice of the Russian czar, which asked for an explanation as to why other parts of the Russian Empire did not need to ban alcohol. The question was especially pertinent because the Finnish territory was relatively sober in contrast to the rest of the Russian Empire. Intellectuals of the temperance movement addressed this question by acknowledging that the Finnish nation did not drink excessively. But they reformulated the question to draw attention to the Finnish drinking style with its emphasis on inebriation. Intoxication-oriented drinking rituals created two problems, they claimed. First, when Finnish men drank, they drank until intoxicated and became violent and unruly.[34] Second, the genetic constitution of the lower classes was such that even small amounts of alcohol affected their brain chemistry and inebriation was inevitable.

In the 1930s, after the repeal of prohibition, intellectuals and

---

[31] Heikki Koski and Esa Österberg, "From Large Projects to Case Consultation – Interaction of Alcohol Research and Policy in Finland," *Addiction*, 88, Supplement (1993), 143–50.

[32] Until 1991, taxes accounted for three-fourths of the price of a liter of pure alcohol. While in most countries, taxes are the smallest components of the price of a liter of alcohol, in Sweden and Finland taxes represent more than three to four times the cost of production.

[33] Harold D. Holder, Eckart Kühlhorn, Sturla Nordlund, Esa Österberg, Anders Romelsjö, and Trygve Ugland, *European Integration and Nordic Alcohol Policies: Changes in Alcohol Controls and Consequences in Finland, Norway, and Sweden* (Brookfield, VT: Ashgate, 1998), 175.

[34] Peltonen, "The Problem of Being a Finn," 183; Erik Allardt, "Drinking Norms and Drinking Habits," in E. Allardt, T. Markannen, and M. Takala (eds.), *Drinking and Drinkers* (Stockholm: Almquist & Wiksell, 1958), 7–109.

administrators had to redefine their views on drinking. Prohibition had been a disappointment and demonstrated once and for all that alcohol could not be banned from society. New thinking emerged that alcohol *per se* was not the main concern. Rather it was the lack of inner discipline or moderation that lay at the bottom of all the drinking troubles. The state had to intervene to deal with binge drinking and intoxicated-oriented rituals while drinking itself should not be a policy target. Public campaigns were considered an effective instrument to re-educate Finns to abandon binge drinking and restrictions on price and physical availability would deter impulse buying and excessive consumption.

For a while, it was not clear that education together with restrictions on availability and price could address the predicament of "hard drinking." Some scientists argued that because the racial/biological constitution of the Finnish ethno-linguistic community evolved in virtual isolation from the rest of the world, its genetic composition accentuated certain negative personality traits, among other things binge drinking and violent drunken behavior. However, most academics and policy officials rejected biological determinism and argued for constructive state intervention.[35]

Once the expansion of the welfare state took off, the government established the Finnish Foundation for Alcohol Studies (1950) to promote and coordinate long-term alcohol research and to provide a deeper understanding of how policy can modify behavior and values. In addition, in 1952, Alko set up a research department, the Social Research Institute of Alcohol Studies, which carried out large-scale empirical projects and included programs managed by the Finnish Foundation of Alcohol Studies. Both institutes employed a large number of social scientists and their publications, reports, and pronouncements received wide coverage in the popular press.[36] Scientific studies displaced religious or cultural exhortations and lent credibility to the overall utility of alcohol control policies. Researchers did not directly influence public policy outcomes because few research findings instantly shaped public policy decisions, but scientists corroborated what public opinion already "knew." Nobody explored whether Finland in fact confronted a major public problem of alcohol misuse. It was a "fact," known by all, that Finns could not handle liquor and the truth did not need to be explored, confirmed, and tested. It was well known that Finns had a problematic relationship with alcohol and science simply reinforced this observation.

[35] Matti Peltonen, "Vekande, makt, sociologi: Debatten 1948 mellan Veli Verkko och Pekka Kuusi om 'det finska ölsinnet,'" *Nordisk Alkoholtidskrift*, 8 (1991), 221–37.
[36] Österberg, "Finnish Social Alcohol Research and Alcohol Policy," 64.

Science also explained why all individuals had to endure high prices and availability restrictions even though it became apparent that only a minority of drinkers (only men, and then not every male person) persisted in binge drinking. Doubts about the whole system of controls arose in the late 1970s once beer replaced spirits as the dominant beverage. Could restrictive drinking measures perhaps be relaxed? The official answer was no, and the establishment embraced a new set of policy objectives to ward off criticism and demands for liberalization. The new goal was to reduce harm, a term so broad that it encompassed everything that could possibly be linked to drinking. Scores of studies soon established a connection between drinking and the incidence of alcohol-related injuries, accidents, violence and assaults, death rates, etc. Alcohol researchers applied a theoretical model, originally promoted by the World Health Organization, which established a causal relationship between on the one hand aggregate alcohol consumption and on the other individual drinking behavior and its consequences for society.[37] This theory, called the Total Consumption Model (TCM), became the main justification for the retention of the elaborate system of buyers' controls, in both Finland and Sweden, after 1980.

Until the early 1970s, most researchers argued that the drinking population fell into two distinct groups. By far the largest group consisted of normal recreational drinkers, alongside whom there was a small minority of alcoholics. The aim of public policy had been to regulate the consumption behavior of heavy drinkers, who seemed to include a large proportion of the Finnish male population according to conventional Finnish wisdom. But by the 1970s, it was difficult to argue that the Finnish people engaged in collective alcohol abuse. Alcohol consumption was low, beer had displaced spirits, and binge drinking (among adults) was chiefly associated with spirit consumption. As the 1970s came to a close, Finnish and Swedish researchers paid renewed attention to a previous theory on alcohol consumption, which had not received much publicity in the 1950s when it was first formulated by the French demographer Sully Ledermann.[38] Statistical modeling on the distribution characteristics of the drinking population, first published in the 1950s, revealed that the proportion of alcoholics or problem

---

[37] Kettil Bruun, *Alcohol Control Policies in Public Health Perspective* (Helsinki: Finnish Foundation for Alcohol Studies, 1975). Others added the social interaction/diffusion mechanism in the model. Ole-Jørgen Skog, "Social Interaction and the Distribution of Alcohol Consumption," *Journal of Drug Issues*, 10 (1980), 71–92 and "The Collectivity of Drinking Cultures: A Theory of the Distribution of Alcohol Consumption," *British Journal of Addiction*, 80 (1985), 83–99.

[38] Sully Ledermann, *Alcool, Alcoolisme, Alcoolisation. Données scientifiques de caractère physiologique, économique et social* (Paris: Presses Universitaires de France, 1956).

drinkers in the general population corresponded to the actual level of alcohol consumption per capita. The higher the level of per capita consumption of alcohol, the larger the number of alcoholics in society. The explanation for this phenomenon was that drinking constituted a social activity and the environment in which it took place influenced overall levels of consumption. Individuals adjusted their drinking habits consistent with prevailing social norms. A milieu of non-drinkers inhibits a person with an inclination to drink while a high-consumption culture encourages this same individual to indulge in alcohol.[39]

The discovery of a single-distribution model with its rigid J-like or lognormal shape suggesting that downward shifts in mean consumption should also result in significant declines in the population's proportion of heavy drinkers appeared at a timely moment. As public opinion questioned the restrictive alcohol control policies in the 1970s, the TCM justified the maintenance of some type of control system while it also vindicated a modest degree of relaxation. The normalization of drinking, however, kindled new questions of whether easy access to alcohol was possible. Here, too, scientists found a way to explain why alcohol policy should remain unaltered. Thanks to new population surveys done in the 1980s, it was discovered that the proportion of hard-core drinkers in the general population was ultimately too small to cause much harm to the rest of society. Instead, regular drinkers because of their numerical size caused most of the problems related to alcohol. The finding became known as the "prevention paradox" – because it suggested that rational prevention policy must aim efforts at the general population of modest drinkers because they amassed the greatest aggregate number of alcohol problems.[40] Researchers urged officials to continue to curb the overall alcohol intake because the regular drinking population was responsible for most of the accidents, injuries, violence, and other public risks.[41] Finally, in the 1990s, further studies introduced the idea of statistical profiles, showing that increased alcohol

[39] Bruun *Alcohol Control Policies in Public Health Perspective.*
[40] Norman Kreitman, "Alcohol Consumption and the Preventive Paradox," *British Journal of Addiction*, 81 (1986), 353–63.
[41] Ole-Jørgen Skog, "Drinking and the Distribution of Alcohol Consumption," and "Implications of the Distribution Theory for Drinking and Alcoholism," in David J. Pittman and Helene Raskin White (eds.), *Society, Culture, and Drinking Patterns Reexamined* (New Brunswick, NJ: Rutgers Center of Alcohol Studies, 1991), 135–57, 576–97; Håkan Leifman, *Perspectives on Alcohol Prevention* (Stockholm: Almqvist & Wiksell, 1996); Ron Roizen, "How Does the Nation's 'Alcohol Problem' Change from Era to Era?" in Sarah Tracy and Caroline Acker (eds.), *Altering the American Consciousness: Essays on the History of Alcohol and Drug Use in the United States, 1800–1997* (Amherst: University of Massachusetts Press, 2000).

intake was associated with increasing levels of risk for one or another sort of alcohol-related problem. Again, the conclusion was that even moderate alcohol consumption could have expensive consequences for society and one's health. Scientific studies, academic conferences, and scholarly exchanges disseminated this knowledge and urged state agencies to stick to a regime of restrictions.[42]

Alcohol consumption was modest in Finland and the elaborate system of controls seemed to be increasingly incongruous until, of course, the prevention paradox explicated how modest personal sacrifices served the greater public good. Since tolerance for drinking was already low, many Finnish citizens, acknowledging the risks of substance abuse, put solidarity ahead of personal gratification. They had all the more reason to do so because scientists pointed out that drinking affects everybody. Abstainers can be killed in DUI (driving under the influence) accidents just as mothers have to deal with their drunken teenage children. The harm caused by misusers is unpredictable and everybody can become an innocent victim. Moreover, the research establishment examined closely the impact of drinking frequency and motivation for drinking on social, physical, and economic consequences. Surveys on drinking frequencies and motivation revealed that many Finns continued to drink sporadically in order to get drunk. The official line was that the harm associated with alcohol was magnified if large quantities of liquor were consumed at once. The public policy objective was to teach Finns to assign a different meaning to drinking and alcohol so that intoxication was no longer considered a mark of having a good time. This objective, apparently, unlike the leveling of aggregate consumption, was much harder to achieve.

How should one interpret the academic discussion on drinking styles or boozing and the Total Consumption Model? A cursory glance at some older surveys on drinking preferences seems to suggest that Finland conformed to a Nordic pattern of drinking, also observable in Sweden and Norway, which revolved around spirits. Table 2.1 raises some questions regarding whether the Finnish drinking style deserved the label "peculiar", whether it was worse than what took place in allegedly more "civilized" countries, and how to assess the putative correlation between alcohol consumption and one of the most obvious proxies for alcohol-related harm, cirrhosis of the liver.

As can be seen from the table, spirits were still popular in all three Nordic countries in the mid-1970s. Yet Finnish observers always

[42] Griffith Edwards, *Alcohol Policy and the Public Good* (New York: Oxford University Press, 1994).

Table 2.1 *The relationship between alcohol consumption, dominant beverage and mortality from liver cirrhosis in selected European countries, 1970s*

	Per capita alcohol consumption[a] (liters of ethanol alcohol) 1975	Liver cirrhosis mortality[b] (per 100,000) 1966–80	Dominant beverage[a] (beer, wine, spirits (% of total) 1975
Austria	14.6	39.4	Beer (47)
Belgium	13.9	15.8	Beer (46)
France	22.5	46.4	Wine (72)
FRG	12.4	32.4	Beer (56)
Italy	17.3	43.3	Wine (81)
Netherlands	11.8	6.8	Beer (45) Spirits (39)
Denmark	11.4	12.3	Beer (63)
Finland	9.3	7.3	Spirits (49)
Norway	5.6	5.7	Beer (46) Spirits (43)
Sweden	7.6	11.8	Spirits (49)

[a] Figures from: Phil Davies and Dermot Walsh, *Alcohol Problems and Alcohol Control in Europe* (New York: Gardner Press, 1983). Per capita alcohol consumption per person aged 15 years or older.
[b] Figures from: Mats Ramstedt, "Liver Cirrhosis Mortality in 15 EU Countries," *Nordic Studies on Alcohol and Drugs*, 16 (1999), 57. Liver cirrhosis mortality is calculated per 100,000 population aged 15 and over.

contended that *Finnish people* embraced a highly destructive style of drinking that set them apart from more advanced nations such as Sweden and Norway.[43] The same researchers also added that anti-drinking restrictions were appropriate because binge drinking intensified the deleterious consequences of ethanol alcohol on the body and mind. But the incidence of cirrhosis of the liver, as a proxy for alcohol-related mortality, more or less corresponded with the actual amount of alcohol consumed. Italy and France evolved so-called "civilized" (moderate and integrated) drinking cultures yet their mortality rates of alcohol-induced diseases were indeed substantially higher than in the professedly unciv-ilized vodka belt.

At the same time, a second examination of this table also reveals that it is hazardous to establish a firm correlation between alcohol consumption and liver cirrhosis. For example, Swedish alcohol consumption was lower than that of Finland, yet its mortality rate of cirrhosis of the liver was higher. Since it is difficult to establish a direct cause and effect

[43] Jussi Simpura and Pirjo Paakkanen, "New Beverages, New Drinking Contexts? Signs of Modernization in Finnish Drinking Habits from 1984 to 1992, Compared with Trends in the European Community," *Addiction*, 90 (1995), 674–75.

between drinking and said outcome, public officials in the rest of the EU hesitate to infer an exact relationship between drinking and problems attributed to alcohol and do not so readily rely on the TCM to formulate policy objectives.[44]

It is essential to view the Finnish *debate* on drinking and spirits as a social construction that hides a host of other concerns, which are subsumed under the label of intoxication-oriented drinking. There is a general fear of substance misuse that also colors much of the Swedish debate on alcohol (and drugs). All Nordic cultures (except for the Danes) distrust the ability of the average person to control his/her appetites for toxic and addictive substances. It could be that the Nordic mentality, being introvert and taciturn, requires a generous dose of alcohol to ease social communication. Having lived for centuries in isolated agrarian communities, the Finnish and Swedish peoples never mastered the fine art of superficial geniality. Customary Nordic melancholy assigned a negative meaning to demonstrations of outward emotions, all of which depress conviviality. In addition, aside from Nordic introversion, Finnish people have this vague sense of unease that they, in contrast to older more established nations, are immature, impulsive, and inconsiderate. Freed of all restraint, they will drink themselves to death and cause much destruction to themselves and others.

The impact of alcohol control policies

Already in the 1970s, social scientists observed a decline in "conflict-prone drunken comportment." But the same social scientists quickly added that "all attempts to remold basic patterns of drinking have more or less failed."[45] This referred to the typical Finnish habit of periodic bouts of heavy drinking. Researchers urged vigilance and a continuation of strict control policies curbing the availability of alcohol to prevent excessive drinking.[46] Yet the drinking habits of the Finnish population have changed remarkably since the 1960s and alcohol control policies

---

[44] Håkan Leifman, "The Preventive Paradox in Light of Problems of Self-Reported Alcohol-Related Behavior," in Leifman, *Perspectives on Alcohol Prevention*, 1–21. For recent criticism of TCM, Jürgen Rehm, "Draining the Ocean to Prevent Shark Attacks?" *Nordic Studies on Alcohol and Drugs*, 16 (1999), 46–54.

[45] Mäkelä et al., "Drink in Finland," 54–55.

[46] Esa Österberg, "The Relationship between Alcohol Consumption Patterns and the Harmful Consequences of Drinking," in Martin Plant, Cees Goos, Wolfram Kemp and Esa Österberg (eds.), *Alcohol and Drugs* (Edinburgh: Edinburgh University Press, 1990), 82–92.

unquestionably work in stabilizing overall alcohol consumption at low levels and in preventing related fatalities, injuries, accidents, and diseases.

In 1948, distilled liquor accounted for 80 percent of the total structure of pure alcohol consumption.[47] In 1982, the consumption of strong liquor had dropped to 40 percent of the total structure of alcohol consumption and this was down to less than 25 percent in 1999. Wine is not very popular and its total share in the structure of alcohol consumption is 20 percent. But beer accounts for more than 50 percent of pure alcohol consumed. The trend away from spirits is permanent because young consumers favor beer and wine over spirits. If vodka played the role of social lubricant and induced intoxicating drinking rituals, Alko and affiliated research establishments succeeded beyond their wildest dreams. Beer is now the favorite alcoholic beverage although rowdy behavior resulting from binge drinking has not diminished.[48]

Another way of assessing the success of decades of alcohol control policies is to compare absolute alcohol consumption per capita. Registered annual consumption of pure alcohol was 6.7 liters per capita in 1996. France recorded an annual consumption of 11.5 liters per capita, Portugal registered 11 liters per capita and Germany consumed annually 10 liters of pure alcohol per person in 1996. Sweden stood at 4.7 liters of pure alcohol in 1996. Adding unrecorded consumption to the official figures, Finnish and Swedish per capita consumption rises by 30 percent, which still places them behind wine-drinking countries.[49] Drinking restrictions existed alongside strict laws against drinking to intoxication. In both Sweden and Finland, the law metes out high penalties for driving under the influence of alcohol and drunken driving is considered a major violation. Here, too, the law has been successful in altering people's behavior.

Although alcohol control policies work by curbing the actual intake of alcohol in the population and by modifying drinking styles, alcohol consumption in Finland has steadily risen over the years. In the 1950s, per capita consumption of pure alcohol was 1.7 liters.[50] Alcohol consumption rose after Alko opened outlets in the countryside and after the legislation of the Medium Beer and Alcohol Act (1969). In addition, as

---

[47] Österberg, "Finnish Social Alcohol Research and Alcohol Policy," 61.
[48] See the article from June 15, 1999 at http://virtual.finland.fi//news/index.html.
[49] Edwards, *Alcohol Policy and the Public Good*, 10.
[50] Österberg, "Finland," 113. The strict controls in the 1950s generated large illicit alcohol production. It was estimated that the actual consumption of alcohol per capita was anywhere between 20 and 40 percent higher. In the 1960s, unrecorded consumption fell to 10 percent.

the moral stigma on drinking faded, more women began to drink wine and beer.[51]

The upward trend in alcohol consumption highlights a critical ingredient without which the whole package of rules and measures to curb alcohol consumption loses its effectiveness. Attitudes and expectations determine the success of alcohol control policy. If individuals accept the ideology and normative values of the alcohol control regime, then it will accomplish its main goal of limiting alcohol consumption. But obedience or compliance itself cannot be enforced by limiting the opening hours of a liquor store or by keeping the retail price of liquor sky high. Rather, consumers must accept the restrictions as true barriers and modify their behavior accordingly. Prosperity has lowered the price elasticity of alcohol because well-heeled middle-class households may still buy costly wines in large quantities.[52] What matters, therefore, more than high excise taxes is whether people believe in the objectives of the policy. Here, Finland has seen a subtle reorientation. Certainly, wine and beer have lost their moral taint in contrast to spirits, which are still perceived with suspicion because of their strong association with binge drinking and intoxication. Nevertheless, in the 1990s, Finnish drinking culture and values moved closer to a Continental model and began to shed some of their specific Nordic qualities.

Conclusion

Anti-alcohol mentality, giving rise to prohibition and alcohol control policy, reflected several major trends and evolutions in Finnish history. Socio-economic pressures in the agrarian economy brought a flood of rural workers into the towns, seeking solace with temperance societies and labor organizations. The banning of home distilling turned many impoverished peasants against manufactured spirits and persuaded dislocated agrarian workers and rural craftsmen to rally around prohibition. Finnish nationalists seized on prohibition as a weapon to oppose the annexation by the Russian Czarist regime and to carve out greater autonomy for the dependent territory. The political left used prohibition and anti-drinking campaigns to bridge the gap between the townships and countryside as social groups tied to diverse local economic structures none the less shared common anti-alcohol views. Alcohol and drinking shaped the constitution of modern Finnish identity. This link

---

[51] Simpura and Paakkanen, "New Beverages, New Drinking Contexts," 674. Whereas 27 percent of surveyed women abstained from alcohol in 1984, the proportion declined to 18 percent in 1992.

[52] Edwards, *Alcohol Policy and the Public Good*, 117.

was further tightened after Finnish intellectuals sought to understand why alcohol and the Finnish population did not mix well. They focused on the putative underdevelopment of Finnish culture and the tendency of the lower classes to turn violent after a few drinks. Common folks, trying to comprehend why they opposed alcohol, absorbed the explanatory framework of the educated elite and expressed a large measure of distrust and apprehension with regards to easy access to alcohol. In the absence of self-control, the state had a duty to impose discipline from above. Coalitions of social democratic and agrarian parties endorsed universal measures to deal with individual failings in order to avoid the stigmatization of vulnerable members of society.

Over time, the moral outrage against manufactured spirits, public intoxication, and drinking in general lessened. Social institutions and researchers increasingly highlighted the public health aspect of alcohol policy intervention and in the process normalized drinking and lifted the moral burden off the drinker. The socio-medical discourse injected new life into anti-drinking regulations and posited a fresh objective of lowering aggregate alcohol consumption. The individual was no longer responsible for his or her actions as most of the attention went to the victim of someone else's drinking. The rhetoric of the deviant drinker was replaced by a discourse on the plight of innocent bystanders who became victims of somebody else's thoughtless actions.

In 1994, on the eve of accession to the European Union, public opinion had already undergone a substantial shift in that table wines and beer were no longer considered risky substances. Distilled spirits continued to be regarded with deep suspicion and strict regulation of their trade and consumption was generally accepted. But the younger generation, born during the first wave of liberalization in the late 1960s, increasingly viewed themselves as capable of handling a glass of wine or beer. At the same time, urban and young Finns are less inhibited by a culture that appreciates introversion and passivity, and are less likely to rely on alcohol to ease interpersonal communication. Self-assured educated Finns no longer buy into the stereotype of the backward uncouth Finn who cannot handle liquor and see themselves as being more in tune with wine-drinking, cultured Europeans. Perceptions of self and collective ideas began to assimilate non-Nordic ideas on drinking with the result that a gap emerged between public attitudes to alcohol and elite preferences. Once Finland joined the European Union, questions arose on the legal compatibility of the alcohol monopoly company and anti-trade discrimination rules set by Community law. This discussion led to fresh scrutiny of the unique style of Finnish drinking habits and opened the way for future steps towards liberalization.

3   Our greatest social problem: anti-alcohol policy in Sweden

A good society, according to Nordic definitions, checks human passions that produce drunkenness, lewdness, and rituals of anti-social behavior. A society that fails to civilize its members confronts self-centered hedonism. Married to a strong belief in social engineering, successive generations of elected officials endeavored to minimize the consumption of alcohol and to ban recreational drug-taking. Sweden, like Finland, was part of the vodka-belt and occasions of sociability were often an excuse to get extremely drunk. For more than a century, this style of drinking provoked little concern although distilled spirits were the subject of a lengthy political struggle between the Swedish monarchy and the peasantry. But the bone of contention was the discretionary right to impose excise taxes on distilled liquor and to sell surplus spirits. The Swedish monarchy depended on alcohol taxes to finance its budget and repeatedly tried to take away from the peasant communities the right to produce and sell vodka. In 1824, the monarchy admitted defeat and the production, sale, and distribution of spirits fell into private hands.[1] By the 1850s, according to the official historiography of Swedish drinking, the nation was succumbing to permanent drunkenness, as each man, woman, and child was said to consume as much as 46 liters of *brännvin* or Swedish vodka per year, which was the equivalent of nearly half a liter of pure alcohol per week.[2] Other figures cited the annual production of 22 million gallons of pure alcohol for a population of 3 million.[3]

Rather suddenly, drinking rituals, which dated from the introduction of spirits in Sweden in the eighteenth century, became a major concern in the late nineteenth century. After 1945, drinking continued to be a

---

[1] Klaus Mäkelä and Matti Viikari, "Notes on Alcohol and the State," *Acta Sociologica*, 20 (1977), 170–72.

[2] Ministry of Health and Social Affairs, *The Swedish Alcohol Policy: Caring about People's Health* (Stockholm: Ministry of Health and Social Affairs, 1993), 2; SOU, *Svensk alkoholpolitik – bakgrund och nuläge* (Stockholm: SOU/Socialdepartementet, 1994), 10.

[3] Jean-Charles Sournia, *A History of Alcoholism*, trans. Nick Handley and Gareth Stanton (Cambridge, MA: Basil Blackwell, 1990), 44.

serious issue although the terms of the discourse moved away from moral depravity to social scientific and socio-medical concepts. Nevertheless, until well into the postwar period, in the matter of alcohol every Swede was guilty until proven innocent.[4]

On the one hand, Sweden and Finland share many traits and characteristics that point to a common drinking past and definition of alcohol use/abuse. Swedish temperance activists focused on intoxication-oriented drinking rituals and evangelical Protestant groups were the first to rally against public intoxication and binge drinking. The emerging Swedish labor movement aligned itself with the anti-alcohol front in order to elevate the standard and quality of living of the laboring classes, and coupled prohibition to political reforms of an archaic political system since "the people" would overwhelmingly vote for a ban on liquor. Swedish organized labor, like its Finnish counterpart, saw a transparent connection between anti-alcohol sentiments in the countryside, an emerging working class in the timber and iron-ore industries, and political emancipation.

On the other hand, as this chapter will demonstrate, there are small yet significant differences between the evolutions of the Swedish and Finnish temperance movements and drinking myths. First, in contrast to the Finnish movement, Swedish temperance organizations succeeded in remaining separate and independent from political organizations and, after the disappearance of the moral stigma against drinking, focused heavily on adult education programs, recreation clubs, youth programs, safe driving programs, insurance companies for non-drinkers, and public campaigns against drugs and alcohol. Second, the Swedish medical community, which was regularly recruited to advise and consult with policy officials, fully embraced restrictive drinking rules and became one of their most persistent defenders. By contrast, in Finland, social scientists carried out most of the research on alcohol dependency and formed a much more heterogeneous community, which did not command the same kind of authority and respect as medical researchers and which was willing to examine the underlying beliefs of alcohol research.

Third, the structure of the state liquor monopoly system differed, with consequences for the push for liberalization in the 1990s. Swedish officials in 1917 decided to create two different state companies to meet two different goals: retailing and production. The state retail monopoly

[4] Attesting to the continued ambivalence towards drinking and intoxication is a sign, found in kitchens, bars, and pubs: "All alcohol consumption is strictly prohibited in this room, except when fish is served. All food except sausage is considered to be fish. Should sausage be served by accident it might also be considered fish."

(Systembolaget) has remained loyal to the old temperance ideology and faithfully alerts consumers to the manifold dangers of alcohol. Vin och Sprit, the state alcohol production company, transmuted into an aggressive market-conscious corporation and engineered the international success of Absolut vodka. In Finland, production, import/export, and retail were housed in the same company with the result that production, with its stress on profitability, brand recognition, and international market expansion, came to dominate the outlook and direction of the entire state monopoly company.

Finally, alcohol control policies in Finland were repeatedly legitimized on the grounds that Finns were backward and uncivilized and hence gravitated towards destructive drinking habits. But the cultural context of Swedish alcohol control policies cannot be traced to a national inferiority complex. Rather, attitudes towards drinking were molded by Christian evangelical ideas, which were then incorporated into the election platform and ideology of the Social Democratic Party. The latter embraced anti-alcohol legislation because it aptly coincided with its own ambitions to improve the lot of the less fortunate. Temperance ideology and social democracy also found common territory in their joint preference for a solidaristic state solution in order to refrain from singling out vulnerable individuals and subgroups in society. In Sweden, therefore, alcohol misuse was mainly a social problem and the treatment of individual deviancy (drinking) was in the interest of the community. Because the community suffered because of non-conformity (i.e. drinking), collective remedies were seen as an appropriate response. Since the mid-1990s, the problem of drinking has taken on a more public health hue in order to convince the European Union to leave the Systembolaget alone. The social aspects are subsequently downplayed.

A detour: why no restrictive drinking measures in Denmark?

At this point, it seems timely to ask why Denmark does not fit the Nordic pattern of alcohol regulation and does not display the typical Nordic obsession with a loss of self-control. While Sweden and Finland (and Norway) embraced a dry alcohol culture, Denmark's was wet. Although Danes drink more alcohol than the Swedes (10 liters of pure alcohol per capita per annum as opposed to the Swedes' 5), Danish coalition governments do not care deeply about alcohol. Yet Denmark shares, at first blush, many things in common with its northern neighbors. So why no history of alcohol control policy in Denmark?

The first difference is that "Anglo-American revivalism," i.e. Methodist and Baptist missionary organizations and Quaker groups, made little headway in Denmark. These dissenting churches formed the backbone of the international temperance movement. More so than other branches of Christianity, the anti-establishment Protestant organizations were obsessed with individual moral responsibility for personal behavior and the loss of self-control in a society with few moral strictures and external control mechanisms. The Danish revivalist movement, by contrast, was pietistic and Lutheran and actually opposed the whole concept of individual self-improvement to achieve salvation. It discouraged attempts to change one's life via concrete action since such activities disclosed a lack of faith.[5] For this reason, the temperance movement never became as strong or consistent in Denmark as in the other Nordic countries. It never entered the mainstream, remaining isolated and therefore unable to sway public opinion. In 1918, after decades of temperance activism, only 15 percent of Danish parishes were dry in contrast to 91 percent of the Finnish ones (in 1900).[6]

A second contrast with Finland and Sweden is the emergence of beer drinking and the political clout of privately owned brewery companies. Inventions in mass manufacturing occasioned the rise of large brewery companies, which joined the debate on temperance by claiming that they intended to "save the Danes" from distilled spirits. They sided with the temperance movement to combat drinking and drunkenness, but repeatedly extolled the wholesomeness of good Danish beer, representative of patriotism and democracy. Beer, they claimed, had been part of Danish culture since antiquity. When conservative landowners in the late nineteenth century sought to impose taxes on strong beer, private brewers formed an alliance with liberal farmers to agitate against this measure. Their opposition to the beer tax was dressed in patriotic language and they drew a clear distinction between distilled liquor, a real evil, and the fine Danish tradition of roadside inns, Danish hospitality, and Danish civilized drinking habits. Despite their opposition, parliament passed a beer tax on strong beer (alcohol content of 2.25 percent and over) in 1892, which split the temperance movement into two, with the majority of local societies permitting the consumption of weak, untaxed beer.[7]

---

[5] Sidsel Eriksen, "Drunken Danes and Sober Swedes? Religious Revivalism and the Temperance Movements as Keys to Danish and Swedish Folk Cultures," in Bo Stråth (ed.), *Language and the Construction of Class Identities. The Struggle for Discursive Power in Social Organization* (Gothenburg: University of Gothenburg Press, 1990), 55–94.

[6] Ernest Hurst Cherrington, *Standard Encyclopedia of the Alcohol Problem* (6 vols., Westerville, OH: American Issue Publishing, 1925–30), vol. III, 793, 991.

[7] Sidsel Eriksen, "The Making of the Danish Liberal Drinking Style: The Construction of a 'Wet' Alcohol Discourse in Denmark," *Contemporary Drug Problems*, 20 (1993), 1–30.

In 1917, the Danish government issued a spirit tax, which raised the retail price of liquor by a factor of ten (a liter of schnapps rose from 0.90 to 11 kroner). Therefore, a third difference with Sweden and Finland was the sudden disappearance of spirit drinking after World War I. Supposedly, the tax preserved precious grain for export to Germany. Just as likely, legislators finally succumbed to the demands of brewery companies since the immediate result of the high spirit tax was that people switched to beer. Since beer contained considerably less alcohol, total alcohol consumption dropped. In addition, Denmark sold its colonies in the West Indies to the USA and the price of rum increased sharply. Altogether, per capita consumption of alcohol fell by 75 percent within two years. After World War II, the consumption of strong beer rose and alcohol consumption increased dramatically but by that time the temperance movement had more or less disappeared.[8]

The Danish workers' movement was concerned about the threat of alcohol to the welfare of the working class. It loudly condemned "beer capitalists," who persuaded workers to spend hard-earned money on liquor. The solution according to the Danish labor movement was to establish a cooperative beer brewery (*Stjernen*) and to implore workers to buy this worthy competitor of Carlsberg or Tuborg beer.[9] In Sweden and Finland, by contrast, the drinking habits of the lower classes led to calls for prohibition.

These cultural, social, and lifestyle differences between Denmark and the other Nordic countries gave rise to the stereotype of the "merry Dane," standing in sharp contrast to the "sober Swede." In the 1990s, the population of Denmark consumed more alcohol and had a higher rate of alcohol-related mortality and morbidity. None the less, official channels and society are less concerned about drinking because alcohol has no specific cultural meanings. Heavy drinking is not singled out as a special activity or a serious social problem and alcoholic beverages are integrated in daily routines with most drinking taking place during mealtimes or just before or after meals.[10]

All three differences – weak evangelical Protestant churches, powerful private brewery companies, and the decline of spirit drinking – must be

---

[8] Peter Schiøler, "Denmark," in Dwight B. Heath (ed.), *International Handbook on Alcohol and Culture* (Westport, CT: Greenwood Press, 1995), 54; Esa Österberg, "Do Alcohol Prices Affect Consumption and Related Problems?" in Harold D. Holder and Griffith Edwards (eds.), *Alcohol and Public Policy: Evidence and Issues* (New York: Oxford University Press, 1995), 152.

[9] Eriksen, "Drunken Danes and Sober Swedes?" 88.

[10] Jussi Simpura, Herman Fahrenkrug, Marita Hyttinen, and Thorkil Thorsen, "Drinking, Everyday Life Situations and Cultural Norms in Denmark, Finland, and West Germany," *Journal of Drug Issues*, 20 (1990), 403–16.

analyzed in light of Denmark's strong liberal tradition and its corresponding firm respect for civil liberties. Early introduction of mass production, the existence of a liberal farming class, the emergence of powerful private companies (Carlsberg and Tuborg), and numerous small towns and cities undermined the general appeal of a "tempered" lifestyle. The liberal legacy of Denmark (like that of the Netherlands) bequeathed an aversion to interference in private life and to curbs on individual self-management.[11] The Danish community like that of the Netherlands stresses individualism and accountability in contrast to the Finnish and Swedish preoccupation with the maintenance of order.[12]

A century of Swedish anti-alcohol activism and debate

Sweden's new constitution of 1809 gave every citizen the right to distill and sell alcohol, and stimulated rising alcohol consumption and public drunkenness. Public authorities tried to outlaw public drunkenness and disorderly conduct and various decrees imposed ever harsher punishment on the lower classes if found drunk. Finally, in 1855, the monarchy banned the private distillation of spirits and production was concentrated in larger units, which could be more easily taxed. Licenses for town distilleries were sold and many municipal governments also tried to control public drinking by creating a private monopoly on off-premise sales. Profits were limited to a certain amount and any excess profits went to the municipal government. Although public drinking, intoxication, and spirits were an important target of local and national control in the nineteenth century, the struggle was more *over* than *against* alcohol as different interests tried to seize control over the liquor revenues and taxation. The spirit reform bill of 1855 was not so much in reaction to temperance activities as an attempt to rationalize taxation and introduce modern manufacturing methods in the production of spirits.[13]

Until 1921, the Swedish political system denied the vast majority of society political participation. Because the formal political system was closed off to 80 percent of the adult male population, voluntary associations began to emerge after the 1840s to form a new civil society

---

[11] Schiøler, "Denmark," 61.
[12] Salme Ahlström-Laakso, "European Drinking Habits: A Review of Research and Some Suggestions for Conceptual Integration of Findings," in Michael W. Everett, Jack O. Waddell, and Dwight B. Heath (eds.), *Cross-Cultural Approaches to the Study of Alcohol* (The Hague: Mouton, 1973), 128–29.
[13] Jan Blomqvist, "The 'Swedish Model' of Dealing with Alcohol Problems: Historical Trends and Future Challenges," *Contemporary Drug Problems*, 25 (1998), 255–58; Karin Nyberg and Peter Allebeck, "Sweden," in Heath (ed.), *International Handbook on Alcohol and Culture*, 280–88.

in which individuals could vent their expectations, frustrations, and need for greater participation in social and political life. All movements provided alongside a common vision numerous social and political activities and the age of popular movements saw the rise of the free church movement, temperance and later teetotaler societies, and the labor movement. Between 1850 and 1920, Swedish society underwent dramatic transformation. Urbanization rose rapidly and the population living in towns increased from 10 to 50 percent. The population itself rose from 3.5 to 5.9 million. Employment in agriculture declined and that in industry and handicrafts increased. Literacy rates improved. In this long period of modernization, popular movements thrived. They concentrated resources in a new leadership to speak up for the mass of excluded citizens and fought to influence the direction of society. Many members and sympathizers belonged to the lower social strata and inhabited parishes in which a mixture of agricultural and industrial activities took place.[14]

The temperance movement of the 1850s was strongly influenced by the example of American and English Baptist, Methodist, and Pentecostal faiths, which condemned excessive pursuit of pleasures, including drinking. At first, local leaders of the temperance societies urged "moderation" because they themselves were not opposed to an occasional glass of wine and only called for abstinence from schnapps. In 1845 the temperance movement counted approximately 100,000 individual members and over 400 member associations. It employed "petitions" to gather the population in support of a ban on distilled spirits and to pressure the king to intervene in the liquor trade. The early temperance movement was not very effective, in part because of a huge social distance between followers and the leadership. Mainly, the rural underclass joined a local temperance association while the leadership came from the established rural upper class.

In 1879, in Gothenburg, the International Order of Good Templars (IOGT) was founded. This new teetotaler movement displaced the earlier temperance societies and agitated for a total ban on drinking and alcohol. It differed from the older temperance societies in several important respects. First, the teetotaling movement attracted a much more diverse membership and coupled a total ban on liquor to an ambitious program of social and political reform. Second, the teetotaler societies aggressively promoted a new civic morality that identified abstinence with personal integrity and virtue. Increasingly, teetotalism became identified with honesty, impartiality, and respect, and many

[14] Sven Lundkvist, "The Popular Movements in Swedish Society, 1850–1920," *Scandinavian Journal of History*, 5 (1980), 219–38.

elected officials declared themselves teetotalers in order to establish their public credentials. Third, as in Finland, the teetotaler movement expressed much greater concern for the strain experienced by agrarian communities facing the arrival of the timber/forestry and iron-ore/steel industries.

The broad agenda of the teetotalers listed measures to address various social issues alongside drinking and the ban of spirits. The fledgling Social Democratic Party formed a fruitful alliance with the teetotaler movement as both strove for a more democratic and just society. The teetotaler movement also appealed to liberals, who on the one hand renounced the social agenda of coupling prohibition to general suffrage yet on the other recognized drinking to be a major scourge and an impediment to the construction of a more productive nation.[15] Eventually, the national umbrella organization – the International Order of Good Templars (Swedish Grand Lodge) – fell apart as the workers' branch adopted the slogan "a sober proletariat is what the ruling class fears."[16] But all the branches of the IOGT focused on practical social issues such as assistance to widows and orphaned children, and ran study circles and folk high schools.

While teetotaler societies represented a broad swathe of society, the authorities were resistant to the idea of prohibition because of its fiscal consequences. The tax on spirits brought in between 12 and 20 percent of state revenues between the 1860s and 1914.[17] In the 1850s, the Swedish monarchy decided to grant each town a monopoly to sell liquor. Local authorities issued liquor licenses to retail establishments and the earnings, plus tax on spirits, financed poor relief projects. Towns and central bureaucracies absolutely resisted a total ban on drinking out of fear of losing critical tax revenues. In view of the local government's defiance, teetotaler activists directed their attention to the state in order to persuade parliament to approve of the local veto to ban alcohol from Sweden. A parliamentary act would then allow local residents of each town to decide whether the town should be dry or not. Since public support for prohibition was high, the local veto would quickly result in a ban on alcohol throughout Sweden. Social democratic supporters also endorsed the municipal veto because they hoped to undermine the entrenched privileges of the upper class, which domi-nated local government by virtue of the fact that property taxes deter-

---

[15] Michele Micheletti, *Civil Society and State Relations in Sweden* (Brookfield, VT: Avebury, 1995), 45.

[16] Micheletti, *Civil Society and State Relations*, 37.

[17] Per Frånberg, "Den svenska supen," in Kettil Bruun and Per Frånberg (eds.), *Den svenska supen: en historia om brännvin, bratt, och byrkrati* (Stockholm: Prisma, 1985), p. 16, table 3.

mined voting rights.[18] In the end, the Upper Chamber repeatedly defeated the local veto option.

While local authorities were unsure how to appease the growing teetotaler movement without losing their fiscal base, the city of Gothenburg stumbled upon a neat solution that served the twin goals of lowering alcohol consumption while preserving tax revenues. Gothenburg replaced working-class pubs with private monopolies for off-premise sales of alcohol. The municipality licensed the semi-public companies and excess profits on the liquor sales disappeared into local government coffers. The main effect of the semi-public retail monopolies was to increase the price of liquor and to destroy public drinking venues, which especially attracted the patronage of the lower classes. The city also created a list of people who were not allowed to buy alcohol because of previous episodes of public intoxication and the shop personnel were supposed to consult these lists. The creation of semi-public retail stores, run by local business leaders, was such a fiscal and social success that the "Gothenburg" system was legislated throughout Sweden in 1905.[19]

During the 1909 labor strike, the teetotaler movement organized an unofficial referendum to gather a petition in favor of banning all alcoholic beverages except for light beer. An impressive 56 percent of adult men and women signed the petition. The teetotaler movement soon counted 450,000 members or 5 percent of the Swedish population. This was the high point of the teetotaler movement and the Social Democratic Party, swept away by the enthusiasm for prohibition, pledged to legislate a statutory ban on alcohol in its party program in 1911.[20] Because teetotalism was a sign of honesty and respect, 144 of the Riksdag's 230 members were self-declared teetotalers in 1911. Over the next years, the proportion of parliamentary teetotalers rose further yet the Upper Chamber repeatedly struck down anti-liquor legislation.

At first, labor leaders publicly condemned the private companies licensed to run liquor stores in various cities as "alcohol capitalists," and proposed a lifestyle of self-improvement and abstinence. However, although the Social Democratic Party inserted the pro-prohibition clause in its program in 1911, the party leadership was ambivalent about the utility of banning liquor from society.[21] The Riksdag faction

[18] Blomqvist, "The 'Swedish Model' of Dealing with Alcohol Problems," 258.
[19] Marquis Childs, *Sweden: The Middle Way* (New Haven, NJ: Yale University Press, 1939), 104.
[20] Hans Lindblad and Sven Lundkvist, *Tusen nyktra: 100 år med riksdagens nykterhetsgrupper* (Stockholm: Sober, 1996).
[21] Per Frånberg, "The Social and Political Significance of Two Swedish Restrictive Systems," *Contemporary Drug Problems*, 12 (1985), 56.

changed its mind after the trade unions mentioned the social costs of closing down bottle factories, distilleries, and breweries and of ruining the catering/tourist industry. In 1920, the Social Democratic Party reformulated its stance on prohibition to leave open whether it would support prohibition or not. In 1922, the referendum on prohibition was finally held. It was defeated by a razor slim margin of 51 percent against and 49 percent for prohibition. It failed because Ivan Bratt (1878–1956), a physician and politician, had proposed in 1916 an alternative to prohibition that would conserve the state's fiscal base yet curb alcohol consumption and reduce public intoxication.[22] As both the left and liberal temperance activists accepted Bratt's middle ground, the passion for banning alcohol from society faded.

Bratt system: 1917–1955

In contrast to many ardent teetotalers, Bratt regarded the alcoholic not as depraved but rather as a weak person. Inordinate drinking was the mark of being unable to set limits. Drinking itself was not the problem; rather it was *excessive* drinking, which spurred human degradation and threatened the nation's productivity. Bratt argued that prohibition was not the solution because it would provoke large-scale bootlegging and could in fact increase the incidence of alcoholism.[23] Rather, building upon the success of the Gothenburg model, he sought to entrust the sale of alcohol to a disinterested party, which derived no extra benefits from the promotion of drinking and eliminated once and for all the private profit motive from the alcohol trade. Education and information under the supervision of municipal temperance boards should teach people how to handle liquor, a lesson that most folks would easily absorb.[24] Each person had to apply for a liquor register, which recorded all purchases, and each register holder could only purchase alcohol up to a personal limit of at the most 4 liters of spirits/aquavit per month (lowered to 3 liters in 1941). No limits were set on beer and wine although their purchases were recorded in the register (*motbok*).[25] All 122 system companies issued registers and local notables (often tee-totalers) made their decision on whether individual applications for a

---

[22] Sven Lundkvist, "Popular Movements and Reforms," in Steven Koblik (ed.), *Sweden's Development from Poverty to Affluence 1750–1970* (Minneapolis: University of Minnesota Press, 1975), 177–93.

[23] Svante Nycander, "Ivan Bratt: The Man who Saved Sweden from Prohibition," *Addiction*, 93 (1998), 17–26.

[24] Pia Rosenqvist, "Nykterhetsnämnderna," in Bruun and Frånberg (eds.), *Den svenska supen*, 163–73.

[25] SOU, *Svensk alkoholpolitik – bakgrund och nuläge*, 14–16.

register were successful and on the upper limit to be applied on each person's register based on proof of one's good moral standing. Marital status, profession, and reputation influenced the decision as to how much alcohol a household/person could purchase.[26]

Increasingly after World War II the Bratt system was seen as contrary to individual and civil liberty.[27] Its class and gender biases were increasingly out of step with new public standards and expectations. Unmarried women were permitted to buy perhaps one liter of liquor *per year*, while married women did not possess a register because only one was issued per household. The design of the system also discriminated against working-class households because tax brackets were increasingly employed to determine alcohol limits.[28] Spirits were also rationed in restaurants, which could serve liquor only at certain times of the day, and only with a meal. Many municipalities had no sales outlet for alcohol at all and prohibited restaurants from serving liquor. Three expert committees with a fair number of teetotaler members therefore proposed to disband the Bratt system to address the inequities of the system, and recommended a steep price increase coupled with restrictions on the opening hours of liquor outlets to curb drinking.[29]

Post-Bratt system: the creation of Systembolaget

The 1955 Temperance Act created the Swedish Alcohol Retailing Monopoly, Systembolaget, or for short, Systemet, which was forged from all the individual system companies. The new corporation was the sole legitimate retail distributor of spirits, wine, and strong beer. It also had a monopoly on the sale of spirits, wine, and imported strong beer to establishments licensed to serve alcoholic beverages. Swedish breweries could sell directly to restaurants. The 1955 Temperance Act laid down that "the sale of alcohol shall be managed in such a way that injuries are prevented as far as possible." Therefore, until recently, the state liquor store advertised alcohol-free wines in its display windows and its national motto was *spola kröken* or, in plain English, "flush it [liquor] down the toilet." It advised shoppers not to abuse their bodies with

---

[26] Kettil Bruun and Lennart Nilsson, "Folkets protester," in Bruun and Frånberg (eds.), *Den svenska supen*, 229–62; Childs, *Sweden: The Middle Way*, 111.

[27] Per Frånberg and Ilpo Koskikallio, "Regionala och lokala varianter," in Bruun and Frånberg (eds.), *Den svenska supen*, 263–86; Frånberg, "The Social and Political Significance of Two Swedish Restrictive Systems," 53–62.

[28] Kettil Bruun, "Kön och klass," in Bruun and Frånberg (eds.), *Den svenska supen*, 298–317.

[29] Nycander, "Ivan Bratt: The Man who Saved Sweden from Prohibition," 21; Blomqvist, "The 'Swedish Model' of Dealing with Alcohol Problems," 268–69.

alcohol and customers were forced to stand in line to place an order with a sales clerk who had to walk to the backroom to pick up the selected beverages. Sales or promotions on liquor were non-existent and the decor of the state monopoly was stark and functional. Initially, the establishment still worried about alcoholics and the problems they were likely to cause if they had unrestricted access to liquor. Systembolaget kept a list with names of known alcoholics and its sales personnel were supposed to ask for identification and then consult the list of names to check whether the buyer should be refused alcohol. Since many System-bolaget employees were negligent and forgot to check the list or to request identification, in 1963 the board of directors decided to install in every store a red light that flashed at regular intervals, at which point the personnel would ask for identification. In this fashion, the personal humiliation was minimized and the task of the sales clerk was eased.[30] In 1977, after complaints about slow and patronizing service, the red light gadget was removed and the blacklist of known alcoholics was phased out.[31]

In the 1990s, many Swedish residents expressed their frustration with the slow service, the long lines on Friday afternoons, and limited opening hours. Nevertheless, Systembolaget resisted the idea of self-service because it was predicted that this would raise turnover by 10 percent if buyers no longer needed to give their order to a clerk.[32] But customer dissatisfaction and complaints forced Systembolaget to convert some large busy stores into self-service. To compensate for the inconveniences of slow services and limited opening hours, System-bolaget began to build a huge inventory of the world's best wines and trained its personnel to become wine connoisseurs. In 1996, System-bolaget had 395 shops and 500 "local agencies" in thinly populated areas. It stocked more than 2,600 brands of alcoholic beverages from dozens of countries. Of course, the prices were and still are exorbitant and a drink at a restaurant can cost a small fortune.[33]

---

[30] Michael Elmer, the Danish advocate-general at the European Court of Justice, published an extremely critical report on Systembolaget in March 1997 and judged the monopoly in conflict with Community law. Many Swedish officials maintained that he held a grudge against Systembolaget because he had been caught by a red light in the 1970s. Humiliated, he took his revenge, according to these sources, by writing a scathing report on Swedish alcohol policy.

[31] Harold Holder, Eckart Kühlhorn, Sturla Nordlund, Esa Österberg, Anders Romelsjö, and Trygve Ugland, *European Integration and Nordic Alcohol Policies: Changes in Alcohol Controls and Consequences in Finland, Norway, and Sweden* (Brookfield, VT: Ashgate, 1998), 83.

[32] Griffith Edwards, *Alcohol Policy and the Public Good* (New York: Oxford University Press, 1994), 132.

[33] Lowest priced wine in an excellent restaurant in 1998 was 230 SEK a bottle. A bottle of

The post-Bratt regime continued to eliminate all private interests from the alcohol trade, with only the brewing industry remaining in private hands.[34] The state monopoly distillery, Vin och Sprit (V&S), founded by Ivan Bratt in 1917, produced the favorite national drink, *brännvin*. V&S was also the only company permitted to import alcoholic beverages with the exception of ordinary beer; the latter could be imported by a beer wholesaler. V&S also controlled the wholesale distribution of spirits, wine, and foreign strong beer and enjoyed an absolute monopoly on the exportation of spirits and wine. It exported 46 million liters of Absolut vodka in 1995.[35] Since Sweden produces no local wines, practically all the wine sold in Systembolaget was imported by V&S, which often bought in bulk and bottled the wines in Sweden.

As soon as the Bratt system was phased out, consumption rose by 25 percent during the first two years and remained close to around 5 liters of pure alcohol per person per annum in the early 1960s. Over the years, various experiments were run that oscillated between greater and lesser relaxation of restrictions and availability of alcohol. In November 1967, an experiment was organized in three counties to allow grocery stores to sell strong beer (approximately 4.5 percent of alcohol content per volume). Sales of beer swelled by a factor of ten and the net effect on overall consumption was a 5 percent increase. The experiment was abandoned after six months. Earlier, in 1965, medium-strength beer (*mellanöl*) with an alcohol content of approximately 3.6 percent by volume had been introduced in grocery stores. When studies showed that beer sales had risen steeply among young people, the product was taken out of circulation in 1977.[36] In the early 1980s, the pendulum swung back to more restrictions and parliament banned all alcohol advertising and closed Systembolaget on Saturdays.

Aside from restricting availability by keeping retail outlets closed on weekends and after 6 p.m., the main instrument of restriction is high taxes. In 1995, taxes on distilled spirits in Sweden were more than three times those imposed by Germany, France, Belgium, and the Netherlands on each liter of hard liquor. Wine was not taxed at all in wine-producing countries (Austria, France, Italy, Spain, Portugal, and

Absolut vodka sold for 309 SEK and a bottle of Chivas Regal scotch cost 464 SEK in Systembolaget in 1998. The exchange rate was 8 SEK to US $1 in 1998.

[34] Tom Nilsson, "Alcohol in Sweden – A Country Profile," in Timo Kortteinen (ed.), *State Monopolies and Alcohol Prevention* (Helsinki: Social Research Institute of Alcohol Studies, 1989), 315.

[35] Richard F. Tomasson, "Alcohol and Alcohol Control in Sweden," *Scandinavian Studies*, 70 (1998), 482.

[36] Light beer has an alcohol content of less than 2.25 percent alcohol by volume and is sold normally in stores. Medium beer has an alcohol content of 2.25 to 3.5 percent and strong beer has an alcohol content of 3.5 to 5.6 percent.

Germany) and was only lightly taxed in Belgium and the Netherlands. Sweden and Finland impose relatively high taxes on beer which in most countries is taxed minimally.[37]

Rationalizing and preserving alcohol control policies

One of the great puzzles is why alcohol continues to be regarded as a major social problem. On the surface, the Swedish people enjoy a long life-span and lead healthy physical lives. Drinking does not seem to tear society apart, or undermine productivity, family life, urban living arrangements, or public health. While binge drinking is still happening and many drunks wander the streets after dark, alcohol-related mortality and morbidity rates are low. Why did Swedes tolerate drinking restrictions and why did the authorities publicly agonize over an "alcohol problem" when comparative studies on alcohol-related diseases painted a very different picture? Sweden was a sober nation and average consumption of absolute alcohol was low by international standards (5 liters as opposed to 12 liters in France in the 1970s and 1980s).

Evidently, the vast network of alcohol policy institutions touched a sensitive chord with many Swedish people because of the existing low societal tolerance for drinking. But this begs the question of why tolerance of alcohol (and mind-altering substances generally) is low in Sweden. To be sure, temperance and the "alcohol" question preoccupied many in Western (Protestant) countries in the early twentieth century yet most governments have relaxed their posture. In Sweden, the temperance mentality persevered even though the conditions under which it originally emerged changed radically. Once again, why do consumers accept the restrictions?

Temperance movements with their backward links to puritan revivalism and forward links to the labor movement ultimately determined the normative standards of Swedish society. As in Finland, abstinence became identified with virtue and honesty. Revivalist Christian concepts of discipline and hard work became the standard for judging proper behavior. Organized labor borrowed indirectly many concepts from evangelical Christianity through its alliance with the temperance movement. A good social democrat did not drink or at most drank modestly. A good social democrat forfeited personal indulgences to work hard for the greater good. Good citizens are rational, in control, organized, practical, and conscientious. In short, they are everything that a drunk is not. The political left assimilated core principles of Protestant-Christian

---

[37] Holder et al., *European Integration and Nordic Alcohol Policies*, 99.

thinking because they coincided with its desire to create a modern individual who would be able to determine his/her destiny. They matched social democratic ambitions to engineer a better society that guaranteed economic and social security.[38] The lawless and inconsiderate behavior of alcohol users/abusers undermined this goal and threatened security.

Yet there is more to this story than the ascendance of the social democratic movement and its absorption of Christian evangelical concepts since the liberal bloc also strongly promoted restrictive drinking rules. A complementary line of inquiry should explore which interests and institutions contributed to the resilience of the alcohol question in the second part of the twentieth century.

Societal and state interests

Four different interest groups actively defended the *status quo* and were instrumental in redefining the goals of alcohol control policies in the postwar era. First, the medical community and social scientists formed a powerful body of opinion in favor of restrictive policy on alcohol. Second, temperance activists together with local social service agencies, charged with the administration of temperance care law, aggressively supported alcohol control policy. Third, important government ministries were committed to preserving the system intact. Finally, the Social Democratic Party has been instrumental in the fine-tuning of restrictive drinking measures to adjust them to new situations.

The political fortune of the Social Democratic Party was tied to the defense of security (*trygghet*), which included military as well as socio-economic security. The Swedish model, as constructed by this party, aimed to protect a homogenous society from external threats and internal disorder. Deviance from social norms was perceived as threatening to the people's home (*folkhemmet*) and drinking (plus drugs) posed such unwanted and unpredictable dangers. The objective of the social welfare state was to promote collectivism and discourage the isolation of individuals or particular forms of behavior, which could undermine social stability. State policy had the twofold objective of stressing communal over individual achievements and of minimizing the stigmatization of individuals who displayed a certain degree of anti-communal or anti-social behavior. To avoid isolating individuals from mainstream society, it was best to avoid even identifying a particular

---

[38] Hugh Heclo and Henrik Madsen, *Policy and Politics in Sweden: Principled Pragmatism* (Philadelphia: Temple University Press, 1987); Bo Rothstein, *The Social Democratic State* (Pittsburgh: University of Pittsburgh Press, 1996).

problem with vulnerable social groups. Thus, anti-drinking measures were universally applicable although only a minority of citizens turned out to be substance abusers. Youth and women's groups, part of the social democratic world, took up the banner of temperance, and together with teetotaler politicians, consistently lobbied for the continuance of restrictions.[39] The left and liberal bloc recruited future politicians from local teetotaler associations and many temperance officials found their way into public service. In 1951, teetotalers accounted for 43 percent of the members of the Riksdag. Their numbers steadily fell after the late 1970s and only 6 percent of the Riksdag members were teetotalers in 1996.[40]

Temperance sympathizers also occupied strategic positions in the Ministry of Social Affairs, Systembolaget, and the National Board of Health and Welfare and directed many state agencies concerned with substance abuse and social care of those dependent on alcohol. Funding for specialized programs dealing with substance abuse has been generous in the past, falling under the Social Services Act, the Act on the Care of Young People, and the Act on the Care of Adult Misusers, and has created a powerful constituency in favor of in-patient substance dependency care.[41]

The third interest that was tireless in its defense of alcohol control policy was practicing physicians who were usually in the employment of local government and did not operate as a powerful independent body of professional interests. But the medical community in Sweden is highly professionalized in spite of the fact that physicians often function like public servants of the state.[42] Various state agencies built a fruitful alliance with the medical establishment, which in turn enabled physicians to enhance their prestige and authority in the vast network of the social welfare programs. Swedish governments relied on non-partisan commissions to advise the cabinet on social and public health questions, and scientists and medical doctors became influential articulators of the "governing images" of alcohol problems. Public money supported their research on alcohol-related questions and thus further confirmed their position as the main repository of knowledge on drinking and substance

[39] Tomasson, "Alcohol and Alcohol Control in Sweden," 497.
[40] Caroline Sutton, *Swedish Alcohol Discourse: Construction of a Social Problem* (Uppsala: Studia Sociologica Upsaliensia 45, 1998), 15; Lindblad and Lundkvist, *Tusen nyktra: 100 år med riksdagens nykterhetsgrupper*, 195.
[41] Arthur Gould, "Pollution Rituals in Sweden," *Scandinavian Journal of Social Welfare*, 3 (1994), 90; Anders Bergmark and Lars Oscarsson, "Swedish Alcohol Treatment in Transition," *Nordic Alcohol Studies*, 11 (1994), 43–54.
[42] Ellen Immergut, *Health Politics: Interests and Institutions in Western Europe* (New York: Cambridge University Press, 1992), 179–92.

abuse. Over time, the medical community forged a consensus and framed the prevailing knowledge on alcohol and drinking. By doing this, they assured themselves a permanent place in the public debate on alcohol and restrictive drinking measures.

Not all physicians are hostile to alcohol. For example, in the USA, it is popular to tout the benefits of moderate wine consumption for preventing coronary heart disease, although Swedish medical experts rejected such suggestions as pure hogwash. Thus, not all medical researchers promote abstinence. The devotion of the Swedish medical community to sobriety is unusual and partly explains why drinking gained the status of a permanent problem with vast institutional connections.[43] The Swedish medical community adopted a unique focus by asking not *whether* a person suffers from alcoholism (diagnostic question) but rather *why* a person copes with an alcohol problem. From the beginning, physicians treated alcohol-related problems in terms of their social consequences and thereby carved an important role for their profession in public debates on social policy.[44]

Finally, various ministries possessed good motives to deflect deregulation of alcohol policy. The Ministry of Social Affairs and Health managed Systembolaget and employed a fair number of teetotalers. The Ministry of Finance collected excise taxes, which yielded anywhere from 4 to 5.7 percent of total central government revenues between 1980 and 1994.[45] The fiscal benefits of alcohol control policies were even more significant if the money saved on health care, injuries, accidents, and lost productivity was added to the actual revenue stream from excise taxes, sales taxes on alcohol, and profits from the operation of Vin och Sprit. Higher consumption levels would have meant higher social and health expenditures on alcohol-related illnesses and injuries.

Ideas: rationalization of alcohol control policy

Institutions do not operate in a vacuum and the ideas they articulate must fall on receptive ears. When pressures began to build to consider relaxation of some alcohol rules, the authorities were able to counter that alcohol restrictions result in a healthier and better society and are successful in quelling discontent. Like their Finnish counterparts, Swedish officials took a keen interest in the use of the total consumption

[43] Holder et al., *European Integration and Nordic Alcohol Policies*, 173.
[44] Pia Rosenqvist, "The Physicians and the Swedish Alcohol Question in the Early Twentieth Century," *Contemporary Drug Problems*, 13 (1986), 503–25.
[45] Holder et al., *European Integration and Nordic Alcohol Policies*, 181. This includes excise taxes on alcohol, income from monopoly, custom duties, and value added tax on retailing alcoholic beverages.

model (TCM) to construct a new ideological framework to justify and explicate scientifically why restrictive drinking rules were indispensable. To reiterate, the TCM links the drinking climate (either wet or dry) to the presence of problem drinking and claims that the level of alcohol consumption determines the size of the group of drinkers at risk for abuse. A corollary assumption is that availability leads to abuse.[46] In the 1990s, the TCM has been further elaborated to address another paradox. Heavy drinkers, because their absolute numbers are so small, cause relatively few alcohol-related problems. Infrequent and modest users of alcohol oddly enough account for a disproportionate number of alcohol-involved traumas (traffic fatalities, drowning, falls, accidental injuries). Thus, measures that restrict aggregate alcohol consumption reduce the total number of alcohol-related accidents and deaths because they influence the consumption pattern of modest drinkers who ultimately are responsible for a large number of alcohol-related social and public health problems.[47]

Most public health analysts, policy officials, and numerous lay observers anywhere in the Western world will readily agree that alcohol carries considerable risks for the individual and society. Yet most societies use informal control mechanisms to condemn *excessive* drinking and aim to limit external causes of death (traffic accidents, suicide, homicide, other kinds of accidents such as drowning, fire, exposure to heat/cold) while generally countenancing drinking. What is unique and different about Sweden in particular and the Nordic societies in general is their readiness to impose restraints on everybody regardless of whether they have evinced a tendency to misuse alcohol. Most public policy officials will argue that the majority of drinkers never develop a problematic relationship with alcohol and that restrictions and control of drinking are arbitrary violations of individual autonomy and self-determination. But the Swedish discourse turns this argument on its head. Restrictive drinking measures exist to protect individuals from the capricious actions of thoughtless drunks who randomly cause harm to law-abiding citizens. It is the duty of the welfare state to guarantee security and stability. Because it is difficult to know who will turn out to cause alcohol-related harm, a universal package of measures prevents anybody from perpetrating harm.

The purpose, here, is not to deny the logic of the total consumption model. Restrictive drinking measures *do* reduce the prevalence of intoxication, alcohol-related fatalities, accidents, etc. Yet researchers and

---

[46] Sutton, *Swedish Alcohol Discourse*, 105.
[47] Harold D. Holder, *Alcohol and the Community. A Systems Approach to Prevention* (New York: Cambridge University Press, 1998); Edwards, *Alcohol Policy and the Public Good*.

policy officials in other countries hesitate to jump to the conclusion that aggregate alcohol consumption affects the extent of alcohol-related harm. Because of the Swedish understanding of the relationship between alcohol, society, and the individual, policy officials make attributions to cause and effect that are not fully accepted by non-Nordic specialists in the alcohol field.[48] A good argument can be made that any connection between drinking and social harm is conditional and probabilistic. If half of all traffic accidents are attributed to drunk-driving, nobody can be sure that these accidents would not have occurred if the driver had been sober. Even fatal diseases such as cirrhosis of the liver cannot be directly linked to alcohol.[49] Since the causal relation is open to interpretation, in countries with a holistic approach to alcohol regulation (Sweden and Finland, obviously), the upshot is often "problem inflation." In other words, the alcohol connection is highlighted as the probable cause at the expense of any other factors also present.

The TCM fell on fertile soil in Sweden because it corroborated existing views on mind-altering substances. Alcohol is dangerous and a threat to society. The TCM "proves" this and justifies universal public policy measures. What is especially "useful" about the TCM is that it explains why drinking restrictions must remain in force after binge drinking and vodka consumption have declined. If earlier policy objectives were centered on weaning the population away from vodka and intoxicating drinking rituals, the new objective is to keep alcohol consumption low. What still needs to be explored is why, of all people, Swedes succumb to alcohol (and drugs).

Part of the explanation rests with the famous taciturnity or "communication anxiety" of the average Swede, which can only be broken thanks to alcohol. When together, Swedes rely on alcohol to facilitate interpersonal communication.[50] Binge drinking was typical during agrarian times and agrarian drinking rituals continued to dominate the culture of drinking since the latter is a learned behavior, shaped by the expectations, mood, mental health, personality, and purpose of the individual. In urban society, binge drinking eases sociability at the same

---

48 Joseph R. Gusfield, *Contested Meanings: The Construction of Alcohol Problems* (Madison: University of Wisconsin Press, 1996), 38–44; Betsy Thom, *Dealing with Drink: Alcohol and Social Policy: From Treatment to Management* (New York: Free Assocation, 1999), 105–33.

49 See, for example, Véronique Nahoum-Grappe, "France," in Heath (ed.), *International Handbook on Alcohol and Culture*, 75–87.

50 Åke Daun, *Swedish Mentality* (University Park, PA: Pennsylvania State University Press, 1996); Jean Phillips-Martinsson, *Swedes, as Others See Them* (Stockholm: Affärsförlaget, 1981).

time as it contravenes middle-class standards of punctuality, discipline, and consideration for others.

To return to the original question, however, considering that the country has been relatively sober for the past fifty odd years, why are drinking restrictions required? To understand this, we must look at the past, which renders an accurate portrayal of what to expect when contemporary Swedes have access to alcohol without any restraints.[51] The darkest period of drinking was in the first half of the nineteenth century after the liquor trade had been totally deregulated. At that time, every Swedish man, woman, and child finished off a liter of strong *brännvin* per week and they were literally drinking themselves to death. This figure, which appears in every text on Swedish drinking, is none the less suspicious. Agrarian societies did not have that much surplus grain to distill spirits and studies from other countries, including Finland, suggest that alcohol was not readily available in pre-industrial societies.[52] Additionally, the Statistical Yearbook of Sweden records annual per capita consumption of alcohol in 1850 as 5.2 liters.[53] Other government publications note that alcohol consumption of *brännvin* (with an alcohol content of 50 percent) stood at around 2.5 liters per capita per year in 1700, rising to 5 liters in 1800.[54] If annual per capita consumption was 5 liters of vodka in 1800 and 5.2 liters in 1850, when did consumption swell to 46 liters of spirits per person per year?[55] Russians, who are the world's largest drinkers, imbibe around 18 liters of pure alcohol a year for each person over the age of fifteen or 15 liters of alcohol for every man, woman, and child.

It is therefore very likely that actual consumption during the period of unregulated distilling was quite temperate. To be sure, at the beginning

---

[51] A good example is the brochure, gratis from the Information Department of Systembolaget, *Systembolaget and the European Union* (Stockholm: Systembolaget, 1995), 5–6.

[52] Patricia E. Prestwich, *Drink and the Politics of Social Reform: Antialcoholism in France since 1870* (Palo Alto: The Society for the Promotion of Science and Scholarship, 1988), 6–19; Susanna Barrows and Robin Room (eds.), *Drinking: Behavior and Belief in Modern History* (Berkeley: University of California Press, 1991). At its highest rate of consumption, which was around 1830, the American population consumed 15 liters of pure alcohol per capita per annum.

[53] Ilpo Koskikallo, "The Social History of Restaurants in Sweden and Finland: A Comparative Study," *Contemporary Drug Problems*, 12 (1985), 24.

[54] SOU, *Svensk alkoholpolitik – bakgrund och nuläge*, 11.

[55] The Swedish language employs at least a dozen different terms to describe the situations in which *brännvin* is drunk. *Jaktsup* implies before the hunt, *körsup* means before driving, *gångsup* before walking, *bäddsup* before going to bed, *slaktsup* before a slaughtering, *kyrksup* before church, a *skåpsup* is drunk secretly from the cupboard, *julsup* is consumed during Christmas, a *flyttsup* before moving, a *tröstsup* for consolation, and a *Helan* (a whole) during ceremonial occasions. Tomasson, "Alcohol and Alcohol Control in Sweden," 483.

of the rise of the temperance movements in the 1840s, drinking was not perceived as an overriding social problem. Originally, the temperance movement recommended "moderation." Only later did the teetotaler movement insist that moderation was impossible and that all drinking was sinful. The temperance focus shifted to the dangers and threats of drinking as more lower-class people gained access to manufactured spirits in public drinking establishments. The successful Gothenburg system of licensed liquor stores arose to destroy the proliferation of pubs in the expanding urban centers. The urban elite did not fear intoxication as much as the congregation of the laboring class in segregated public spaces. During the next fifty years, as values changed and the temperance movement became a genuine popular cause, consumption of alcohol steadily declined. By the time that the Bratt system was in place, Sweden no longer had to cope with an alcohol problem.[56] It is therefore more appropriate to say that *tolerance* for drinking diminished after 1850, which made "normal" (pre-industrial) drinking behavior no longer acceptable.

The mid-nineteenth century is for most Swedes far removed from their collective consciousness because it pre-dates the formation of modern Sweden. Therefore, observers point to more recent events to warn against liberalization and deregulation. Consumption surged by 25 percent in the first two years after the abolition of the Bratt system and cirrhosis of the liver increased fourfold, until liquor prices were substantially raised and consumption fell again. An even more recent example of excessive drinking after restrictions had been relaxed was during the decade of drinking liberalization, namely 1965 to 1977. In 1965, the idea was conceived of selling medium-strength beer in grocery stores. Alcohol consumption rose by 15 percent during those years. Even more shocking was that many underage youngsters bought beer in grocery stores because sales clerks were remiss in checking their ages. A more limited experiment, tried in 1967, also documented the dangers of relaxation. In that year, strong beer was made available in grocery stores and bars. The experiment was supposed to have lasted for twelve months but was cancelled after six. The consumption of strong beer jumped while the consumption of wine and spirits remained stable. The net effect on overall alcohol consumption was estimated to be 5 percent.[57]

Without disputing these figures, recent events are none the less open

---

[56] Pia Rosenqvist and Jukka-Pekka Takala, "Two Experiments with Lay Boards: The Emergence of Compulsory Treatment of Alcoholics in Sweden and Finland," *Contemporary Drug Problems*, 14 (1987), 15–38.

[57] Edwards, *Alcohol Policy and the Public Good*, 133, 136.

to more than one interpretation. During the Bratt system, a lively black market existed where persons without the right to buy spirits obtained their quota of alcohol. The rise in registered consumption after 1955 could equally well be attributed to the end of black market trade and the ability of individuals, previously denied a *motbok*, to buy legal alcohol. Similarly, the increase in underage drinkers in the 1960s must be contrasted with the fact that many students dabbled in home production. The introduction of medium-strength beer took away the incentive to brew at home. Because the authorities kept silent about the existence of home distilling, home brewing, and individual travelers' imports of alcohol, the actual consumption of alcohol has always been higher than registered consumption. The removal of some restraints results in an increase in registered consumption as people move away from illicit sources of alcohol.

Ultimately, the reason or justification for alcohol control policy goes back to some intangible quality of the Swedish people. In contrast to other people, they cannot be trusted with mind-altering substances, which produce nothing but chaos and disorder. This fear of turmoil is magnified by the fact that postwar Sweden has placed much faith in constructing a fair and equitable society in which the state assumes responsibility for social and economic security. Anti-drinking rules play a special role in the preservation of economic and political stability.

In 1993, when EU membership suddenly became a real option, Swedish researchers published alarming studies on what would happen if Sweden was forced to adopt an EU-like regulatory regime.[58] Table 3.1 summarizes the projections of the Swedish research community if alcohol is sold in food stores, if it is sold in a monopoly system but at lower prices (perhaps equivalent to Danish prices), if the state alcohol monopoly is abolished and prices lowered, and if prices fall steeply (to prices perhaps similar to those in Germany).

Policy officials and knowledgeable insiders were troubled by the idea of having to phase out restrictive drinking measures. To defend the monopoly system, officials from the Ministry of Social Welfare and Systembolaget emphasized the public health dimension of Swedish alcohol policy because Sweden wanted to prevail on the Commission and other member states to keep the current regime of alcohol regulation intact. They also reversed a decades-old argument. Rather than

---

[58] The November 1993 report, *Assessment of Consequences Resulting from the Elimination of the Swedish Alcohol Retailing Monopoly*, was published as Harold Holder, Eckart Kühlhorn, Sturla Nordlund, Esa Österberg, Anders Romelsjö, and Trygve Ugland, "Potential Consequences from Possible Changes to Nordic Retail Alcohol Monopolies Resulting from EU Membership," *Addiction*, 90 (1995), 1603–18.

Table 3.1. *Rises in consumption and their consequences predicted as the result of alterations to the Swedish alcohol control policy*

Scenario	Predicted rise in consumption (liters)	Predicted increase in the number of alcohol-related deaths	Predicted increase in the number of cases of assault
Monopoly is abolished but prices remain the same	1	600	3,000
Monopoly is retained, Danish prices adopted	1.5	1,000	5,000
Monopoly is abolished, Danish prices adopted	2.5	1,800	10,000
Monopoly is abolished, German prices adopted	5	4,000	22,000

Source: Swedish National Institute of Public Health, *Swedish Alcohol Policy* (Stockholm, 1995), 42.

emphasizing that the weak character of the Swedes who could not control themselves necessitated consumer restrictions on alcoholic beverages, the post-accession argument accents the terrible drinking habits of other European countries. France and Denmark are depicted as frightful examples of what might happen if Sweden is forced to Europeanize.

Conclusion

Temperance-influenced societies connect drinking with social harm and with "externalities" affecting others as well as the drinker. In earlier Swedish thinking, the drinker faced a large moral responsibility that was used to punish and isolate the individual. By contrast, the social democratic version of alcohol policy promotes collectivist or universal measures to abstain from stigmatizing problem drinkers. In many European societies drinking has become normalized and drinking problems are relegated to the private sphere. In Sweden, and to a lesser extent Finland, drinking has not been normalized and the discourse is characterized by fearful rhetoric. Vigilance by the authorities is justified on the grounds that drinking causes unimaginable tragedies and that everybody can potentially cause harm.

At the same time, it should be clear that the Swedish and Finnish fixation with alcohol is not shared by the rest of Europe, with the exception of Iceland and Norway. It follows that the Nordic applicants to the European Community encountered difficulties when they approached Brussels to discuss the future of their state alcohol monopolies. The entire discourse and the tone of the alcohol control debate are alien to the bureaucrats in Brussels. In addition, a core feature of the postwar alcohol control policies is the suppression of private agents by the operation of a vast state monopoly on the production, distribution, trade, and retail of alcoholic beverages. The monopoly system itself triggered alarm bells in Brussels.

While the authorities readied themselves to defend the institutions of the alcohol control regime, opinions on drinking in Sweden (as in Finland) became more Danish or Continental. An increasing number of middle-class consumers resented state interference in the alcohol market especially as many urban and educated households primarily drank light alcoholic beverages such as wine and beer. They wanted the convenience of being able to buy wine and beer in ordinary stores at affordable prices. The conflict with Europe disclosed the widening gap between the official position on alcohol regulation and new attitudes among Finnish and Swedish consumers. To some extent, prior to accession to the European Union, Swedish and Finnish drinking patterns and attitudes already resembled those of Continental Europe. However, until EU accession, the gap between public opinion and elite preferences could be ignored and any mention of liberalization could be quickly dismissed by the policy community as irresponsible, dangerous, and thus out of the question.

4   Nordic morality meets the European Union

As soon as Finland and Sweden joined the European Union, the state alcohol monopoly companies – Alko and Systembolaget – encountered a whole set of fresh challenges. By 1995, political and social pressure against drinking restrictions had already been growing and European Union membership intensified public impatience with the state monopoly companies. Finnish and Swedish citizens were acquainted with non-Nordic regulatory regimes and increasingly came to value the concept of the sovereign individual with autonomous decision powers. State regulations to direct consumption publicly were seen as a violation of this treasured autonomy. Until quite recently, it was considered normal for the state to tell people what makes them happy. But with the new mood since the late 1980s, Nordic people prefer to tell the government what makes them happy. Accession to the European Union only deepened the new ideological orientation towards individualism and personal responsibility, as seen in many different political economy domains.[1]

The expert community contributed to the Europeanization of drinking attitudes. Specialists emphasized science and applied theoretical models to whole populations thereby lifting the moral burden off the drinker. No longer did public servants pretend to identify specific risk groups or individuals and no longer did they pass moral judgments on drinking *per se*. Only the consequences mattered and individuals were encouraged to assess the costs of their actions independently. The public health perspective normalized drinking, and subsequently, convinced people to demand less state intervention.[2]

Nevertheless, genuine reform, let alone the abolition of state

---

[1] Christine Ingebritsen, *The Nordic States and European Unity* (Ithaca: Cornell University Press, 1998); Trygve Ugland, "European Integration and the Corrupting Gaps in the Systems," in Pekka Sulkunen, Caroline Sutton, Christoffer Tigerstadt, and Katariina Warpenius (eds.), *Broking/en Spirits: Power and Ideas in Nordic Alcohol Control* (Helsinki: NAD, 2000).

[2] Pekka Sulkunen, "Ethics of Alcohol Policy in a Saturated Society," *Addiction*, 92 (1997), 1117–22; Christoffer Tigerstedt, "Det finns inte längre någon alkoholpolitik," *Nordisk alkohol- & narkotikatidskrift*, 16 (1999), 79–91.

monopolies, was not on the agenda in the 1980s. Many critical observers anticipated enormous parliamentary resistance to proposals for limited deregulation and privatization and thus dismissed the possibility of altering the *status quo*. Until the question of EU membership forced a fresh assessment, alcohol policy itself was simply not publicly debated. European Union membership jolted the consensus on drinking restrictions and emboldened proponents of the neo-liberal model to challenge the repository of knowledge espoused by the research community, the medical profession, and social welfare policy officials.

Accession itself was also accompanied by institutional reforms of the state alcohol monopolies. Finland and Sweden were asked to de-monopolize the production and foreign trade parts of the state companies. New private sector agents have therefore appeared, which now compete alongside the state alcohol monopoly in the production and wholesale distribution of alcoholic beverages. The private sector closely identifies with the Commission's hostility towards monopolies and takes advantage of European prejudices and the legal superstructure to urge national administrations to institute further reforms. Since many consumers are in any event no longer tied to the historical forces that gave birth to temperance and alcohol control policies, "normalization" of alcohol policy is, according to the private sector, overdue.

State alcohol monopolies are, furthermore, threatened by a third outgrowth of accession to the European Union. New rules on personal travelers' imports, dictated by membership in the EU, spurred a massive surge in cross-border trade and resulted in an increase of 20 to 40 percent in unregistered alcohol consumption. Elimination of border controls piques the interest of organized crime, which is involved in the transport of illegal spirits and the production of moonshine. The dramatic increase in travelers' imports and smuggling undermines the public health claims of the authorities and hurts the state-owned network of retail stores financially. The growing size of unrecorded consumption diminishes the rationale for anti-drinking restrictions and governments cannot arrest the cheats without violating common democratic principles. Moreover, the widespread practice of deception is indicative of shifts in attitudes and perceptions. Alcohol tourism removes the protective veneer on a sensitive topic.

The Nordic countries and the application to join the European Union

Most questions with regard to the integration of the Nordic economies into the EU were discussed and partly resolved during the previous negotiations on the European Economic Area (EEA) arrangements. The accession negotiations with Brussels covered areas not included in the EEA agreement such as home and justice, agriculture, and regional policy. At no point during the discussions on either the EEA or EC membership did alcohol policy occupy a central place. Swedish governments published various studies examining the consequences of European Free Trade Association (EFTA) and EC membership on Sweden and none of them included a discussion on the future of alcohol control policies. Knowledgeable insiders, such as the director of Systembolaget, were optimistic about the future of the state retail monopoly as late as 1989 when Sweden had already entered into the final phase of the negotiations on the European Economic Agreement. So long as the retail monopoly did not discriminate against foreign products, claimed Systembolaget director Gabriel Romanus, it would be compatible with the EEA agreement.[3]

Alcohol control policies were not directly covered in the EEA negotiations but the governments of the Nordic countries issued a joint declaration, which was attached to the EEA agreement signed in May 1992. This unilateral declaration recalled the social and health foundations of the alcohol policy but left the exact status of the state alcohol monopolies undecided, to be determined by the future EFTA Surveillance Authority or its court of justice.[4]

Social welfare officials and politicians took comfort in a much earlier exchange of letters between the Norwegian government and the Brussels Commission with regard to the position of the Norwegian alcohol monopoly. In 1970, the Norwegian government submitted a memorandum to investigate the status of the Vinmonopolet (Norwegian state alcohol monopoly) in case it decided to proceed with an application of membership to the European Community. The Norwegian government argued that Vinmonopolet was the foundation of its alcohol policy and that its purpose was to satisfy social policy objectives. The reply of the Commission at that time validated the assertions of Norwegian alcohol policy and Brussels declared that, except for its exclusive rights concerning the importation and distribution of foreign beer, Vinmonopolet was indeed compatible with Community law. More than two decades later, Finnish and Swedish delegations pointed to that earlier opinion to silence any qualms

[3] Svante Nycander, *Svenskarna och spriten: Alkoholpolitik 1855–1995* (Malmö: Sober, 1996), 276.
[4] SOU, *Svensk alkoholpolitik bakgrund och nuläge* (Stockholm: SOU/Socialdepartementet, 1994), 66.

surrounding the compatibility of the state alcohol monopoly company with the legal constitution of the EC.[5]

Public scrutiny of whether Nordic alcohol policies had a place in the EC was thus absent. In both Finland and Sweden, the debate on membership came down to two broad issues. How would it mesh with the legacy of neutrality or non-alignment and how would it affect the economic recession?[6] Economic or market-related topics had already been ironed out during the negotiations on the European Economic Area at which point all EFTA countries were asked to accept the provisions regarding the four freedoms (capital, goods, services, and people) and EC rules on competition and state aid. Basically, the EFTA countries were told to accept the bulk of the *acquis communautaire* and some related policies with the result that few derogations were either requested or granted.

Sweden was the first EFTA country to decide that the free trade agreement was not what it had sought and the Social Democratic Party announced its intention to seek full EC membership in October 1990.[7] The Finnish elite wanted to wait for the national parliamentary elections in March 1991 and the completion of the Intergovernmental Conference in Maastricht (December 1991) to decide on full membership. Once Finland decided to follow Sweden, it signaled its intention to embrace the Maastricht package without reservations. The Finnish application was simple and short, and had no conditions attached.[8] The enlargement negotiations began in 1993 and Finland put a few critical items on the agenda that dealt with the transitional problems of financial support to adjust agriculture to EU rules, regional policy, and free trade arrangements with Baltic countries. Sweden emphasized social and environmental policy derogations and transparency in EU decision-making and its budgetary contributions.[9]

---

[5] Peter Germer, "Alcohol and the Single Market: Juridical Aspects," *Contemporary Drug Problems*, 17 (1990), 481–96.

[6] Both countries experienced the steepest postwar recessions in the late 1980s and early 1990s. Sieglinde Gstöhl, "The Nordic Countries and the EEA," in Lee Miles (ed.), *The European Union and the Nordic Countries* (New York: Routledge, 1996), 55.

[7] Lee Miles, *The Nordic Countries and the 1995 EU Enlargement* (New York: Routledge, 1996), 64–65; Nikolaj Petersen, "The Nordic Trio and the Future of the EU," in Geoffrey Edwards and Alfred Pijpers (eds.), *The Politics of European Treaty Reform* (Washington, DC: Pinter, 1997), 159–64.

[8] Thomas Pedersen, *European Union and the EFTA Countries* (New York: Pinter, 1994), 89–99.

[9] Miles, *The Nordic Countries and the 1995 EU Enlargement*, 68; Francisco Granell, "The European Union's Enlargement Negotiations with Austria, Finland, Norway, and Sweden," *Journal of Common Market Studies*, 33 (1995), 117–41.

The alcohol question in the EU

Commission officials were from the beginning suspicious of Nordic claims of preserving public health standards through a state monopoly. Certainly, the confusion in Brussels was more than a clash of principles. In Brussels, alcohol is either an industrial or an agricultural product. Beer, including strong ales and porters, falls under the mandate of national governments because of its connection to national tax regimes. Brussels considers wine an alcoholic beverage but its production and distribution are directed by the Directorate-General for Agriculture, whose main concern has been to raise wine consumption in and outside Europe. If anything, the Commission expressed its disappointment with the "underconsumption" of wine in the applicant states.[10] Distilled spirits are regarded as alcoholic beverages. But the production of spirits is controlled by gigantic international beverage companies, which lobby hard to keep the market free of restrictions and impediments. In 1992, this sector warned the Commission that it employed 650,000 people directly and no less than 2.25 million indirectly.[11]

Individual member states use a variety of laws to control sales to minors, to minimize intoxicated driving, to screen liquor advertising and opening hours of liquor stores, and to oversee the retail distribution of distilled spirits. But it is fair to say that non-Nordic countries do not possess an authentic alcohol control policy and the term itself is foreign in the public policy discourse of other member states. Selected national ministries in some member states have special interdepartmental divisions to deal with alcohol-related questions.[12] Yet overall, compared with the Nordic countries, the non-Nordic member states are liberal when it concerns drinking. The Council's social action program singles out drug addiction, smoking, and infectious diseases for special attention. Alcohol and drinking go unmentioned.[13] Article 152 (formerly Article 129) of the Treaty establishing the European Community

---

[10] Nycander, *Svenskarna och spriten*, 277–78.
[11] The Amsterdam Group, "The Socio-Economic Impact of the European Alcoholic Drinks Industry," *Alcoholic Beverages and European Society* (The Amsterdam Group, 1993), 3; see, also, Jussi Simpura, "Alcohol and European Transformation," *Addiction*, 92 (1997), 33–41.
[12] Hermann Fahrenkrug, "Alcohol Control Policy in the EC Member States," *Contemporary Drug Problems*, 17 (1990), 497–524; Christoffer Tigerstedt, "The European Community and Alcohol Policy," *Contemporary Drug Problems*, 17 (1990), 461–79.
[13] Harold D. Holder, Eckart Kühlhorn, Sturla Nordlund, Esa Österberg, Anders Romelsjö, and Trygve Ugland, *European Integration and Nordic Alcohol Policies: Changes in Alcohol Controls and Consequences in Finland, Norway and Sweden* (Brookfield, VT: Ashgate, 1998), 26.

(TEC) covers public health. Yet alcohol-related diseases are not singled out, in contrast to health problems flowing from drug misuse. Earlier, in 1993, the Commission published a report on "common issues" faced by all member states and drew attention to public health trends. Again, the Commission did not flag alcohol and drinking as special problems common to all member states.[14]

After Sweden submitted its application for membership, the Commission took a year to reply. Its opinion, sent to the Swedish government in July 1992, highlighted a few problem areas, among other things, the state alcohol monopoly and neutrality. In the Bulletin of the European Communities, the alcohol monopoly was described as "the most worrying" and the Commission suggested that other means "less obstructive of competition" could fulfill equally well the goals of public health.[15] All state monopolies with a commercial character were considered as violating Article 31 (formerly Article 37) on free competition. Sweden's response was to reiterate the public health objective of combating alcoholism.[16] In addition, the Swedish negotiators mentioned Article 30 (formerly Article 36) of the Treaty establishing the European Community, which leaves room for public state monopolies to pursue overriding social goals such as combating alcoholism, and they cited the campaign by the European regional office of the WHO to decrease consumption of alcohol by 25 percent by the year 2000 to back up its public health considerations.

The Commission's interpretation of Article 30 was more circumspect. It pointed to a 1987 ruling by the European Court of Justice that any form of discrimination was only legitimate if absolutely no other means or measures could fulfill the same function (*Commission v. Germany* Case 178/84). If the goal of alcohol control policies is to safeguard the population from alcohol-induced diseases and harm, the Nordic authorities must prove beyond doubt that other measures with fewer barriers on free trade fail to meet the target. The Commission even questioned the legality of a state alcohol *retail* monopoly. Proportionality was the key term in that the contentious measures must be commensurate with the goal to be achieved. The Commission doubted that the institutional

[14] Caroline Sutton, *Swedish Alcohol Discourse: Construction of a Social Problem* (Uppsala: Studia Sociologica Upsaliensia 45, 1998), 125; Trygve Ugland, "Europeanization of the Nordic Alcohol Monopoly Systems: Collisions between Ideologies and Political Cultures," *Nordic Studies on Alcohol and Drugs*, 14 (1997), 10.

[15] European Policy Advisory Service/Euro Pas, *State Alcohol Monopolies and the Accession of the Nordic Countries to the EC* (Brussels: Euro Pas, 1993), 2; Sutton, *Swedish Alcohol Discourse*, 59.

[16] Pedersen, *European Union and the EFTA Countries*, 92.

network of state monopolies was proportional to the public health goals of the Nordic countries.[17]

In early 1993, the real negotiations for membership began and the Nordic countries discovered that the Commission was indeed opposed to the alcohol monopoly systems. It told Sweden that the existence of all monopolies (alcohol, natural gas, electricity, and pharmaceuticals) obliged it to revise its current legislation. The Commission invited all three countries (Norway included) to exchange letters on how to resolve this outstanding issue. Sweden agreed to enter a dialogue with the Commission and Finland had already determined that Alko needed restructuring. Norway refused to respond to the Commission's invitation.

The Finnish government set up a working group under the Ministry of Social and Health Affairs to propose radical changes in the organization of Alko in early 1992. In part, the initiative came from Alko itself, which realized that it had to secure its own future because the Commission would not grant unlimited derogation and the Finnish government did not place much priority on protecting Alko from Brussels. Thus, Alko's management came out in favor of de-monopolization in order to avert even more dramatic organizational restructuring.[18]

Both Finland and Sweden agreed in late 1993 to remove the institutional link between the monopoly on alcohol production and the off-premise retail monopoly on alcoholic beverages. Production and wholesale distribution were deregulated while Systembolaget and Alko continued to be the only retail distributors. In effect, the state alcohol monopoly was de-monopolized and the private sector could produce, import, and distribute alcoholic beverages. Sweden retained the state-owned Vin och Sprit, but each public company now faced competition from the private sector. The Commission was satisfied with this outcome and claimed that it "does not see any reason to proceed on its own initiative, either now or after the Swedish accession to the Union, against the maintenance of the retail monopoly on the basis of current *acquis*."[19] Swedish and Finnish governments hailed the agreement as a major achievement and delayed a public announcement for a month to make a grand statement at the end of the year in December 1993.[20]

[17] Nycander, *Svenskarna och spriten*, 282.
[18] Holder et al., *European Integration and Nordic Alcohol Policies*, 33, 184; Christoffer Tigerstedt and Pia Rosenqvist, "The Fall of a Scandinavian Tradition? Recent Changes in Scandinavian and Finnish Alcohol Policy," *Nordic Alcohol Studies*, 12 (1995), 91.
[19] Ugland, "European Integration and the Corrupting Gaps in the Systems."
[20] Miles, *The Nordic Countries and the 1995 EU Enlargement*, 72. A more emotional issue was the possible ban on snuff, a sort of chewing tobacco consumed by 20 percent of the Swedish adult male population. This product is banned in the rest of Europe because

The Commission also yielded on the issue of travelers' personal imports. The existence of quotas on travelers' imports was inimical to the Single Market and a borderless Europe. Years ago, the Commission declared that an EU citizen could import for personal use 10 liters of spirits, 90 liters of table wine, 20 liters of fortified wine, and 110 liters of beer. These limits are arbitrary and larger quantities can be imported if the person can show that there is no commercial purpose. The point is that citizens of the EU can buy goods anywhere in the EU so long as it is for personal use. If it is for resale, then the goods fall under the tax regime of the country of destination. Otherwise, the tax regime of the country of origin prevails. But until 1995, Sweden and Finland restricted travelers' imports to 1 liter of spirits, 1 liter of wine, and 2 liters of beer. The Nordic applicants could not accept EU rules on travelers' imports because this would destroy the alcohol monopoly system, considering that local residents could bring back enough alcohol on one trip to last for a year or more! Swedish and Finnish negotiators requested a derogation because the EU rules were in contradiction with existing social policy and because they needed a transition period to introduce higher ceilings to avoid total chaos. The compromise solution was to raise the maximum to 1 liter of spirits, 5 liters of table wine, and 15 liters of beer.[21]

During the debate on the EU membership referendum, alcohol control policies did not figure prominently. Other issues were of greater concern and, if anybody did wonder what would happen to the elaborate system of controls on drinking, Finnish and Swedish officials assuaged any worries. The alcohol retail system would be unaffected and the Commission, according to Finnish and Swedish legal experts, could not unilaterally abrogate the derogations granted on personal travelers' allowances. They drew the analogy with Denmark, which was also granted special derogations on travelers' imports, and argued that pricing and excise duties were fiscal matters and that each member state had a veto with regard to national taxation.

The Finnish referendum took place in October 1994 and the turnout was 74 percent of the voters. Of these, 57 percent voted in favor of and 43 percent against joining the EU. The Swedish referendum was scheduled to be held after the Finnish one. Throughout 1994, the "no" side could claim a plurality with many undecided voters. The refer-

of health hazards and the rumor that the Commission would take this national product away provoked enormous anguish, anger, and annoyance. In the end, the Commission backtracked.
[21] Esa Österberg and Juhani Pekhonen, "Travellers' Imports of Alcohol into Finland: Changes Caused by Finnish EU Membership," *Nordic Alcohol Studies*, 13 (1996), 23.

endum was held in mid-November and 52 percent of the electorate approved of accession. The turnout was very high at over 83 percent, and half of the social democratic voters voted against membership. Again, alcohol control policies were subsidiary.

After membership

The agreement on alcohol control policies was presented as a victory by the governments of the Nordic states. The retail monopoly stayed intact, pricing policy was unchanged, and the adjustments to higher ceilings on travelers' imports were well below the EU norm. It is certainly ironic that one of the immediate results of membership was not lower food prices, as promised and predicted by politicians and business leaders, but multiple stress factors on the alcohol policy regimes. One way or another, the negotiators had failed to predict the impact of the relaxation in the rules on travelers' imports and of the free movement of goods and people on the alcohol control policies. There had always been a fair share of undeclared imports of duty-free or taxed alcohol and there was a long tradition of legal home brewing and illegal home distilling in Sweden. Entry into the European Union magnified and multiplied the flow of personal imports and the incentives for smuggling and illicit distilling. Stark price differentials created enticing opportunities for "alcohol" arbitrage.

Finns imported 3.5 million liters of beer in 1994 and this amount rose to about 30 million liters in 1995. In that year, Finnish tourists also imported 7 million liters of distilled spirits and wine, up from 3 million in 1994. Alcohol imports by tourists accounted for about 17 percent of aggregate alcohol consumption in 1995. Although registered alcohol consumption remained stable between 1994 and 1995, it rose in fact by 10 percent thanks to cross-border shopping. Alko outlets in the areas near the border with Russia suffered a 30 percent decline of turnover in 1995 while food stores, which also carried medium-strength beer, experienced a sharp decline in sales. Generally, all Alko stores except for those located in the northern regions saw a drop in sales.[22] In May 1996, Finland restored pre-accession time restrictions on travelers' imports. Finnish travelers returning home from non-EU countries can bring duty-free beverages only if their stay is longer than 20 hours. Citizens of countries outside the EU or Nordic passport area must stay

---

[22] Esa Österberg, Kari Haavisto, Raija Ahtola and Maija Kaivomurmi, "The Booze Rally on the Eastern Border, Alcohol Consumption and Problems Caused by Alcohol" (originally published as "Itärajan viinaralli, alkoholin kulutus ja alkoholihaitat," *Alkoholipolitiikka*, 61 (1996), 325–35).

at least 72 hours if they want to bring duty-free goods. Subsequently, the amount of alcohol bought in from Russia or Estonia dropped by approximately half. Time limitations do not apply to EU visitors, to visits to EU countries or to travelers arriving by air.

Sweden has a larger domestic market and a tradition of home distilling. In the mid-1980s, it was thought that 100,000 illegal stills were operating in Sweden.[23] The combination of a sizable domestic market and a tradition of illegal home distilling encouraged organized crime to enter the smuggling business. This smuggling comes in two forms. Either criminal syndicates arrange for the transport of bottled liquor to be dropped off at a warehouse in Sweden and then sold through "gray channels" to the consumer or they import ethanol alcohol to produce moonshine vodkas. Each method is extremely remunerative and the national custom agency confiscated nearly 500,000 liters of alcohol in December 1996 compared with 80,000 liters in 1995 and 63,000 liters in 1993.[24] In the meantime, Systembolaget suffered sharp drops in sales and lost tax revenues in total of 462 million SEK in 1996.[25]

As is the case in drug trafficking, the incentives are so attractive that it is virtually impossible to stamp out alcohol smuggling. One solution is to change the paper trail and documentation requirements in the EU so that it is less easy to claim a load for a third country and then disappear somewhere in the EU, evading value added taxes. But Swedish customs officials are virtually powerless because EU rules prevent them from erecting border controls. Finland and Sweden ratified the Schengen Convention of 1985, which obliged them to ease border controls between contracting parties. Customs officials are supposed to do visual checks on private vehicles but cannot require drivers to stop their cars. Neither are customs officials allowed to perform random checks to apprehend tourists carrying more than the allowable quota of alcohol.[26] Moreover, prison sentences and punishments are light for apprehended smugglers, most of whom are recruited from East European countries by Swedish criminal organizations.

---

[23] Jean-Charles Sournia, *A History of Alcoholism*, trans. Nick Handley and Gareth Stanton (Cambridge, MA: Basil Blackwell, 1990), 192.

[24] Sven Ohlsson, "Alkoholsmuggling till Sverige" (Stockholm: Generaltullstyrelsen/ Kontrolbyrn, 1997), 2. As a rule, around 10 percent of the smuggled goods are caught at the border. That means that the amount of illegal alcohol brought in is around 5 million liters.

[25] Ohlsson, "Alkoholsmuggling till Sverige," 3. In early 2000, sales by Systembolaget were sharply up by an average of 12 percent. Part of the reason was stronger police and customs operations against illicit distilling and alcohol smuggling. "Kraftigt ökad försäljning av alkohol," *Dagens Nyheter* (www.dn.se), March 10, 2000.

[26] Holder et al., *European Integration and Nordic Alcohol Policies*, 44–46.

Assuming that the smuggling problem can be brought under control, Sweden is still not out of the woods. In 1995, 15,000 bottles of (legal) Danish pilsner entered Sweden *per hour* during the weekend. The trade in Danish beer has cut sales in retail outlets in southern Sweden and sales of spirits and beer have dropped by 20 percent.[27] The cross-border trade with Denmark hurts Swedish brewers. At least Finnish tourists bring home Finnish beer brewed in Tallinn. But Swedish tourists visit Denmark and buy non-Swedish products and all revenues are lost to the Swedish economy. In 1997, Swedish taxes on strong beer dropped by 39 percent and retail prices fell 20 percent to counter the rising complaints of private brewing companies. Subsequently, legal beer consumption rose by 8 percent.[28]

Travelers' allowances plus smuggling, all of which are the direct outcome of joining the European Union, impose considerable strains on the system of alcohol control. Swedish brewery companies released a report, in late 1997, claiming that unregistered consumption was equal to 40 percent of registered consumption.[29] Ironically, the surge in undocumented alcohol consumption could have been foreseen by Finnish and Swedish officials. Denmark, the only Nordic country to join the European Community in 1973, adjusted excise taxes to promote light alcoholic beverages. In 1972, Danish beer cost as much as Swedish beer but by 1995 it cost only half as much as Swedish or Finnish beer, mainly because of competition from tourist imports. Danish consumers shopped in Germany, and Danish food stores and brewery companies finally forced the Danish government to keep the country's prices for alcohol, cigarettes, and chocolates no more than 20 percent higher than German prices for these items.[30]

Danish authorities had to adjust price levels closer to those of the nearest European country in part because alcohol was sold in private stores. Private interest groups lobbied ferociously to stem the loss of revenue on liquor sales and were impossible to ignore in the long run. In Finland and Sweden, the private sector is hampered by the fact that state-owned companies control the retail distribution. But the rise in

---

[27] *The Economist*, "Temperate Nordic Climes" (August 10, 1996), 38.

[28] Holder et al., *European Integration and Nordic Alcohol Policies*, 45, 146. Sweden also agreed with the Commission to apply a uniform tax rate according to the alcohol percentage of the beverage. Excise taxes on wine decreased in Finland by 17 percent and the retail price dropped by 10 percent on January 1998. Greg McIvor, "Sweden Cuts Tobacco Tax by 27 Percent," *Financial Times* (April 15, 1998), 1.

[29] "Stort mörkertal i alkoholstatistiken," *Aftonbladet*, September, 17, 1997 (www.aftonbladet.se).

[30] Anders Milhøj, "Structural Changes in the Danish Alcohol Market," *Nordic Alcohol Studies*, 13 (1996), 33–42; Susanne Bygvra "Border Shopping Between Denmark and West Germany," *Contemporary Drug Problems*, 17 (1990), 595–611.

unregistered consumption and the free market rhetoric of the EU have certainly emboldened the Swedish and Finnish private sectors to attempt to push governments to institute further reforms. Their allies, they believe, are the Commission and the Court of Justice.[31]

The Commission views the concessions granted during the negotiations for accession as temporary or transitional measures. It was never the intention to award permanent derogation, in part because the Nordic members agreed to accept the *acquis communautaire* in its entirety. Moreover, the Commission is keen to consolidate the progress made in freeing the movement of goods and services, people and capital. Alcohol control policies, regardless of how they are defined or construed, contradict the fundamental principles of the Single Market. Harry Franzén, a grocery store owner in southern Sweden, seized upon the latent tension between Community intention and national objectives to challenge Swedish rules by selling wine in his private store. Once the Swedish authorities decided to prosecute Mr. Franzén for illegally selling wine, Mr. Franzén claimed that he had not committed any crime because Article 28 of the TEC (formerly Article 30) prohibits restrictions on the importation of goods and Article 31 (formerly Article 37) guarantees that state monopolies shall not impede trade or foster discrimination. *Allmänna Åklagaren vs. Harry Franzén* (C-189/95) arose after the Swedish district court requested a preliminary ruling on whether the alcohol retail monopoly was in compliance with the Treaty of Rome. In June 1995, the *Landskrona Tingsrätt* sought clarification on three questions:

1 Is the monopoly in line with Article 30 of the Treaty of Rome (free importation of goods from other member states)?
2 Does a legal monopoly such as Systembolaget violate Article 37 and if so must it be abolished or are there ways to adapt it to Treaty requirements (trade barriers erected by state monopolies)?
3 If Systembolaget violates Article 37 does there exist a period of transition and adaptation beyond January 1, 1995?

The ECJ took two years to reach a judgment.

Court case: Allmänna Åklagaren vs. Harry Franzén (C-189/95)

The report of Michael Elmer, a Danish advocate-general, appeared in March 1997 and the Court made its final judgment in October 1997.

---

[31] Case E-1/94 *Ravintoloitsijain Liiton Kustannus Oy Restamark*, Case E-6/96 *Tore Wilhelmsen AS vs Oslo Kommune*, and Case E-1/97 *Fridtjof Frank Gundersen vs Oslo Kommune* also touched on the issue of legal compatibility.

Elmer, in his report, argued that Systembolaget was contrary to Article 30 and Article 37 for the following reasons. Foreign producers or importers must purchase a license if they want to sell their alcoholic beverages in Sweden. But the license does not guarantee that the state retail company will sell the products of the foreign licensed producers/importers/distributors through its retail outlets. Although the Swedish government de-monopolized alcohol distribution and imports, Systembolaget ultimately decides what Swedish consumers can buy. Elmer therefore argued that Systembolaget functions like an import monopoly since private importers cannot freely sell their products in the Swedish market.[32]

As to the question of whether overriding health considerations justify limited trade restrictions, Elmer cited various scientific studies suggestive of another possible link between moderate drinking and health. Red wine had a possible positive health impact so that the Swedish restrictions on trade, on the grounds of protecting public health, could be considered disproportionate.[33] With regard to the transition period, Elmer stated that Sweden was never granted permanent derogation for its retail system and a transition period was simply not discussed. Rather, the only correspondence that he could find to corroborate the acquiescence of the Commission to a state monopoly on alcoholic beverages consisted of a unilateral declaration by the Nordic applicants on the importance of safeguarding public health. Such a declaration has no legal standing.[34]

The negative report provoked obvious consternation in official Swedish circles and received extensive criticism. Many commentators ridiculed the advocate-general for citing medical scientific data of which he knew nothing and could claim no expertise. Social welfare officials and Systembolaget officials argued that Elmer had totally misunderstood the procedures of the monopoly. Finally, numerous commentators privately dismissed the report on the grounds that Elmer was a Dane, and therefore anti-Swedish, and had lost scores of cases in front of the Court of Justice.[35]

The Court made its decision public in late October 1997. To the

[32] In the first eight months of 1996, Systembolaget received 12,576 requests for inclusion in its retail system. It already carries a large selection of alcoholic beverages from throughout the world. Elmer, *Allmänna Åklagaren contre Harry Franzén Affaire C-189/95* (March, 1997), 15.

[33] Elmer, *Allmänna Åklagaren contre Harry Franzén*, 42.

[34] Elmer, *Allmänna Åklagaren contre Harry Franzén*, 45.

[35] Elmer was considered anti-Swedish not only because he was a Dane but also because he had had bad experiences with Systembolaget during a visit to Stockholm. He was one of the customers at a Systembolaget store in the mid-1970s who was caught by the "red light" and asked for identification papers.

enormous satisfaction of the Swedish establishment, the Court considered the distribution system of the alcohol monopoly non-discriminatory and not liable to put imported products at a disadvantage. Despite the restricted number of sales outlets, the monopoly is structured in such a fashion as to offer customers a wide range of choices of domestic and foreign beverages. It does not promote domestic over foreign products and its overall arrangements do not amount to selection bias. But the method of licensing agents to import alcoholic beverages hindered trade between member states because this created additional costs for imported beverages. Such a measure was not permissible for the sake of protecting public health because this aim could be achieved by measures less restrictive of intra-Community trade.[36] But the Court construed the case mainly as a matter of trade discrimination and did not refer to any of the public health arguments used by either the Swedish government or advocate-general's report.

Domestic trends and external pressures

Despite the favorable outcome of the Franzén case, the long wait for the ECJ decision permanently changed the national assessment of Sweden's alcohol control policy. Paradoxically, this legal victory turned into a major political debacle. The legal case, and the long wait for its final resolution, all at once made the abolishment of Systembolaget a real possibility. Until 1995, consumers griped about the hassles of cheerless and pricey state-owned liquor stores; the press repeated these complaints and suggested modifications such as more self-service stores to alleviate some of the inconveniences, and the private sector played up the public's vexations to effect further reforms. Yet it seemed inconceivable that the authorities would in fact redesign the entire network of institutions to permit wine and beer to be sold in ordinary grocery stores or, even more farfetched, that they would dismantle Systembolaget. The Swedish association of grocery stores, a group which had been extremely critical of Systembolaget for years and which had financed Franzén's legal costs, originally espoused such radical ideas. Invariably, the authorities dismissed their objections on the grounds that ordinary grocery stores did not represent "the people" and that their plan for System-bolaget would hurt Swedish society in the long run. Candid speculation on the fate of the retail monopoly, which dominated the debate in the popular media during the long wait for a final ECJ ruling, gave new

---

[36] Ylva Nilsson, "Nya bra-ok väntar om alkoholpolitiken," *Svenska Dagbladet* (October 24, 1997); "Dom gäller omedelbart," *Svenska Dagbladet* (October 29, 1997) (www.sd.se).

legitimacy to otherwise far-out scenarios with respect to the future of Systembolaget. The public debate itself raised further expectation of alcohol policy liberalization and fed into demands for reforms.

Until the Franzén case, most observers believed that no real alternative existed because parliament would veto any legislative moves that contradicted a basic aspect of the Nordic construction of the welfare state and was so intimately tied to definition of Nordic identity.[37] But the ECJ deliberations invoked much uncertainty on the actual compatibility between the state alcohol company and Community law and enabled opponents to take charge by introducing an entirely new frame of reference in the public debate on the future of the alcohol control policy. Private actors re-drew the debate in terms of private versus state responsibility and in terms of free trade versus state monopolies. It was in the interest of the consumer, the private sector claimed, to create and maintain free trade and competition. Since efficient and fair markets benefit consumers, the monopoly could be seen as hurting the very same people that the Swedish and Finnish governments were said to be protecting.[38]

Protest parties on the right joined the fray and advanced the ideas of cultural competence and negative consequences of excessive regulation. High taxes/prices force consumers to resort to moonshine, which can be more deadly than what is sold on the retail market. Since alcoholic beverages are prohibitively expensive, consumers drink at home and fail to learn how to incorporate alcohol into everyday life. Right-wing politicians blamed the authorities for causing unnecessary pain because artificial restrictions in the alcoholic beverage market nurtured the growth of unsupervised black markets of home-made liquor. Such radical ideas were even espoused by establishment figures. The managing director of Vin och Sprit, Kjell-Olof Feldt, appealed for laxer rules to arrest the popularity of smuggled spirits and moonshine. He suggested more stores, weekend opening, and the advertising of legal liquor to enable it to compete with the popularity of black market spirits. Likewise, the mainstream conservative party (*Moderate* party) argued that alcohol policy should focus on public opinion building and measures to reduce alcohol abuse among the young and vulnerable. Lower prices in restaurants would, moreover, promote sound drinking habits.[39]

---

[37] Sturla Nordlund, "Holdningsendringer og Vinmonopolets framtid," *Nordisk alkohol- & narkotikatidskrift*, 15 (1998), 223–33.

[38] Sutton, *Swedish Alcohol Discourse*, 138.

[39] Nycander, *Svenskarna och spriten*, 281; Sutton, *Swedish Alcohol Discourse*, 141. Feldt is on record as favoring liberalization since the mid-1990s. His appeal for relaxation to

Price and availability restrictions on alcoholic beverages were accepted by the population with a certain measure of resignation because it was believed that it was the duty of the state to tame the human passion for risky behavior and that it was the obligation of citizens to accept universal restrictions on drinking for the sake of a better society. Scientists and public officials who elucidated over and over again how unrestricted drinking would bring about unmitigated disasters further emphasized this message. But tourist imports and the emergence of an alternative repository of knowledge question the validity of the scientists' specialized knowledge of alcohol problems. Opponents point out that actual consumption figures are unreliable because they are drawn from reported sales through the state-owned retail monopoly and that illegal alcohol is especially popular among heavy drinkers from low-income households. If the consumption figures are suspect and if problem drinkers are more likely to resort to illicit liquor, the monopoly system cannot be considered effective in moderating alcohol intake.[40] Opponents also argued that other member states did not seem to experience outsized alcohol-related problems and relied on information, public campaigns, and internal control mechanisms. If Sweden confronted terrible drinking problems in spite of restrictive rules then it is perhaps time to introduce a liberal Continental model.[41]

This debate on free markets versus restrictive drinking rules takes place primarily in Sweden. By and large, officials and the research community in Finland have distanced themselves from the whole temperance legacy. Evidence of this is an alcohol regime that is comparatively liberal. Grocery stores have been allowed to sell medium-strength beer (alcohol content of up to 4.7 percent) since 1969, which is why beer consumption has rapidly increased in Finland. Other light alcoholic drinks with an alcohol content of 4.7 percent or less are also available in grocery stores. Alko has converted many of its stores into self-service and it downplays public health campaigns. The Finnish private sector is also in a different situation compared with that in Sweden. The Finnish food sector is opposed to private imports (from Estonia) because shoppers also purchase other items in addition to liquor once they are abroad. But Finnish brewery companies do not fully support deregulation since beer is available in thousands of shops,

combat the black market was reprinted in "Spritreklamen måste återinföras," *Sverige Nytt* (May 4, 1998), 2.

40 Holder et al., *European Integration and Nordic Alcohol Policies*, 135.

41 Caroline Sutton, *The Swedish Alcohol Discourse: From Inappropriate Behavior to "Our Greatest Public Health Threat"* (Stockholm: Stockholm International Studies, 2, 1996), 65–67.

gas stations, and newspaper kiosks while wine and distilled liquor are only available in 255 state monopoly shops.[42]

In general, drinking opinion is more liberal in Finland. The popular press began to demand better services and less bureaucratic control in the alcohol distribution system in the mid-1980s. It also asked for cheaper and better wines, more cheerful store decor, and fewer restrictions on the restaurant trade. Many newspaper articles criticized the whole monopoly system for being worthless and a major nuisance.[43] Partly in response to this barrage of criticism, Alko transformed itself into a business enterprise with a strong focus on brand management, market expansion, profits, and customer service. The business outlook of Alko was both the impetus for and the consequence of greater involvement of private interests in the alcohol debate. Retail trade, hotels, restaurants, and tourist boards have been active in the effort to influence alcohol policies. Their main objective is of course not to stabilize consumption or decrease health risks. They want to capture some of the liquor revenues or they want to use alcohol to compete in other market sectors. At the other end of the spectrum, very few social groups or organizations exist to defend alcohol policy. Voluntary associations (temperance and health interests), municipal administrations, and professionals (physicians and social workers) have undertaken no new initiatives in the past two decades to reframe the alcohol question. In the absence of any institutional commitment on behalf of the full set of alcohol control policy instruments, Finnish public opinion expresses considerable support for liberalization. Reflecting this sentiment, 101 of the 200 Finnish members of parliament signed a petition in early 1997 asking the government to increase the availability of wine and strong beer in general food stores. In a similar vein, Ilkka Suominen, former leader of the Conservative Party and former director-general of Alko, proposed to abolish the state monopoly and open the market to competition in the summer of 1997. His reasoning was that freer trade and open borders were putting a strain on the state monopoly and that state control over the alcohol trade was based on a myth about Finnish drinking patterns.[44]

It is important to remember that cultural values and public opinion had already adopted a more liberal stance before EU accession. Consumer trust in self-control and recognition for cultural competence, that

---

[42] Holder et al., *European Integration and Nordic Alcohol Policies*, 187.

[43] Pekka Sulkunen, "Alcohol Policies fin de siècle," *Health Policy* 7 (1987), 331, and "The Conservative Mind. Why Does the New Middle Class Hate Alcohol Control?" *Addiction Research*, 1 (1994), 295–308.

[44] Greg McIvor, "Call to Scrap Finland's State Alko Monopoly," *Financial Times* (August 1, 1997), 3.

is, the ability to decide for oneself what to buy and how to consume, have risen in Finland and Sweden. Cohorts born in the 1960s and during the waning years of the temperance movement are more liberal than previous generations of voters. The post-temperance generation increasingly rejects the right of others to define the good life because, they allege, this is a private matter. In spheres where the public and the private intersect, such as consumption risks of alcohol, universal rules no longer work because they set rigid norms unacceptable to self-directed individuals. Thus, values and attitudes already began to converge to European, majority-supported norms, diluting the distinctiveness of typical Nordic temperance values in the 1980s.[45] Opinions on drinking and alcohol mirror a trend away from collectivism although there is still plenty of support for the basic entitlements of the welfare state; there is, however, also a yearning for greater individual autonomy.

The liberalization or Europeanization of drinking attitudes is best captured through public opinion surveys. In 1981, 96 percent of Swedes regarded alcohol as a serious problem compared with 99 percent who considered the drug problem to be a grave hazard. In 1994, 91 percent of Swedes still thought drugs were a serious problem in contrast to 66 percent who felt the same about alcohol.[46] Other studies show that the percentage of the surveyed population who defined the alcohol problem as *very serious* (as opposed to just *serious*) fell from 66 to 13 percent between 1981 and 1994 in spite of a noticeable increase in alcohol consumption.[47] As consumers begin to minimize the risks of alcohol misuse, they want alcohol to be more easily accessible. A majority of Swedes want grocery stores, alongside Systembolaget, to sell wine and beer. In 1980 and 1988, about 38 percent of the Swedish population favored wine sales in grocery stores. But during the debate on EU accession in 1993, this figure climbed to 75 percent. In the late 1990s, some of the initial enthusiasm for privatization waned and 55 percent of Swedes wanted wine sales in grocery stores. In urban areas, however, wine sales in grocery stores still enjoyed the support of over 70 percent of Swedish respondents in a small-scale survey done in 1997.[48] In all

---

[45] Bo Rothstein, *Just Institutions Matter: The Moral and Political Logic of the Universal Welfare State* (New York: Cambridge University Press, 1998), 192–200; Jo Saglie, "Attitude Change and Policy Decisions: The Case of Norwegian Alcohol Policy," *Scandinavian Political Studies*, 19 (1996), 309–27. The proportion of workers with a strong attachment to individualism and autonomy rose from 39 to 53 percent between 1981 and 1990.

[46] Holder et al., *European Integration and Nordic Alcohol Policies*, 200–01.

[47] Cited in Richard F. Tomasson, "Alcohol and Alcohol Control in Sweden," *Scandinavian Studies*, 70 (1998), 497.

[48] Lars Söderberg, "Skrota bolaget, ministern," *Aftonbladet* (March 6, 1997) (www.aftonbladet.se).

age groups, aside from those over the age of 65, the free sale of alcohol is the favored option and the overwhelming majority of conservative voters (*moderata*) favor the "other stores" option (72 percent).[49]

Compared with Swedish consumers those in Finland express even stronger support for liberalization.[50] In 1981, Finns were asked for the first time if they supported the current alcohol policy regime or favored more restrictive or more liberal measures. At that time, 46 percent of the interviewees supported stricter measures, 40 percent were content with existing regulation, and 10 percent called for liberal reforms. In 1990, 40 percent of the population wanted more liberal rules while only 20 percent desired to see more restrictions.[51] In 1998, when the alcohol field had been greatly liberalized, a third of the Finnish population still wanted to see more liberalization, half accepted the current regime, and only 16 percent desired to see greater restrictions.[52] By the late 1990s, access to alcohol had been made easier, the number of self-service stores had expanded, prices had come down, and restrictions on advertising had been loosened. Nevertheless, a sizable majority still supports further steps of deregulation. Liberalization, at this stage, involves the sale of table wines and beer in ordinary grocery stores. In 1984, 24 percent of Finnish respondents agreed with the idea of selling wine in grocery stores, in 1988, 54 percent were in favor and by 1999, 75 percent approved.[53]

Opinions on drinking are thus more liberal or Continental in Finland than in Sweden. One explanation is that the Finnish community of experts is more heterogeneous and less unified than the Swedish one and is thus more willing to examine underlying beliefs and cultural biases. Finnish researchers did not display the same kind of passion and moral certitude as the medical community in Sweden. Another factor was that Alko itself was divided on how to frame alcohol control policies. The tension inside Alko was created by its growing inclination to act like a commercial business enterprise and for management to emphasize profits over public health. The strain has been largely overcome after the retail branch was placed directly under the aegis of the Ministry of Social and Health Affairs in 1998. Systembolaget, which is separate

---

[49] Tomasson, "Alcohol and Alcohol Control in Sweden," 498. Fifty percent of social democratic voters favor the "other stores" option.

[50] Sulkunen, "The Conservative Mind," 295–308.

[51] Salme Ahlström and Esa Österberg, "Changes in Climate of Opinion Concerning Alcohol Policy in Finland in the 1980s," *Contemporary Drug Problems*, 22 (1992), 437–38.

[52] Holder et al., *European Integration and Nordic Alcohol Policies*, 200.

[53] Esa Österberg, "Changes in Public Attitudes towards Alcohol Control in Finland," paper presented at the 38th International Congress on Alcohol, Drugs, and Other Dependencies, Vienna, August 16–20, 1999.

from and independent of Vin och Sprit, continued to work to restrict alcohol availability by maintaining its Saturday closing, disseminating alcohol information, resisting self-service, and refusing to sell curiously named, packaged, and labeled products.[54]

But Finland's break with the anti-alcohol legacy is also connected to the ebbing relevance of the historical narrative on abusive drinking. Binge drinking is now a "myth" and no longer a powerful characterization of the idiosyncratic behavior of the average Finnish male. Boozing was always closely linked to perceptions of cultural inferiority and was equated with ignorance. Finnish per capita consumption of pure alcohol was much higher in the 1990s than it had been at any time since the end of prohibition, yet concern for alcohol misuse dropped appreciably. The explanation for this changed perception is self-evident. Tolerance of alcohol is higher because drinking is no longer considered a symptom of backwardness.[55] Inasmuch as Finnish consumers hold reservations on the wisdom of alcohol liberalization, they still advocate the sale of wine in ordinary food stores. Wine is not very popular in Finland and accounted for 13 percent of total alcohol consumption in 1998. Approximately 80 percent of Finnish consumers feel that wine in food stores would lead to increased consumption among underaged and problem drinkers. Regardless, Finnish consumers want to see wine in food stores as this signifies, for Finnish consumers, a modern lifestyle in congruence with the rest of Europe.[56]

Is the alcohol monopoly system then doomed to extinction? Not if it were up to the Ministers of Finance and Social Welfare. They are fully committed to the preservation of quotas on travelers' duty-free allowances and high excise taxes, which amount to over 6 percent of state revenues in Finland and 3 percent in Sweden. Already, tax revenues will be less than half owing to pressures to conform to EU price structures, and further liberalization will probably mean higher alcohol consumption and more money spent on dealing with a higher prevalence of alcohol-related problems.[57] The Ministry of Finance is otherwise very pro-market oriented, but it fears the fiscal implications of alcohol liberalization.

---

[54] Holder et al., *European Integration and Nordic Alcohol Policies*, 173.

[55] Ahlström and Österberg, "Changes in Climate of Opinion concerning Alcohol Policy in Finland in the 1980s," 438; Jussi Simpura and Pirjo Paakkanen, "New Beverages, New Drinking Contexts? Signs of Modernization in Finnish Drinking Habits from 1984 to 1992, Compared with Trends in the European Community," *Addiction*, 90 (1995), 679.

[56] Ingebritsen, *Nordic States and European Unity*, 188

[57] Esa Österberg, Sami Kajalo, Kalervo Leppänen, Kari Niilola, Timo Rauhanen, Jukka Salomaa, and Iikko B. Voipo, "Alkoholkonsumtion och–priser i Finland till å 2004. Fyra scenarier," *Nordisk alkohol- & narkotikatidskrift*, 15 (1998), 212–22.

In addition, mistrust of spirits is still high. The Finnish population still believes that distilled liquors pose a public health threat and should not be available in grocery stores. In 1999 only 20 percent of Finnish and Swedish respondents approved of spirits being made available in food stores.[58] Consumers still see a role for state-owned alcohol monopolies in public policy because binge drinking, though less frequent than a hundred years ago, is still an expressive ritual for certain classes of people (residents of rural areas, people with less education, and young adults). There is also enormous support for extremely tough anti-drunken driving rules. In Sweden, drunken driving is perceived to be as serious as a bank robbery. Legal alcohol limits in Sweden are the lowest in the OECD with a limit of 0.02 percent (in the USA the limit for gross alcohol-impaired driving is 0.10 percent and thus five times as high).[59] Thus, the misuse of alcohol and its potential costs to society are still taken seriously.

Regardless of how much state officials would like to retain the entire complement of policy tools, the Commission announced in late 1999 that Sweden must phase out all restrictions on personal alcohol imports by June 30, 2000. Earlier, in 1996, Finland had agreed to eliminate quotas by December 2003. At that time, Sweden still believed that it could perhaps persuade the Commission to grant a permanent exemption. Fritz Bolkestein, Commissioner for Internal Market, was adamant that Sweden must conform to EU rules in late 1999 and dismissed reports by Swedish public health experts that, after the abolition of limits on personal travelers' imports, the number of alcohol-related deaths would increase by between 1,000 and 3,000 per year. After visiting Stockholm in early 2000, Bolkestein granted Sweden the same terms as Finland with the result that both countries have until December 2003 to adjust to EU rules whereby a traveler can bring back 10 liters of spirits, 90 liters of wine, and 110 liters of beer.[60]

An interesting detail is the reaction of the Swedish population. In 1994, various pundits claimed that Brussels' interference in Sweden's hallowed alcohol policy would influence voters to say no to the referendum on accession to the EU. Less than six years later, 60 percent of

---

[58] Holder et al., *European Integration and Nordic Alcohol Policies*, 207; Österberg, "Changes in Public Attitudes towards Alcohol Control in Finland," 5. Even representatives of the supermarket chains and conservative politicians argue that spirits should only be available in non-profit state stores.

[59] Tomasson, "Alcohol and Alcohol Control in Sweden," 497–99. Support for anti-drunken driving campaigns is high because measures are effective, involve minimal personal burden, and clearly address a serious alcohol-related harm.

[60] Christopher Brown-Humes, "Brussels Stands Firm on Sweden's Alcohol Import Restrictions," *Financial Times* (March 7, 2000), 2, and "Swedes Accept Limits on Drinks Import Curbs," *Financial Times* (March 14, 2000), 4.

the adult population favored the same rules in effect in the rest of the EU and the Conservative Party argued for an immediate abolition of the restrictions unless this would cause too much hardship.[61] E-mails and letters from Swedish citizens, the overwhelming majority of whom urged an end to the import restrictions, inundated Bolkestein's office.[62] An informal electronic opinion poll on the website of *Aftonbladet* revealed that 92 percent of the nearly 8,000 respondents opposed an extension of the import curbs on alcohol.[63]

In preparation for the big moment when the special rules will be phased out, the Swedish government raised the personal limits on wine from 5 to 20 liters in July 2000 and will permit further increases in personal imports in 2001 and 2003 for both beer and wine. Prior to the quarrel with the Commission, the Swedish authorities had already undertaken another small step towards liberalization by allowing selected stores in the northern part of the country to be open on Saturday. The Finnish authorities recognized years ago that import rules would have to adjust to extant EU rules and Alko is urging the government to lower prices of alcoholic beverages by 25 to 30 percent to ward off competition from tourist imports.[64] It should be noted that nobody proposes an immediate end to the public monopolies. Rather, the main focus is on preparing the state monopoly for increased competition, which will mean lower prices (and excise taxes) and of course, higher registered consumption of alcohol.

Conclusion

A wide range of preventive strategies was adopted to reduce the prevalence of harm related to alcohol consumption. The working assumption was that alcohol, though available in retail outlets, is unlike any other legal commodity and must be subject to a distinct set of commercial principles. The state monopoly systems were a compromise between the temperance-led call for prohibition and private sector desires for free circulation of alcoholic beverages. The distinctive model of alcohol regulation was tied to national discourse, symbols, and value system. A virtuous person was sober and temperate. A worthy state

---

[61] "Regeringen backar om alkohol," *Svenska Dagbladet*, February 23, 2000 (www.sd.se). The survey was done by Sifo and Temo.

[62] Cina Rönn, "EU-kommissionären chattade med läserna på aftonbladet.se," *Aftonbladet* (March 6, 2000) (www.aftonbladet.se).

[63] "Är det bra att Sveriges undantag från införselreglerna förlängs?" *Aftonbladet* (March 13, 2000).

[64] Kerstin Stenius, "Lugnet efter stormen inom Alko. Intervju med Reijo Salmi," *Nordisk alkohol- & narkotikatidskrift*, 16 (1999), 387.

imposed universal solutions to address individual failings on behalf of the community. A just society checked members from succumbing to intoxication and abuse.

Changes in attitudes and values were already afoot in the 1980s as the temperance–social welfare ethos began to wear off and urban, educated middle-class consumers favored greater self-responsibility and control. The national symbols of an immature nation no longer resonated with the post-1960 generation in Finland yet the peculiar Finnish drinking style was regularly attributed to ignorance and backwardness. The European Union accelerated value shifts because it brought in its wake organizational reforms of the state monopoly and liberalized tourist imports. In this new climate, attention focused on the negative externalities of state alcohol monopolies and availability restrictions. The private sector emerged as a stronger actor thanks to partial de-monopolization of production and imports. Conservative voices and private sector interests skillfully appropriated EU language and symbols to dispute the expert medical opinion on alcohol.

In the 1980s, public opinion turned against invasive regulation of consumer choices but voters had few opportunities to translate their resentment into policy action. Obviously, alcohol control policies, which impose a particular moral framework and normative mindset, only work if society condemns alcohol and is willing to subject itself to restrictions and barriers. As the moral stigma of drinking vanished, socio-medical theories replaced the earlier justification for the institution of the regimes. But more and more consumers regard drinking as a regular activity and ignore the social and medical warnings against moderate intake of alcohol. In fact, they probably are familiar with the American debates on the beneficial impact of a moderate consumption of red wine. Ultimately, Swedish and Finnish consumers no longer are so sure that they are truly very different from other European people. If other Europeans know how to drink and can purchase wine and beer in ordinary food stores, what prevents Finns and Swedes from acquiring this knowledge and being in control of their own consumption decisions? There is no real answer to this question unless you believe that Swedes and Finns are more prone to substance abuse than citizens of other Western nations.

Does this mean that the Finns and Swedes are shedding their alcohol neurosis? If beer and wine are normal commodities, spirits still provoke fear and anxiety. Finland and Sweden continue to hold slightly different views on alcohol and view strict regulation of spirits as a national priority. In the foreseeable future, the drinking cultures and attitudes of the two Nordic countries will continue to differ from those of Denmark or southern Europe. The tough anti-drinking road laws, the many restrictions on advertisements and selling to minors, the presence of a state alcohol monopoly, and the cultural acceptance of binge drinking differentiate Sweden and Finland from the rest of the EU. But the distance between the uniquely Nordic conceptualization of drinking and that of the rest of Europe is narrowing. At the same time, the definition of what it means to be Finnish or Swedish – introvert, shy, and awkward in social gatherings – is also under revision.

5   Permissive pragmatism: drug control policy in the Netherlands

In spite of its notoriety, Dutch drug[1] control policy resembles that of many other advanced industrialized countries. Emma Bonino, the former Commissioner for Consumer Policy and for Humanitarian Affairs of the European Union came out in public in favor of Dutch-style decriminalization of cannabis, after the European Drugs Observatory issued a report showing "little relationship" between strict prohibitionist policies and reductions in the number of drug offenses.[2] Nevertheless, the Netherlands is known as Europe's drug Mecca. The aim of this chapter is to highlight how Dutch drug policy diverges from conventional standards, why this particular form of intervention is representative of Dutch collective self-identity, and how institutions and interests interpret and rationalize the Dutch way of doing things.

The Netherlands deviates from the rest of Europe in that it views the circulation of illicit drugs as a public health issue rather than a law and order crisis. Like Nordic alcohol policy, Dutch drug policy aims to reduce harm to the individual and society so that assistance and prevention go hand in hand with detection and prosecution of punishable offenses. Three government departments are involved in drug policy deliberation and implementation: Interior, Justice, and Public Health. The latter is in charge of overall coordination.[3] Of course, as every tourist will testify, the most striking facet of Dutch drug policy is the coffee shop. This establishment sells small amounts of hashish and marijuana for personal use alongside ordinary refreshments. First opened in Amsterdam, coffee shops are now found across the country.

---

[1] Drugs refer to illegal substances that are said to be addictive and dangerous to society and the individual.

[2] "EU Commissioner Urges Drugs Liberalization," *Agence France Press*, October 9, 1996.

[3] Report of Minister van Volksgezondheid, Welzijn, en Sport, Minister van Justitie, Staatsscretaris van Binnenlandse Zaken, "Het Nederlandse drugbeleid; continuïteit en verandering," in T. Blom, H. de Doelder, and D.J. Hessing (eds.), *Naar een consistent drugsbeleid* (Deventer: Gouda Quint, 1996), 258; Dirk J. Korf, Heleen Riper, and Bruce Bullington, "Windmills in their Minds? Drug Policy and Drug Research in the Netherlands," *Journal of Drug Issues*, 29 (1999), 451–72.

The easy availability of soft drugs and tolerance for open drug scenes is for many commentators the strongest indication that the Netherlands is soft on drugs generally.

It is important to stress at the beginning of this chapter that the Netherlands simply belongs to the *less* prohibitionist EU countries. Roughly two-thirds of the total budget allocated to the drug problem is spent on criminal action.[4] Dutch authorities make an exception for the personal possession and consumption of drugs and for the retail trade in soft drugs. Decriminalization of soft drugs is part of the harm reduction strategy to prevent youngsters from falling prey to drug-peddling criminals.

All drug control systems arose from years of experiences filtered through cultural, legal, and political perceptions. Like alcohol control policies, the boundaries and objectives of drug policies reflect a particular line of thinking on public health, deviant behavior, the judicial system, and state-society relations. In every country, the public discourse on drugs articulates abstract ideas on the origins of the epidemic, its challenge to society or the state, and the relative risks of anti-social activities in advanced welfare states. The debate and attendant policy measures communicate society's tolerance for behavior incongruous with the work ethic, self-discipline, and ethical individualism. The Dutch, apparently, are willing to accept, within limits, private lifestyle choices at odds with middle-class sensibilities.

The Dutch see themselves and are viewed by others as morally permissive. Various studies have identified the Danes as the most morally permissive people in Western Europe, followed by the Dutch and the French. While the Danes were especially tolerant with respect to behaviors in the personal-sexual domain (divorce, abortion, and euthanasia), the Dutch were tolerant across the board in areas related to personal-sexual morality, self-interested morality (cheating on taxes, buying stolen goods, lying in one's own interests) and legal/illegal morality (under-age sex, political assassination, joyriding).[5] The European Value Systems Study labeled the Netherlands as the most permissive country in 1981 and 1990 followed by France, Germany, and Belgium.[6]

This chapter will examine why tolerance emerged as the dominant

---

[4] Marcel de Kort and Ton Cramer, "Pragmatism versus Ideology: Dutch Drug Policy Continued," *Journal of Drug Issues*, 29 (1999), 477.

[5] Stephen Harding, David Phillips, and Michael Fogarty, *Contrasting Values in Western Europe: Unity, Diversity, and Change* (London: Macmillan, 1986), 9–18.

[6] Loek Halman and Ruud de Moor, "Religion, Churches, and Moral Values," in Peter Ester, Loek Halman, and Ruud de Moor (eds.), *The Individualizing Society: Value Change in Europe and North America* (Tilburg: Tilburg University Press, 1993), 56–60.

anti-drug strategy. In the conclusion, the tensions and ambiguities in the current drug policy regimes will be described. The first step, however, before delving into the mysteries of Dutch drug control policy, is to discover why Dutch Calvinism, which is a more austere version of Lutheranism, did not give rise to a prohibitionist mentality and corresponding repressive sanctions to suppress drug-taking.

Detour: Protestant nations and intoxication

Although the Netherlands has always possessed a sizable Catholic minority, Calvinism shapes its culture. Calvinists dominated the state elite until the arrival of mass politics, and cliques of Calvinist merchants ruled universal suffrage, with strong anti-papist feelings, and the richest province, Holland. Social historians attributed to this Calvinism the "proverbial phlegm of the Dutch," the lack of passion and open emotion and a certain degree of circumspection. Thriftiness (if not stinginess) and domesticity together with cleanliness were other traits attributed to Calvinism. Generally, Protestant cultures stress self-control and associate excessive eating or drinking with moral failure, sloth, and impulsiveness. Successful temperance movements emerged in the English-speaking world (the USA, Canada, the UK, Australia, and New Zealand) and the Nordic societies of Finland, Sweden, Norway, and Iceland because they were Protestant and favored hard liquor (vodka, gin, rum, or whiskey).[7]

The Netherlands in the nineteenth century falls into this category. Calvinism and the popularity of *jenever* (Dutch gin) gave rise to a temperance movement more or less at the same time as in Finland and Sweden. None the less, although the Dutch were known to be serious drinkers and academic descriptions published in the prewar era mentioned heavy drinking and dullness or awkwardness in personal relationships as typically Dutch, the temperance movement made no lasting impression on the state.[8] A smallish temperance movement emerged first in the 1840s to agitate for the reduction of consumption of *jenever* and was eclipsed by a larger working-class teetotaler movement in the 1880s, which urged abstinence in order to raise the social and material status of the poor. But the state refused to legislate any real limits on alcohol production and retailing in spite of a petition, gathered in 1914,

---

[7] Harry G. Levine, "Alcohol Problems in Nordic and English-speaking Cultures," in Malcolm Lader, Griffith Edwards, and D. Colin Drummond (eds.), *The Nature of Alcohol and Drug Related Problems* (New York: Oxford University Press, 1992), 17.

[8] Bart van Heerikhuizen, "What is Typically Dutch? Sociologists in the 1930s and 1940s on the Dutch National Character," *Netherlands' Journal of Sociology*, 18 (1982), 107.

with almost 700,000 signatures (or 25 percent of the adult population). The petition called for the introduction of the local option or veto to enable municipalities to issue their own rules for on-premise sale of alcohol. While parliament was willing to contemplate some curbs on the alcohol trade, the Upper House blocked every piece of legislation until 1931. By then, consumption of distilled spirits had dropped considerably and *jenever* was no longer the dominant alcoholic beverage.[9]

Why would the Netherlands not be more apprehensive about alcohol and drugs than Sweden, considering that Calvinism belonged to the more ascetic branch of the Christian faith? Why does Swedish social democracy take a much more restrictive view of intoxicants than Dutch Christian democracy? Swedish authorities regard drug usage as deviant behavior and seek to isolate its presence in society. The Nordic hostility towards drugs is partly related to the cultural legacy of its Protestant mentality, which has been very influential in shaping certain aspects of the social welfare state. But how does *this* explanation account for the pragmatic tolerance of mind-altering substances in another Protestant nation such as the Netherlands?

As in Denmark, evangelical anti-establishment churches failed to attract a substantial number of followers. This deprived the temperance movement of an important ally. Moreover, the Calvinist view of the state and state power differed significantly from that of official Lutheranism. Calvinism was more suspicious of state power and intervention than was the Lutheran church, which historically was absorbed into the state structures of centralizing monarchies in Sweden (and Finland, which was part of Sweden until 1809). Lutheran churches became an extension of state power and the clergy was converted into a corps of ecclesiastical officials subject to crown authority. Their opposition to state intervention in the social and familial spheres was muted. But Calvinism upheld the ideal of a Church-civilization and refused to cede authority to civil governments even in matters of state. The end result was that Calvinism and the state entertained a more fractious relationship and this engendered a tradition of distrust of state interference in societal affairs.[10] It would have been out of character for the Calvinist

---

[9] Jan de Lint, "Anti-Drink Propaganda and Alcohol Control Measures: A Report on the Dutch Experience," in Eric Single, Patricia Morgan, and Jan de Lint (eds.), *Alcohol, Society, and the State* (2 vols., Toronto: Addiction Research Foundation, 1981), vol. II, 86–96.

[10] John T.S. Madely, "Politics and the Pulpit: The Case of Protestant Europe," *West European Politics*, 5 (1982), 149–71; Monica Claes and Bruno de Witte, "Report of the Netherlands," in A.-M. Slaughter, A. Stone-Sweet, and J. Weiler (eds.), *The European Court and National Courts* (Oxford: Hart Publishing, 1998), 171–94.

church to join a popular movement to pressure the state to expand its regulatory scope.

It is also important to remember that the Netherlands like Denmark underwent a different political economy trajectory. Agriculture became commercialized early on and the mythic struggle of the Swedish or Finnish peasant against the elements, which forged a psychology of taciturnity and self-reliance, hardly typified the early modern history of the Netherlands. Not only was the climate more benign but agriculture was never the single largest economic activity and always existed along-side commerce and shipping. Extensive international contacts, which built an economy dependent on trade, cultivated a "mellow" attitude towards strange customs, odd habits, and different cultures. Dutch religious tolerance and political pluralism grew out of the need to engage in commerce while its small size, its location in the center of Western Europe, and its dearth of natural resources, motivated various Dutch groups to get along with more powerful neighbors.[11] The official culture, at least at home, granted equal status to contending religious views and espoused official tolerance in the face of diversity. Catholics were officially discriminated yet were informally at liberty to construct their own parallel world. So long as they built places of worship in private, out of sight of the Dutch Reformed Church, they could hold Mass. The dogmatic Calvinist church recognized that religious mino-rities, who sought shelter from persecution in other countries, brought skills, expertise, and wealth to the Dutch Republic. It made sense to seek accommodation with people of other faiths.[12]

Other factors seem to account for why the political culture espoused tolerance. The weakness of organized labor in a mercantile economy strengthened respect for civil liberties and dissuaded the state from regulating private consumption habits. Labor movements in Sweden and Finland politicized drinking in part to appeal to recent migrants from the countryside and in part to improve the quality of life of the industrial working class. Organized labor in the Netherlands was from the beginning divided into separate religious and socialist communities and working-class leaders de-emphasized class identity. Late and scat-tered industrialization kept the working class numerically weak also. Sweden industrialized late as well but once its timber and iron-ore industries took off, the rise of the labor movement was rapid. Since Finland and Sweden were typical agrarian countries with widely

[11] J.C.C. Voorhoeve, *Peace, Profits and Principles: A Study of Dutch Foreign Policy* (The Hague: Martinus Nijhoff, 1979).
[12] Thomas R. Rochon, *The Netherlands: Negotiating Sovereignty in an Independent World* (Boulder, CO: Westview Press, 1999), 26–29.

dispersed populations and few towns, attachment to civil liberties was less strong, even after the countries industrialized. The combination of an underdeveloped tradition of pre-industrial civil liberties with a strongly activist labor movement yielded belief in social engineering for the sake of the public good.

Although state agencies refused to implement laws to solve an alleged drinking problem, the population demanded state action to reduce gin consumption. But state agencies preferred to rely on education and public information to alter consumer behavior. The moral restraint exercised by central government agencies arose from Calvinist state theology, a fragmented labor movement, a strong attachment to civil liberties, and a desire for contact with different cultures and mores. But there is an additional factor, which is not frequently mentioned, that accounts for the mellow approach to alcohol and drugs: the Netherlands was deeply involved in the colonial trade of opium and cocaine.

Dutch merchants began trading opium in the early seventeenth century. In 1685, the amount of opium sold by the United Dutch East India Company (a public monopoly) was over one hundred thousand kilograms. In the 1790s, the United Dutch East India Company was disbanded, its employees became Dutch civil servants, and the opium trade fell into the hands of the state. Profits from opium exceeded those from coffee, sugar, and tin and the colonial government prohibited the private cultivation of opium poppies in order to restrain competition. After 1830, in need of more state revenues, the Dutch began to lease the right to sell opium to the highest bidders, most of whom were Chinese merchants. Between 1834 and 1895, opium profits accounted for around 10 percent of all colonial income.[13] Profits declined in the late nineteenth century in part because Chinese merchants were apparently involved in massive smuggling operations. To limit smuggling, the government decided to switch to a monopoly production regime where a colonial state agency ran large factories to process the opium to be sold in special state stores. Between 1893 and 1913, the state opium monopoly accounted for 15 percent of the total income from colonial possessions.[14]

Aside from the importation, preparation, and distribution of smoke-

[13] Ewald Vanvugt, *Wettig Opium* (Haarlem: In de Knipscheer, 1985), 414; also, Jan-Willem Gerritsen, *De politieke economie van de roes: De ontwikkeling van reguleringsregimes voor alcohol en opiaten* (Amsterdam: Amsterdam University Press, 1993), 60–62.

[14] Marcel de Kort, "A Short History of Drugs in the Netherlands," in Ed Leuw and I. Haen Marshall (eds.), *Between Prohibition and Legalization: The Dutch Experiment in Drug Policy* (New York: Kugler, 1995), 7; Marcel de Kort and Dirk J. Korf, "The Development of Drug Trade and Drug Control in the Netherlands: A Historical Perspective," *Crime, Law, and Social Change*, 17 (1992), 124–27.

able opium, the Dutch government was also active in the extraction of cocaine from coca leaves. It took years of experimentation to improve the quality of the coca leaves. By 1913, the Dutch East Indies finally managed to produce 1.4 million kilograms of coca leaves. Dutch officials claimed that most of the cocaine was for medical usage.[15] But the demand for medicinal cocaine was estimated to be around 12,000 kilograms in 1922 while the Dutch colonial production was over 1.2 million kilograms![16] It was at this point that the League of Nations branded the Netherlands as one of the most important drug-producing countries.

Distinguished Dutch parliamentarians, civil servants, and mission-aries campaigned against opium smoking in Dutch East India but did not believe that the Dutch state could and therefore should put a complete halt to this ingrained custom. Rather, they pressured the state to minimize the economic influence of Chinese organizations by taking over the entire opium industry. But Dutch interest groups were indif-ferent to the opium habits of the Javanese and other inhabitants of the Indonesian archipelago. American delegations played a much larger role in forcing the Netherlands to pass new legislation to control the manufacturing, sale, processing, transport, and trade of cocaine, and opium and its derivatives in 1919 (Opium Act). The invasion and occupation by the Japanese Imperial army ended the Dutch state opium monopoly, especially after the USA blocked any further prospects of resuming opium production after the liberation of Dutch East India in 1945.[17]

The examples of *jenever* and opium smoking show that the Dutch state has historically taken a decidedly non-interventionist attitude towards the consumption of intoxicating substances. The philosophical orientation of the elite was to discount the regulation of private behavior and to shun highly moralistic agendas. Obviously, there is no direct mechanical connection between past efforts to root out particular forms of intoxication and contemporary drug policy. Yet looking at the past, a "national drinking problem" was successfully overcome notwith-standing the failure to pass stricter alcohol legislation. Per capita consumption of alcohol fell from around 5–7 liters to 2 liters between

---

[15] H. Richard Friman, *NarcoDiplomacy: Exporting the US War on Drugs* (Ithaca: Cornell University Press, 1996), 18–34.

[16] The Netherlands (with Java) was singled out, together with Peru and Bolivia, as one of the main states engaged in coca production in a lengthy Joint Resolution (HJR 453) of the US Congress in 1923. David F. Musto, *The American Disease: Origins of Narcotic Control* (New Haven, NJ: Yale University Press, 1973), 198.

[17] Marcel de Kort, *Tussen patiënt en delinquent: Geschiedenis van het Nederlandse drugsbeleid* (Hilversum: Verloren, 1995), 53.

1830 and 1920, demonstrating the positive impact of education and information on moral choices and consumer behavior.[18] When drugs appeared in Dutch society, their use or misuse did not tap primordial fears of moral decay since the Dutch state had earned large revenues from the opium trade for centuries. It was not strange for Dutch agencies to rely, again, on information and education to warn against drug addiction since that fitted with its past orientation. None the less, it would be very misleading to draw a direct causal link between an anti-alcohol movement in the past, middle-class anxiety about substance abuse in general, and the emergence of a repressive drug regime decades later except to conclude that the Dutch central government administration was unaccustomed to prohibit the private consumption of just about anything.[19]

This predilection of shutting one's eyes against troubling forms of private behavior is as essential to the definition of Dutch collective self-identity as is the Nordic definition of taming human passions to produce a better society to Nordic self-identity. This does not mean that anti-social behaviors are accepted; it would be more apt to say that they are tolerated. Tolerance, however, flows from the decision of Dutch state agencies to shun moralizing agendas. Central governments, whether on the left or right of the political spectrum, recognize individual autonomy in the realm of personal morality. This attitude even characterized government bureaucracies at the peak of social welfare state activism.

Why would Dutch state institutions demonstrate such restraint in the wake of non-conformist, questionable anti-middle-class activities during a period of greatly enlarged state responsibility for the social wellbeing of its citizens? Part of the answer is mentioned above. But another piece of the puzzle is the division of Dutch society into competing self-contained socio-cultural blocs, all of which insisted on autonomy to guide the lives and moral values of their followers. Once the loose federation of the Dutch Republic gave way to the unified Kingdom of the Netherlands in 1815, outwardly the new kingdom adopted all the trappings of other European nation-states. In reality, state-building went hand in hand with the emancipation of different religious groups. Rather than forging an assertive nationalist ideology to back up claims of unity and homogeneity, the state dampened its natural tendencies to impose a common cultural and normative framework on society. Social control and the forging of a modern political identity were the domain of

[18] Gerritsen, *De politieke economie van de roes*, 88–92.
[19] Henk F.L. Garretsen and Ien van de Goor, "The Netherlands," in Dwight B. Heath (ed.), *International Handbook on Alcohol and Culture* (Westport, CT: Greenwood Press, 1995), 193.

tightly organized subcultures of Catholics, Protestants, and the secular working class, which structured most aspects of political, social, and personal life in the Netherlands. Called *zuilen* or pillars, leaders of each bloc exercised control over the rank and file and subsequently created viable political parties to compete in general elections.[20] The socio-cultural organizations relegated the state to a subsidiary role in conflict management and social integration in order to shape the vital spheres of family, education, and religion/culture. A fourth minority, moreover, remained disorganized precisely because it occupied a dominant position in society. The liberal bloc directed state agencies, shaped the economy, and determined relationships between competing churches. Because of its political and economic supremacy, it experienced fewer pressures to form cohesive organizations yet the liberal faction also upheld the concept of subsidiarity of central state institutions to social organizations. Even the smallish Calvinist bloc, because of its association with classical liberal capitalism, favored sovereignty for its own community.[21]

The electoral reforms of 1917, which introduced direct proportional representation, consolidated the influence of competing subcultures in social life and politics. Each organizational network was relatively autonomous and entered elections with its own political party. Catholics and Protestants put limits on state intervention since the leaders of the confessional blocs claimed to uphold the natural order of society.[22] The fragmentation of society into competing socio-cultural blocs each with its own political elite described the era of pillarization between 1917 and 1967. The parliamentary election of 1967 marked a turning point as the three (two Protestant and one Catholic) confessional parties lost their combined parliamentary majority which they had enjoyed for fifty years. The largest loser was the Catholic party, which lost nearly half its seats in less than ten years while the Labor party also registered in 1967 its lowest support since it started competing in elections. Instead, new anti-establishment parties came from nowhere to capture votes from the political mainstream. The remarkable 1967 elections accelerated the crumbling of the pillars. As the system of social control fell apart in the

[20] Arend Lijphart, *The Politics of Accommodation: Pluralism and Democracy in the Netherlands* (Berkeley: University of California Press, 1975) and his "From Politics of Accommodation to Adversarial Politics in the Netherlands: A Reassessment," in Hans Daalder and Galen Irwin (eds.), *Politics in the Netherlands: How Much Change?* (London: Frank Cass, 1989), 139–53.

[21] Kees van Kersbergen, *Social Capitalism: A Study of Christian Democracy and the Welfare State* (New York: Routledge, 1995), 195.

[22] Ken Gladdish, *Governing from the Center. Politics and Policy-Making in the Netherlands* (London: Hurst, 1991).

late 1960s, state agencies faced a difficult dilemma. They could either step into the vacuum and assert moral leadership or they could hold back and allow society to find its own moral center. Eventually, the choice fell for the latter and state agencies accepted different lifestyles, cultural values, and unorthodox behavior. The political elite opted for this decision because the personal morality sphere provoked sharp and irreconcilable disagreements cutting across the usual left–right split. Its choice also flowed from the recent legacy of minimal state involvement in moral-educational issues.[23]

Toleration was also convenient because it freed state agencies and politicians from having to define and then defend a new moral code, contested by either the confessional or the secular bloc. After years of debate, it was decided to label drugs an illicit good while omitting to prosecute their private possession and consumption.[24] Drug usage was sanctioned, together with scores of non-traditional socio-ethical mores, although the lack of consensus held back the alteration of existing laws. Critical in the evolution of this strategy of expediency (officially omitting the prosecution of punishable acts) was law enforcement and the criminal justice system. Police officers and the courts were averse to playing the role of moral adjudicator, which would erode their institutional effectiveness and legitimacy.

Institutions: law enforcement and drug policy in the 1970s

The Dutch Police Act of 1957, revised in 1993, defined the duty of the police as maintaining the legal order and providing assistance to any who may require it. The administration of the police was delegated to the Ministry of Home Affairs and the mayor. Small towns had a state police, which was placed under the competence of the Ministry of Justice. Five years of German occupation deepened the natural Dutch distrust of law enforcement, and until the new Police Act of 1993, the Dutch police lacked, by all accounts, strong crime-fighting capabilities.[25] In view of the unwieldy structure of law enforcement, justice officials and chiefs of police quickly reached the conclusion that they could never hope to win the war against drugs. By 1968, therefore,

---

[23] Joyce Outshoorn, *De politieke strijd rondom de Abortuswetgeving in Nederland 1964–84* (The Hague: VUGA, 1986); Rochon, *The Netherlands*, 77–96, 141–42.

[24] De Kort, *Tussen patiënt en delinquent*, 184–223.

[25] Trevor Jones, *Policing and Democracy in the Netherlands* (London: Policy Studies Institute, 1995), 40–70; L. Outrive and Cyrille Fijnhout, "Police and the Organization of Prevention," in Maurice Punch (ed.), *Control in the Police Organization* (Cambridge, MA: MIT Press, 1983), 47–59.

prominent police chiefs called for the legalization of cannabis to cut down petty criminality and to free police resources to combat drug trafficking. During that time, sensational (and unreliable!) studies documented the enormous popularity of cannabis as 20 percent of high school students claimed to smoke hashish or marijuana.[26] In light of these findings, the Ministry of Justice relinquished its duties of ensuring compliance with the Opium Act and began a campaign to define cannabis possession/consumption as a mere violation rather than a felony crime. In 1971, relevant officials in the ministry came to the conclusion that alcohol and tobacco were more dangerous than cannabis and that the Opium Act should not apply to soft drug users.

Training at police academies also stressed the weighty responsibilities of police organizations in a democratic society and many senior police officers contended that it was better to limit policing powers than to open the door to potential police abuses.[27] Certainly, the majority of Dutch police officers, in the early 1970s, believed that the war against drugs could not be won. At the same time, the Office of the Public Prosecutor was directly involved in the punishment of cannabis possession/consumption. Under Dutch law, the Public Prosecutor enjoys a large degree of discretion to waive trials. The 1926 Code of Criminal Procedure stated that the Public Prosecutor could decide to drop proceedings against a defendant for reasons of public interest. In the 1970s, the surge in violations of the Opium Act and the lack of manpower in the criminal justice system reversed the reasoning of the 1926 Criminal Code when the public interest served as a reason *for* prosecution. Even if cases came to court, judges assessed the severity of the crime and the conditions in which it was committed before meting out a sentence.[28] Not receiving much guidance from the government, the Public Prosecutor had to evolve its own directives on investigative priorities and punishment. Gradually, new guidelines emerged in which occasional cannabis users were not placed under arrest at all and regular drug users were judged according to whether they were productive members of the community or trendsetters and dealers. Hard drug users received harsher treatment though it was clear that they, of all drug users arrested by the police, were the most likely to be in need of medical attention. By 1972, courts were no longer seeing cannabis users

[26] De Kort, *Tussen patiënt en delinquent*, 210–11.
[27] David Downes, *Contrasts in Tolerance: Postwar Penal Policy in the Netherlands, and England and Wales* (New York: Oxford University Press, 1988), 132.
[28] Constantijn Kelk, Laurence Koffman, and Jos Silvis, "Sentencing Practices, Policy, and Discretion," in Phil Fennell, Christopher Harding, Nico Jörg, and Bert Swart (eds.), *Criminal Justice in Europe: A Comparative Study* (Oxford: Clarendon Press, 1995), 325–28.

or hard drug addicts because none of them were deemed to be a danger to society.[29]

Other state agencies also advocated leniency and tolerance. The Ministry of Culture, Recreation, and Social Work, established in 1965, was responsible for youth welfare and noticed a rapid spread of drug usage in youth centers and night clubs. Ministry officials counseled indulgence and attributed the drug fad to adolescent rebellion against parental and state authority. Legalization of drugs seemed to be the best answer to protect young users from a life of crime. The Ministry of Culture was therefore also on the side of either legalization or decriminalization of drugs. The most conservative voice was the Ministry of Public Health, unconvinced about the overall impact of drug liberalization. But a Social Democrat at the head of the Ministry of Health, after the election of the Den Uyl cabinet (1973–77), changed the agency's outlook. By 1974, the Ministry of Culture, Recreation, and Social Work advocated decriminalization of all drugs while the Ministry of Public Health suggested the decriminalization of personal consumption of all drugs, and Justice urged a differentiation between hard and soft drugs.

Revision of the 1919 Opium Act in 1976

The Biesheuvel cabinet of Christian democrats and liberals had requested an extensive report on the increased prevalence of illegal substances in 1968. The Baan Report finally appeared in 1972 and summarized the current state of the art research on drugs. Its conclusion adopted the following viewpoint. The report claimed that the risk posed by a particular drug should determine the extent to which the authorities become involved in its regulation and prosecution. The Baan Report recommended that the authorities should differentiate between soft and hard drugs, or between drugs with acceptable and unacceptable risks.[30] Because the Single Convention on Narcotic Drugs (1961) pre-empted any deliberation on legalization of drugs, the authorities were left with the alternative of decriminalizing soft drugs (cannabis products), which proved to possess acceptable risks to the user and society. Further justification for the separate treatment of soft and hard drugs came from medical research that had raised doubts as to the damaging physiological effects of hemp products and as to the validity of the so-called stepping

---

[29] Jones, *Policing and Democracy in the Netherlands*, 40–42.
[30] Henk Jan van Vliet, "A Symposium on Drug Decriminalization: The Uneasy Decriminalization: A Perspective on Dutch Drug Policy," *Hofstra Law Review*, 18 (1990), 723.

stone theory with its contention that individuals would move on from soft to hard drugs.

Soon after the report appeared new elections brought the Netherlands' most progressive government to power. The Labor-led cabinet of Joop den Uyl (1973–77) included the Catholic party and one of the Christian-Protestant parties (ARP). Although the Christian and Catholic parties were opposed to decriminalization of cannabis use, the rapid diffusion of heroin altered the focus of the debate since it was generally recognized that heroin with its ties to organized crime posed a much greater threat to society than did cannabis. As the cabinet contemplated new measures to address illicit drug usage, the emphasis switched from regulating the demand-side of the drug market to regulating the supply-side. Originally, lenient treatment of cannabis users was justified on the grounds that the state sought to prevent the isolation and stigmatization of youthful drug users who otherwise lived perfectly proper middle-class lifestyles. The consequences of criminalization, so it was argued, would be the growth of a subculture of addicts, divorced and separated from society, caught in a world of violence and anomie. After 1974, the public debate centered on how to differentiate between harmful and less harmful drugs in the supply-side of the market. A political compromise was now possible because new legislation would not eliminate all penalties against drug possession but rather impose differential penalties for different kinds of drugs to deter drug dealers from specializing in heroin. Cannabis users, then, would buy their drugs from dealers who had no involvement with hard drugs. Thus, while at first the objective was to protect the individual user from the allures of heroin, in the end the law encouraged drug entrepreneurs to shun hard drugs. This strategy satisfied the governing confessional party because increasing the punishment for heroin dealing compensated for the lessening of penalties for cannabis dealing.[31]

The 1976 amendment to the Opium Act increased punishment for hard drug trafficking and proposed stricter prosecution of dealers while it decriminalized the possession and consumption of small quantities of cannabis (up to an ounce).[32] Penalties for possession of drugs with unacceptable risks (hard drugs) were raised to a maximum of 4 years imprisonment and a fine of 50,000 guilders and international trafficking and dealing could lead to 12 years of imprisonment and a fine of 250,000 guilders. Possession of small quantities of hard drugs for

---

[31] De Kort, *Tussen patiënt en delinquent*, 233–34.
[32] Sebastian Scheerer, "The New Dutch and German Drug Laws: Social and Political Conditions for Criminalization and Decriminalization," *Law and Society*, 12 (1978), 595–97.

personal use could lead to a year's imprisonment and a fine of 20,000 guilders. By contrast, the trade, possession, and production of cannabis were linked to a maximum sentence of 2 years of imprisonment and a 20,000 guilder fine. The possession of up to 30 grams (one ounce) was demoted to a violation and was subject to a maximum of a month's imprisonment and a 10,000 guilder fine.

By the time that the Opium Act was amended in 1976, the actual situation on the street had altered again. Many Dutch cities subsidized youth centers or clubs. From the beginning, these public youth centers were scenes of drug exchange and consumption. The directors of some centers, to keep out unscrupulous dealers, appointed a "house dealer," a trusted person who sold cannabis to young people at the center. Local city authorities requested clarification from the Office of the Public Prosecutor on the legal status of the "house dealer" who received a cash advance from the center to buy marijuana. City officials had to know whether this dealer, who carried more than 30 grams of cannabis, was committing a felony punishable with a long jail sentence and a sizable fine. The Office of the Public Prosecutor decided that the legal status of the house dealer should be determined in consultation with the chief of police, the mayor, and chief officer of justice at the locality. The Office added, however, that it saw no harm in designating one particular person to be a house dealer because it helped exclude criminals, deterred hard drug consumption, and hindered the sale of adulterated and dangerous drugs. Their activities were seen as socially responsible and free from prosecution.[33] In 1980, the Justice Ministry published new guidelines, which stated that police would only interfere in the retail trade of cannabis if dealers acted provocatively and openly advertised their business (or pushed drugs).

Harm reduction in the 1980s

The Dutch constitution encourages a great degree of power decentralization. Local governance authorities, formally responsible for public order and safety, are vested with considerable autonomy to determine police priorities and modes of operation. The guidelines of the Ministry of Justice stipulated that retail trade of cannabis would be permissible so long as the dealers did not aggressively push their wares. The local mayor in consultation with the chief of police and chief public prosecutor, moreover, should make decisions regarding prosecution of the

---

[33] A.C. 't Hart, "Criminal Law Policy in the Netherlands," in Jan van Dijk (ed.), *Criminal Law in Action* (Arnhem: Gouda Quint, 1986), 77–78.

retail trade of cannabis.[34] Establishments like the coffee shops already existed before 1980 but the new guidelines authorized non-action with regard to retail outlets that sold cannabis. Amsterdam was the first city to ignore the operation of coffee shops and other cities soon followed suit. The gradual growth of official sales points for cannabis forced the Ministry of Justice to elucidate the term "provocatively" and new guidelines appeared in 1987. Coffee shops had to comply with three iron-clad rules: retail sales could not exceed 30 grams, there was to be no advertising, and no selling to people under the age of 16.[35] Of course, coffee shops also could not sell hard drugs. City governments decided whether to permit the opening of a coffee shop or not and whether the establishment had to comply with additional rules.

In the 1980s, most of the policy debate dealt with soft drugs and the legal position of the coffee shop. But a core of hard drug addicts appeared to be impervious to all social agency efforts to cure them of their addiction. Social workers and local agencies began to ponder what to do about these unrecoverable addicts. A 1985 government report, *Drug Policy in Motion*, brought attention to the dilemma of the unrehabilitated drug addict. The report proposed that a more fruitful approach, rather than enforced detoxification, was to normalize drug usage so that (unwritten) rules existed to distinguish normal from irresponsible drug behavior. Next, once drug usage took place within certain rules, addicts could be held responsible for their behavior. Government agencies printed brochures and leaflets to help parents, teachers, and counselors to educate young people on the hazards of drug experimentation and on how to test their limits and use drugs responsibly. Rather than exhorting them never to use drugs, official rhetoric called for accountable drug behavior and focused on "cultural integration" of drug problems.[36] The new focus grew out of the realization that a core group of life-long drug addicts would always be there. If a cure for addiction remained elusive, the next best thing was to reduce harm by minimizing rampant criminality and marketing of impure drugs. After 1985, harm reduction, risk reduction, and harm minimization became the guiding policy slogans. The harm reduction focus

[34] Van Vliet, "A Symposium on Drug Decriminalization," 731–32.
[35] A.C.M. Jansen, "The Development of a 'Legal' Consumers' Market for Cannabis: The 'Coffee Shop' Phenomenon," in Leuw and Marshall (eds.), *Between Prohibition and Legalization*, 174.
[36] Jack T.M. Derks, Marten J. Hoekstra, and Charles D. Kaplan, "Integrating Care, Cure, and Control: Drug Treatment System in the Netherlands," in Harald Klingemann and Geoffrey Hunt (eds.), *Treatment Systems in an International Perspective: Drugs, Demons, and Delinquents* (Thousand Oaks, CA: Sage, 1998), 86–87; de Kort and Cramer, "Pragmatism versus Ideology," 482–83.

stimulated the expansion of extramural programs such as methadone provision, counseling, open-door crisis centers, and projects aimed at specific ethnic groups (Moroccans and Surinamese) or certain categories of clients (prostitutes addicted to heroin or children of addicted mothers). The objective was to guide the addict to a conventional lifestyle and reduce the secondary effects of drug abuse such as AIDS or violence.

As before, academic studies did not directly influence new policy thinking but research findings justified a reassessment of current government measures. A growing volume of studies established a very complex relationship between formal and informal control. Informal controls – sanctions and rituals – are more effective if acceptable formal controls exist. Formal controls are exercised by the law and social institutions and must to some extent be intelligible to the individual. This is why most institutions do not condemn drinking but do censure drunkenness. Most individuals, in turn, accept the restrictions on excessive drinking. After 1985, more effort was made to create a norm for judging appropriate drug consumption and for inculcating informal limits. The objective became to prevent dysfunctional use of drugs while recognizing some form of normal drug use. But the aim was mainly to normalize the drug problem, not to normalize drug use.

Effectiveness of drug policy

A large unresolved question is of course whether the Dutch are correct that a lenient non-coercive approach to drug use benefits society. By all accounts, Dutch officials can justly be proud of their results. The number of hard-core addicts is more or less stable at 25,000, or 1.7 per thousand inhabitants. France and the United States, which adopted the "war on drugs" model, recorded the equivalent of 2.6 and 12.2 addicts per thousand inhabitants respectively in 1995 (totalling 147,000 and 3,050,000). Although research shows that the number of Dutch school-aged children of 12 years and older who smoked cannabis occasionally rose from 4.8 percent to 15 percent between 1984 and 1997, the percentage of problematic cocaine or heroin users stabilized at 1.7 per thousand while the European average was closer to 2.7 per thousand.[37] Dutch addicts also tend to be older than other European addicts on

[37] Marja Abraham, "Illicit Drug Use, Urbanization, and Lifestyle in the Netherlands," *Journal of Drug Issues*, 29 (1999), 565–86; C.W. Maris, "Dutch Weed and Logic: Part II: The Logic of the Harm Principle," *International Journal of Drug Policy*, 7 (1996), 144. Lifetime prevalence of cannabis among the population aged 12 years or older was 33 percent in the USA and 9 percent in Sweden.

average because the availability of low-threshold methadone programs keeps heroin abusers alive and out of prison.[38] Because of the existence of numerous maintenance programs and treatment centers, the Netherlands also registers relatively low percentages of HIV-positive or AIDS-infected drug addicts.[39]

The extensive involvement of health care officials and social service agencies has also had a positive effect on the number of drug fatalities. The Netherlands registered 31 deaths due to drug overdoses in 1993 or 1 death per thousand addicts. France recorded a total of 454 deaths, which is equal to a rate of 3 per thousand addicts and the American figures were substantially worse, namely a death rate of 10 per thousand addicts.

All in all, the strategy of harm reduction seems to work, confirming that the contemporary drug crisis is manageable and that the American "war on drugs" model is a poor alternative. In the 1990s, however, in spite of the positive medical picture and the widening interest among officials of other European countries in the workings of the Dutch model, Dutch drug policy has come under increased criticism and scrutiny. Part of the reason for the more critical tone is the friction with the European Union and neighboring, prohibitionist countries (France, Germany, and Sweden). But the actual catalyst for a re-examination of an apparently successful and stable policy regime was the formation, in 1994, of a brand new coalition government that for the first time in eighty years did not include a confessional political party. The new coalition had agreed beforehand to re-evaluate the current situation with the view of liberalizing drug policy by legalizing the cultivation and trade of Dutch-grown marijuana (*nederwiet*). The coalition wished to revisit the policy measures of the 1980s because the entire package of piecemeal responses to illicit drug consumption was riddled with some blatant inconsistencies. The greatest absurdity was that the authorities ignored the retail trade in cannabis while its commercial supply was subject to harsh penalties. Politicians coined the term front-door and back-door to illustrate the dilemma. Front-door commerce was condoned (*gedogen*) while back-door supply was prohibited and subject to prosecution. Since prohibition still marked core aspects of the drug business, the Netherlands coped with the same problems as other countries in that soft drugs retailers and suppliers operated in a gray

[38] Wim van den Brink, Vincent Hendriks, and Jam M. van Ree, "Medical Co-Prescription of Heroin to Chronic, Treatment-Resistant Methadone Patients in the Netherlands," *Journal of Drug Issues*, 29 (1999), 588.

[39] Stichting Toekomstscenario's Gezondheidzorg, *Verkenning Drugsbeleid in Nederland* (Zoetermeer: STG, 1998), 9.

zone of criminality. Decriminalization of soft drugs fed into the expansion of vast criminal syndicates, which supplied the coffee shops with illicit merchandise. The center-left's solution was simple yet bold: decriminalize (if not legalize) the supply of soft drugs, and especially, legalize the Dutch cultivation of *nederwiet*.

The contradiction between front- and back-door had evolved slowly as the number of coffee shops and other retail points for cannabis literally exploded. The retail trade in cannabis moved from the control of amateurish dealers to actual business establishments. In turn the existence of numerous (1,200) coffee shops plus other sorts of outlets (900) nourished the import and cultivation of hashish and marijuana. The estimated total value of the soft drugs industry in the Netherlands, including domestic consumption, export, and re-export, was roughly around 6.5 billion guilders in 1994.[40] At first, law enforcement paid scant attention to the growth of the soft drugs business, uncertain of how to reconcile decriminalization of retail trade with prohibition of wholesale supply of soft drugs. Professional ambivalence led the police to place very low priority on the trafficking of soft drugs (not hard drugs!). By the time that Dutch law enforcement agencies had come to the realization that the Netherlands was quickly becoming Europe's distribution center for marijuana, it faced a serious shortage of manpower, training, resources, and organization to combat organized soft drug trafficking.[41] Originally, the proposal of the cabinet in 1994 was to consider the legalization of Dutch marijuana by allowing private individuals to possess up to six marijuana plants, which would be sufficient to meet the entire demand for Dutch-grown cannabis.[42]

This proposal did not get very far. In 1993, just prior to the election of the new cabinet, a major criminal investigation crisis broke out. The affair involved the unsupervised operations of a group of enthusiastic police detectives who went after the ostensible big names of the drug underworld. The criminals under surveillance, realizing that the organization with which they dealt was a police front, exploited the gullibility of the police detectives to move massive volumes of marijuana into the Netherlands to the extent that the market price of cannabis fell. The denouement of this affair, widely discussed in the Dutch media, brought

---

[40] Report of Minister van Volksgezondheid, Welzijn, en Sport, Minister van Justitie, Staatsssecretaris van Binnenlandse Zaken, "Het Nederlandse drugbeleid; continuïteit en verandering," 284. This figure does not include other drug categories nor the amounts of drugs controlled by Dutch groups abroad.

[41] C.J.C.F. Fijnaut, "Gedoogbeleid en bestrijding van de drugshandel: een inconsistentie in het drugsbeleid," in T. Blom et al. (eds.), *Naar een consistent drugsbeleid*, 36.

[42] 'Justitiele werkgroep pleit voor legale winkels voor hard drugs," *De Volkskrant* (August 19, 1994).

to light the existence of dozens of Dutch professional crime syndicates and spoke volumes of the weak supervision exercised by elected officials over complicated police operations.[43]

In this atmosphere, the bold promises of the new cabinet to end the intolerable hypocrisy of the differing attitudes to retail and wholesale sales of soft drugs by legalizing Dutch marijuana cultivation was overtaken by sensationalist accounts of organized crime, bribery and corruption in the police force, and voters' fears for their personal safety. Conservatives, who had always felt ambivalent with regard to the Netherlands' reputation as Europe's drug Mecca and its indulgence of all kinds of questionable activities (not only drugs but rave parties, porn shops, and open prostitution) seized on the disarray in Dutch law enforcement to put an end to all further discussion on liberalization of drug laws. In the meantime, it became apparent that Dutch citizens never fully embraced the sophisticated analysis and corresponding policy measures of the expert community.

Contradictions and ambiguities

Supposedly, the attitudes of the state mirror popular demands for action. In the Netherlands, however, in the field of drug policy, the state elite is more permissive or tolerant than the electorate. Generally, the Dutch policy process de-emphasized popular participation of the electorate in the decision-making process. Expert committees of prominent citizens balanced the wide range of interests and dominated the policy process. In addition, civil servants played an influential role in policy drafting and Dutch civil servants regarded themselves as policy-makers to a much greater extent than elsewhere in Europe. When the authorities deemed it advisable to drop the prosecution of acts that remained punishable, the voter was not consulted.[44] Dutch people are permissive, but they never liked drug-taking. From the beginning, therefore, there was a tension between elite strategies to mitigate the development of a potential social disaster and the view of the average person on the street. As decriminalization of personal use of drugs yielded real benefits in terms of public health and order, much of the criticism against expediency disappeared. Real support, however, for this particular form of state intervention was shallow.[45]

[43] H.C. Ossebaard and G.F. van de Wijngaart, "Purple Haze: The Remaking of Dutch Drug Policy," *International Journal of Drug Policy*, 9 (1998), 266. A huge parliamentary investigation followed; see the report, *Inzake Opsporing: Enquêtecommissie opsporingsmethoden* (The Hague: Sdu, 1996). The report is also called *Van Traa Rapport*.

[44] Rochon, *The Netherlands*, 133–38.

[45] Anton van Kalmthout, "Some Aspects of New Dutch Drug Policies: Continuity and

Table 5.1. *Justifiability of "morally debatable" behaviors in selected Western European countries, 1981*

	Abortion	Euthanasia	Homo-sexuality	Under-age sex	Lying in your own interest	Buying stolen goods	Tax fraud	Taking marijuana	Average score on 22 issues
NL	4.35	5.43	5.64	4.70	3.33	1.57	3.14	2.05	3.11
Ireland	1.70	2.12	2.72	1.42	2.55	1.54	3.35	1.62	2.12
France	4.89	4.71	3.16	3.78	3.32	2.09	3.22	1.76	3.17
Spain	2.63	3.11	2.82	2.42	3.21	2.13	2.80	2.08	2.68
UK	4.01	4.36	3.42	1.77	2.72	1.86	2.69	1.73	2.62
FRG	3.88	4.27	3.51	2.63	3.15	1.53	2.51	1.39	2.64

Note: Scale runs from 1.00 to 10.00 and a higher score indicates greater tolerance. The survey posed twenty-two questions on "morally debatable" behaviors.
Source: Stephen Harding, David Phillips, and Michael Fogarty, *Contrasting Values in Western Europe: Unity, Diversity, and Change* (London: Macmillan, 1986), 8–9, Table 1.2.

For example, a public opinion survey in 1969 revealed that 69 percent of the population advocated a total prohibition of all drugs and only 20 percent supported some version of decriminalization.[46] In another poll, taken in 1971, 45 percent of the Dutch favored severe punishment for drug use and a negligible 4 percent of the population believed that no intervention would be the best of all options.[47] From 1970 until 1991, anywhere between 54 and 71 percent of the population believed that smoking hashish and marijuana should be severely punished.[48] Yet when it comes to abortion, homosexuality, euthanasia, or divorce, the Dutch seemed to hold fewer qualms.

As expected, the Netherlands scored high on a cluster of questions related to sexual morality. Dutch respondents were also more willing to accept marijuana than other Europeans because its score, together with that of Spain, was the highest of nine countries.[49] However, compared with the broad willingness to accept personal-sexual autonomy, drug-taking received a much lower rate of approval and taking marijuana is considered more "morally debatable" than abortion and tax cheating.

Change," in Helge Waal (ed.), *Patterns on the European Drug Scene* (Oslo: National Institute for Alcohol and Drug Research, 1998), 17.

[46] De Kort, *Tussen patiënt en delinquent*, 313, n. 72.

[47] Scheerer, "The New Dutch and German Drug Laws: Social and Political Conditions for Criminalization and Decriminalization," 586, n. 1.

[48] Sociaalen Cultureel Planbureau, *Social and Cultural Report 1992* (Rijswijk: Sociaal en Cultureel Planbureau, 1993), 332.

[49] The study compares attitudes in Belgium, Denmark, Spain, France, the UK, Holland, Ireland, Italy, and West Germany. It also includes Northern Ireland, which is of course not a country.

Why did the harm reduction strategy fail to win over a skeptical electorate? No precise answer is possible but several explanations come to mind.

Sexual morality truly belongs in the private sphere. Same-sex partnerships and abortion are typical activities that can be hidden from outside scrutiny and are purely private matters with few, according to conventional Dutch interpretation, public ramifications. Drug-taking, however, with the growth of drug scenes and roaming drug addicts, has become a highly visible activity and has greater social ramifications, considering that drug usage is closely identified with youth culture. Many (adult) individuals may hold different standards for young people than they do for themselves. While adults are considered mature enough to enter into consensual sexual relationships or to engage in self-abuse, the same rules need not apply to defiant adolescents. The animosity towards drugs may therefore conceal a double standard: one standard for adults but a very different set of values and expectations for youngsters. It should also be remembered that the Dutch population mobilized on behalf of temperance and anti-drinking measures in the early part of the century. Temperance concerns may also color views on drugs. Both the confessional (Protestant and Catholic) and labor movements once possessed large temperance wings.

Probably, the policy establishment itself should be blamed for the shallow support for harm reduction. Nowhere in the ongoing discussion on drug policy did Dutch officials declare drugs to be unproblematic, on par with, say, milk and butter. In fact, the package of rules and regulations that govern the drug field are much more severe and limiting than those that regulate alcohol and tobacco. What voters heard is that drugs are dangerous but the best way to diffuse their risks is to normalize their use. Never did the authorities proclaim that cannabis and hard drugs are ordinary consumer items. Drugs are a major threat to society; the question is how to deal with that threat. Referring to the Netherlands' vaunted tradition of pragmatic permissiveness bridged the gap between elite and voters. Officials proclaimed that decriminalization and tolerance of drug users "fits" the Dutch mold, which is probably true except that permissiveness was always predicated on a careful assessment of costs and benefits. For a while, the harm reduction strategy did appear to yield better outcomes than the sort of repressive strategies employed by neighboring countries. After all, it shielded end users from police harassment and protected them from a criminal milieu. Maintenance programs and treatment centers lowered drug-related mortality rates and enabled addicts to live relatively normal lives. From a socio-medical perspective, Dutch drug policy was a success in that it protected users from disease and death. Critics, when pressed, found it difficult to come up with an alternative anti-drug program. Police deployment to prosecute more or less law-abiding citizens is alien to Dutch culture and ideology.

In the early 1990s, however, the achievements of harm reduction no longer silenced the growing number of skeptics and detractors. Harm reduction was a stepwise response to deal with new developments but constraints both in and outside the Netherlands produced a policy fraught with inconsistencies. International obligations and domestic opposition kept the wholesale distribution and production of soft drugs a punishable offense. In turn, owners of coffee shops were forced to deal with the criminal world in order to obtain supplies and the latter grew increasingly rich. As trafficking in soft drugs took off, many Dutch exploited the Netherlands' unparalleled expertise in horticulture (usually confined to plants such as tulips!) to crossbreed an extra potent variety of marijuana.[50] This led to yet more trafficking and money-making schemes and prompted widening alarm as the Netherlands emerged as Europe's main conduit for soft drugs. In addition, thanks to the country's geographic location and large underground drug economy, the global manufacture of synthetic drugs (ecstasy and amphetamines) was also found in the Netherlands.

Decline of support for drug toleration also mirrored growing public doubts concerning the variety of local treatment strategies to aid hard drug users. As part of the containment/normalization strategy, local authorities insisted on police leniency to keep addicts above ground and within the reach of social welfare assistance. Local city councils and police forces accepted the advent of public drug scenes and the existence of open places in which hard drugs (heroin) were sold in order to forestall losing the drug user to the netherworld of crime. An open drug scene was seen as part of a successful public health approach because it prevented criminalization and deviancy. But such places drew other marginalized groups such as the homeless, alcoholics, and prostitutes whose visible presence in downtown areas or train stations intimidated and angered working people and lowered public tolerance for addicts.[51] Many voters regarded drug-taking as socially disruptive, associated with an alleged surge in robberies, thefts, and harassment. They demanded firm action by city councils to cleanse the streets of addicts. Local police and city officials tried to explain that drug users have the right to occupy

---

[50] De Kort, *Tussen patiënt en delinquent*, 256.
[51] Police ignore possession of cocaine or heroin not exceeding 0.5 grams. Tim Boekhout van Solinge, "Dutch Drug Policy in a European Context," *Journal of Drug Issues*, 29 (1999), 514.

public space and cannot be picked up simply because they are loitering next to the train station and looking unkempt. Such answers did not fully satisfy local residents.

Conclusion

Dutch policy-makers are concerned about the pattern of drug use in society. But they have consistently avoided a moral panic whether it concerns drugs or alcohol. Temperance movements failed to translate their philosophy into state action and the lucrative state monopoly in opium did not mobilize outraged middle-class citizens. After the 1960s, the drug epidemic unleashed harsh views among the population but law enforcement and social welfare agencies counseled caution and urged a differentiation between hard-core addicts, dealers, traffickers, and occasional recreational drug users. Over time, the police left all end users alone and addicts fell under the care of the social welfare state.

Harm reduction accords with a historic pattern of state action that shuns highly moralistic agendas and desists from enlisting state resources for the sake of an overriding good. Historically, Dutch state agencies did not need to provide moral leadership because the comprehensive socio-cultural pillars exercised control over society. When the pillars began to crack in the late 1960s, political divisions on moral issues stymied an assertive state strategy in response to the cultural turmoil. The final compromise, applied to many controversial issues, was to refrain from prosecuting punishable acts that had been embraced by large subgroups in society. Professional interest groups such as physicians, law enforcement officers, scientists, and social welfare officials preferred to employ relatively scarce resources on the most egregious and unacceptable forms of drug dealing – large-scale trafficking in hard drugs. The solution to the drug issue matched a typical Dutch mode of thinking and action. In turn, a non-prohibitionist drug policy underscored the Dutch tolerance for uninhibited lifestyles and set the Netherlands apart from the rest of the EU.

In the Netherlands, as in Sweden and Finland, the left and right, with small differences, endorsed the route chosen by various national cabinets at particular points in time. Nordic and Dutch governments select panels of experts, from different walks of life, to deliberate on large social questions and to propose a set of solutions. It is striking that the Swedish medical community advocated restriction, coercion, and punishment to tackle drug usage while the Dutch one called for integration and treatment. This suggests that different national communities of academic experts articulate existing beliefs in society and that scientists validate national perceptions, norms, and preferences. In the Nordic countries, this perpetuated alcohol control policies and repressive drug laws in the postwar period. In the Netherlands, researchers and scientists promoted the opposite strategy of incorporating deviancy into mainstream society to rob the activity of its special attraction to rebellious groups and young adults.

Both the Nordic model of alcohol regulation and the Dutch model of drug control clashed with prevailing norms and ideas dominant elsewhere in the European Union. The arrival of the Single Market coupled with the end of the Cold War has Europeanized drug policy. Classical military threats have given way to new perils related to international crime, which call for the strengthening of the member state's policing capacity. The deployment of law enforcement to fight new enemies such as drug cartels fits uncomfortably with the Dutch philosophy of overlooking the personal possession of drugs. At the same time as drug policy becomes a topic for European coordination, the Dutch public asks for measures to halt the inflow of foreigners who take advantage of the country's relaxed drug environment. The combination of internal and external pressures invites a second look at some of the core principles of the country's anti-drug policy.

6   Harm reduction meets the EU: from public health to public order

A 1992 report by the European Parliament made the allegation that the power of criminal organizations was growing at an alarming rate and was having serious effects on society and on the political institutions of the member states. It continued to note ominously that organized crime undermined the foundations of the legitimate economy and threatened the stability of the states of the Community.[1] In this ongoing debate on international crime, much attention is given to the aberration of Dutch drug policy with its open retail trade in cannabis and tolerance for the petty trade in hard drugs. At the same time, many member states have in fact incorporated selected features of the Dutch method into their own systems. In 1994, the German Federal Court urged the *Länder* to differentiate drug offenses according to the nature of the stimulant. Belgium, Denmark, Italy, the United Kingdom, and Spain have also dropped the US-style "war on drugs" model.[2] Chiefs of government, however, are hesitant to openly endorse a moderate anti-drug approach, as opposed to local authorities, which are willing to experiment with new anti-drug methods. Of course, there is a core group of countries (France and Sweden) that unconditionally rejects drug toleration and they carry the upper hand in official EU deliberations since the EU itself perceives drugs as an internal security challenge.[3]

Internal security dominates the official discussion on drugs in Brussels and at intergovernmental meetings because European cooperation arose from numerous attempts to deepen policing, custom, and judicial cooperation. In other words, drug policy coordination falls under the remit of the Ministers of Home Affairs and Justice. Anti-drug action is

---

[1] Cited in Bill Hebenton and Terry Thomas, *Policing Europe: Cooperation, Conflict, and Control* (New York: St. Martin's Press, 1995), 158.

[2] Ethan Nadelmann, "Commonsense Drug Policy," *Foreign Affairs*, 77 (January/February 1998), 125; Tim Boekhout van Solinge, "Dutch Drug Policy in a European Context," *Journal of Drug Issues*, 29 (1999), 522–26.

[3] Georges Estievenaert (ed.), *Policies and Strategies to Combat Drugs in Europe: The Treaty on European Union: Framework for a New European Strategy to Combat Drugs?* (Boston: Martinus Nijhoff, 1995).

barely mentioned in the Community sections of the Treaty of Rome and European-wide public health initiatives with respect to drug addiction are negligible. Former Article 129 (now Article 152 of the Treaty Establishing the European Community) briefly alludes to drug dependence in the context of public health and calls for cooperation among the member states. The new version of Article 152, which came into force in May 1999, expands the scope of EU activity for improving public health and is the first legislative instrument supplied to the Commission (Consumer Protection) to "assess the health impact of the implementation of other policies." The Amsterdam Treaty extends qualified majority voting to public health protection and permits co-decision making by the European Parliament. Nevertheless, public health protection gained greater prominence in the wake of the bovine spongiform encephalopathy (BSE) scandal and the threat of spreading HIV/AIDS through contaminated blood transfusions, and most discussions on illicit drugs take place in the so-called third intergovernmental pillar on "police and judicial cooperation in criminal matters."[4]

That the EU considers drugs to be mainly an internal security concern also stems from the role played by various United Nations international treaties in forming the legal groundwork for specific European efforts in this field. The UN Single Convention on Narcotic Drugs (1961) advises the contracting parties to adjust national legislation, to supervise and monitor licit drugs, coordinate preventive and repressive actions against illicit traffic, and provide treatment for drug addiction and abuse. This is followed by the 1971 Vienna Convention on Psychotropic Substances (amphetamines, barbiturates, and tranquilizers) and the 1988 UN Vienna Treaty on Narcotics and Psychotropic Substances, which binds the parties to cooperate in the combat against drug trafficking. The first major European treaty on border cooperation, police coordination, and anti-drug measures is the Schengen Convention and Article 71.1 urges the contracting parties to abide by the three separate UN treaties on drugs and narcotics. Since the UN treaties aim to eradicate drug production and trade for recreational use, the EU dialogue, based on these international agreements, is also steeped in the language of a drug-free society.

International arrangements and European coordination constrained Dutch drug control policy from the beginning. The original drug memorandum of the Den Uyl cabinet in 1974 mentioned the possibility of legalizing the supply and production/cultivation of cannabis. Because the 1961 International Convention on Narcotics would not permit such

---

[4] Michel Petite, *The Treaty of Amsterdam* (Cambridge, MA: Jean Monnet Working Papers 2/1998) (*www.law.harvard.edu/programs/JeanMonnet/papers/98/98-2-.html*).

a measure, Dutch politicians sought, unsuccessfully, to amend the Convention. It is fair to say, therefore, considering the international commitments entered into by the Netherlands in the past forty years that the EU is simply yet another international hurdle in the pursuit of an independent drug policy. But it hardly constitutes a major impediment. Progress in judicial cooperation, criminal, customs, and police matters has been painfully slow due to a series of political complications and delay tactics. The deliberate pace of constructing a common policing and border control space has been beneficial to Dutch drug control policy because concrete pressures for adaptation to "conventional norms" are modest. Since the Netherlands is a full-fledged participant in the deliberations to create a common judicial and policing space, it can of course influence the final outcome of any intergovernmental agreement and veto arrangements in apparent conflict with paramount national goals and interests. Thus, formal integration and intergovernmental treaties are not the main source of frustration for advocates of drug legalization or bold cannabis/heroin experiments. Of greater concern are the unending complaints by specific member governments and the free movement of people, which is the root cause of much of the criticism directed against the Dutch policy of harm reduction.

As in Finland and Sweden, however, exogenous constraints are only one, albeit significant, element of the story. There are and always were organizations, interests, and agents at home which opposed the operation of coffee shops and tolerant treatment of end users of soft and hard drugs. Such opponents made the persuasive argument that successive Dutch cabinets themselves drew a distinction between various intoxicants by permitting the free sale and consumption of alcohol while regulating the use of recreational drugs closely. These critics were not only conservative "law and order" types but were found across a broad spectrum of society and included religious people and socialist temperance sympathizers. Yet proponents of a harsher anti-drug approach found it difficult to alter the course of the debate and the direction of policy action. Much of what has been decided in the past twenty years grew out of actions taken by local city councils and by the Office of the Public Prosecutor. In truth, central governments were invariably several steps behind the decisions of local authorities and at the same time blocked the rise of a united counteroffensive. Opponents also faced the dilemma of what could possibly be a superior alternative to expediency and decriminalization. American-style repression and punitive measures were out of the question since this kind of state reaction was absolutely irreconcilable with Dutch culture and institutions, and so, the opposition remained fragmented and isolated.

Critical voices remained marginalized although it is important to remember that public opinion held more repressive views than did civil servants and politicians. But the obvious benefits of harm reduction in minimizing the social pathologies and medical complications associated with aberrant drug use muted any vehement objections to the nation's drug policy until the late 1980s. Harm reduction also fits the culture of the Netherlands, which is deeply wedded to the idea of tolerance. The Dutch believe themselves to be tolerant and are perceived by others to be so. Since 1990, however, growing European fears of crime and criminals have also contaminated the Dutch political discourse and open drug use is blamed for a deterioration in public order and personal safety. In addition, neo-liberal ideas on social responsibility and individual accountability also tinged Dutch views. While in the 1970s hardcore drug users evoked sympathy, they were now blamed for lacking civility, control, and self-management.

Domestic complaints have divided the political leadership and the cross-party consensus on national drug policy collapsed in the nineties as the neo-liberal conservative party (VVD) and Christian democratic bloc stepped up their criticism.[5] Conservative voices repeatedly admonished the center-left cabinet (under the leadership of Wim Kok) not to deviate too far from European norms. One of the ironies of the nineties was therefore that local officials in many European countries eased their posture towards personal consumption of drugs yet Dutch drug policy was turning ever so slightly more punitive. The Dutch Ministry of Justice is receptive to complaints from abroad and at home. Drug policy coordination rests with the Ministry of Health, Wellbeing, and Sport. But the Ministry of Justice represents Dutch drug policy in Brussels and in the Council of Ministers. There it confronts classic "law and order" deliberations and liaison officials from the Ministry of Justice have become more attuned to the idea of curbing domestic "excesses."

Constraints by Europe on national drug policy

The end of the Cold War eliminated the looming threat of a nuclear Armageddon yet has stimulated growing concerns about internal destabilizing forces. The opening up of Eastern Europe intensified the heightened sense of vulnerability as criminal organizations seemed to flourish in the new democracies. New kinds of threats – infectious diseases, information warfare, religious fanaticism, smuggling of people,

[5] Saskia Gaster, "Drugdebat in Tweede Kamer," *Amsterdams Drug Tijdschrift*, 1 (1996), 3–7.

stolen art and antiques, and of course drugs – have blurred the distinction between societal and national security and galvanized European leaders to invest in better judicial coordination. The 1991 intergovernmental conference, the first in the new post-Cold War era, placed internal security high on the agenda and established a decidedly intergovernmental structure to foster and promote cooperation in justice and home affairs. The next intergovernmental conference in 1997 led to Title IV (Area of Freedom, Security, and Justice) of the Treaty Establishing the European Community (TEC). It carries responsibility for visas, asylum, immigration, and other policies related to the free movement of people. During the transition period (until 2004), unanimous decision-making prevails while the European Parliament plays a marginal role, making progress uncertain in the terrain of coordinating internal security. Provisions for police and criminal justice cooperation remain within the truncated third intergovernmental pillar.[6]

Cooperation in internal security grew out of an early intergovernmental experiment to remove border controls and build a real borderless Europe. In 1985, the five governments of the Netherlands, Belgium, West Germany, France and Luxembourg signed the Schengen Treaty to abolish all border controls between those states. The removal of border controls required at the same time new compensatory measures. The Schengen group set out to create a study group to work out how to deal with free movement of people and goods. Negotiations took place in various working groups dealing with police and security, movement of people, transport, and movement of goods. The Schengen Convention contains provisions for the pursuit of criminals across national borders, a common asylum policy, illegal immigration, resolution of the status of refugees, joint action against drug trafficking and terrorism, and a computerized information system (SIS) for the exchange of personal data. Schengen has been incorporated into the Community legal order by means of a protocol annexed to the TEC. Freedom of movement issues fall under the Community legal base in contrast to policing or criminal matters, which remain intergovernmental. The European Court of Justice received limited jurisdiction over law and order or security matters in the remaining pillar on police and judicial cooperation in criminal matters.

The sum of the various European initiatives and treaty agreements has fostered a more institutionalized form of cross-border police cooperation. The Netherlands has been from the beginning a staunch advocate of granting the European Court of Justice jurisdiction over

---

[6] Desmond Dinan, *Ever Closer Union* (Boulder, CO: Lynne Rienner, 1999), 439–51.

home affairs and internal security.[7] Dutch negotiators argued that an active role for European Union institutions would safeguard the personal rights and freedoms of Europe's citizens. At the same time, the formation of European structures to address security deficits constrains national autonomy to implement measures to reduce drug addiction or dependency. To bridge these incompatible goals, Dutch governments have pursued a two-pronged strategy. They aim first to divorce national drug control policy from Communization and then to press for the regionalization of the Justice and Home Affairs (JHA) pillar generally. During the Amsterdam summit, the Benelux countries together with Germany lobbied strongly (with the support of the European Parliament and the Commission) to move Schengen into the *acquis communautaire* and transfer all matters relating to the movement of people to the first pillar. This strategy produced awkward moments since the Netherlands' position on a strong presence of Community law and institutions in the area of freedom, security, and justice is not easily reconciled with accusations that it obstructs effective European-wide cooperation on internal security.

To be sure, European cooperation on policing barely interferes with the pursuit of a harm reduction strategy. Article 71, paragraph 2 of the Schengen Convention obliges the contracting states to prosecute the sale, distribution, and supply of drugs. This clause squarely contradicts the essential aim of the Dutch policy regime to avoid the criminalization of low-level trade in soft drugs. To resolve this inconsistency, the Netherlands argued vehemently for an additional paragraph, which explicitly stated that the contracting parties were free to choose whatever strategy they decided to halt the spread of illicit drugs. Other chiefs of government went along reluctantly and thus validated Dutch harm reduction by formally agreeing that the criminal prosecution of sale, distribution, and supply of drugs can be dropped if a contracting state judges other kinds of policy instruments equally effective in minimizing the use/misuse of illicit drugs. In return, the relevant member state(s) had to take extra efforts to collaborate with neighboring countries to intercept the trade of soft and hard drugs.[8]

A more recent example of the Dutch ability to protect its national drug control system from harmonization or convergence is the *Action*

---

[7] Martin Baldwin-Edwards and Bill Hebenton, "Will SIS be Europe's 'Big Brother'?" in Malcolm Anderson and Monica den Boer (eds.), *Policing across National Boundaries* (London: Pinter, 1994), 150.

[8] C.F. Rüter, "De grote verdwijntruc," in T. Blom, H. de Doelder, and D.J. Hessing (eds.), *Naar een consistent drugsbeleid* (Gouda: Quint, 1996), 18–19; H.C. Ossebaard and G.F. van de Wijngaart, "Purple Haze: The Remaking of Dutch Drug Policy," *International Journal of Drug Policy*, 9 (1998), 267.

Commune launched by President Chirac in the fall of 1996. In June 1995, the Cannes summit issued a declaration to the effect that drug addiction and trafficking constituted a major threat to the citizens of Europe. A five-year plan adopted in 1995, which ran until 1999, contained two goals. The first step was to reconcile existing, divergent national practices and to consolidate them into common legislation where possible. The second step was to overcome the fragmentation of socio-medical approaches and law enforcement philosophy in the member states.[9] The Dutch prime minister signed the declaration to placate France and pledged, under the aegis of the JHA, to strive for the harmonization of drug legislation and enforcement practices in November 1996. When the declaration was discussed in the Dutch parliament, politicians from across the political spectrum rejected the *Action Commune* on the grounds that it endangered Dutch policy because it obliged amendment to Dutch law with regard to legislation and practices against drug production and trafficking. The Dutch government altered the declaration by adding a sentence on the need to guarantee national independence of drug policy, which was accepted at the Council meeting in December 1996.[10] Just as previous German attempts to use Schengen to bring the Netherlands into conformity failed, France's plan to summon the authority of Europe to pressure the Netherlands went nowhere. In fact, the Dutch delegation added an inoffensive sentence to Article 152 (1) to the effect that the "Community shall complement the Member States' action in reducing drugs related health damage . . ." This was the first time that the constitution of the European Union described drugs in terms of their public health impact. The French, apparently, were distracted during the small hours of June 18, 1997 and failed to pick up the addition of this sentence.

In short, the formal structures of the old JHA and new Article IV on "progressive establishment of an area of freedom, security, and justice" do not directly challenge national autonomy in drug policy thanks to timely political intervention by national authorities and careful

---

[9] Gordon Cramb, "UK Poll May Curb Dutch Ambitions," *Financial Times*, December 19, 1996, 2; Dan Kaminski, "The Transformation of Social Control in Europe: The Case of Drug Addiction and its Socio-Penal Management," *European Journal of Crime, Criminal Law, and Criminal Justice*, 5 (1997), 128, n. 21.

[10] Paul H.H.M. Lemmens and Henk F.L. Garretsen, "Unstable Pragmatism: Dutch Drug Policy under National and International Pressure," *Addiction*, 93 (1998), 158. Chirac persuaded former Chancellor Kohl to visit Prime Minister Kok to discuss Dutch drug policy in 1997. The health ministers of eight of the fifteen German federal states wrote a letter to their Dutch counterpart to express their support for Dutch drug laws, embarrassing Kohl. The visit was eventually cancelled.

negotiations. A far greater predicament is the free movement of people and goods and the extent to which the cross-border trade in drugs infuriates local residents as well as foreign governments.

Diplomatic tension and drug tourism

Pressures from EU institutions can be diffused because policing, judicial cooperation, and customs harmonization are still decided by member governments themselves and the influence of the Commission or the European Parliament is limited. The Netherlands can use or threaten to use its right of veto to halt or redirect the next step in multinational cooperation. Few member states in the EU are ready to relinquish one of the last symbolic vestiges of national sovereignty: policing and law enforcement. Undoubtedly, the international system constrains domestic drug policy but the immediate problem for Dutch policy officials and supporters of decriminalization/legalization is the increased circulation of people in Europe and the differences in price and quality of identical drugs in adjacent national markets. Greater availability, less risk to dealers and customers, and the market mechanism of supply and demand of common drugs ultimately determine the price and quality of illicit goods. Excellent prices and quality of common drugs have turned the Netherlands into a veritable drug supermarket. European drug users and couriers, being rational agents, prefer to buy their supplies in the Netherlands if the cost and length of travel are reasonable. Many German, Belgian, or French users are often no more than a couple of hours away from Europe's most exciting drug market. The aggregate result of many rational decisions by cost-conscious or profit-maximizing drug users is a persistent inflow of people whose main destination is the coffee shop or sites where hard drugs are openly sold.

Drug tourism is not a new phenomenon for the Netherlands.[11] From the 1970s, heroin addicts, drawn to the less repressive climate, easy access to drugs, and sympathetic containment programs, sought out the Netherlands.[12] The difference between then and now, however, is the absolute number of people entering the Netherlands and their concentration in downtown areas, low-income neighborhoods, and border towns. Second, in contrast to previous generations of drug users, this wave of visitors does not mingle with the local drug scene and thus it

---

[11] Walter R. Cuskey, Arnold Klein, and William Krasner, *Drug-trip Abroad. American Drug Refugees in Amsterdam and London* (Philadelphia: University of Pennsylvania Press, 1972).

[12] A.C.M. Jansen, *Cannabis in Amsterdam: een geografie van hashish en marijuana* (Muiderberg: Coutinho, 1989), 29–47.

creates a specific tourist problem. Third, compared with the early years of the 1980s, drugs are more available as the number of cannabis retail sites has exploded and the locations at which hard drugs are sold have multiplied. Back in the early 1980s, the retail sale of soft drugs was in the hands of "idealists," people who had grown up in the more laid-back days of the sixties and ran a "coffee shop" out of conviction that it is better for society to make cannabis products legally available. Since those innocent days, the retail trade in soft drugs has grown into a highly competitive venture with many different outlets such as house dealers (700 to 2,200), community centers (500 to 1,000), and coffee shops (1,200 to 1,500). In 1991, in all, there were between 2,400 and 4,700 cannabis outlets or 1 per 2,600 or 5,200 of the population over 15 years of age. In 1995, the actual number of outlets was assessed to be only around 2,000.[13]

Aside from coffee shops, hard drug users also visit the Netherlands for the quality and price of heroin. A gram of heroin sold for 100 guilders in the Netherlands as against 250 guilders in France and 175 guilders in Belgium in 1993.[14] Dutch drug entrepreneurs exploited the foreign interest in the local heroin market by evolving a sophisticated network of drug guides to escort tourists to sites of drug dealing. The spectacle of open street scenes and drug guides, who stationed themselves along the highway into Rotterdam, firmed up the country's reputation as the "narcotics capital of Europe."[15]

Of course, the Netherlands is a major port of entry into Europe for many licit goods and drugs simply ride along with the flow of international trade. Rotterdam is the world's biggest seaport, serving the whole of Europe. Although government policy is blamed for the large flow of drugs in and out of the Netherlands, the country's centrality in Europe's transportation network also plays a prominent role in its emergence as a major drug center. Of the approximately 2,200 tonnes of hashish and marijuana that passed through the Netherlands in 1995, with a street value of around 19 billion guilders, over 95 percent was

---

[13] Jack T.M. Derks, Marten J. Hoekstra, and Charles D. Kaplan, "Integrating Care, Cure, and Control: Drug Treatment System in the Netherlands," in Harald Klingemann and Geoffrey Hunt (eds.), *Treatment Systems in an International Perspective: Drugs, Demons, and Delinquents* (Thousand Oaks, CA: Sage, 1998), 82.

[14] D.J. Korf, "Drugtoerisme in de grenstreek: mogelijkheden voor beheersing," in Blom et al. (eds.), *Naar een consistent drugsbeleid*, 228.

[15] Marcel Dela Haije, "Drugsrunners en drugtoeristen: criminaliteit, overlast en onveiligheidsgevoelens in de grote stad," unpublished MA thesis, Erasmus University 1995; R. Bless, D.J. Korf, and M. Freeman, "Open Drug Scenes: A Cross-National Comparison of Concepts and Urban Strategies," *European Addiction Research*, 1 (1995), 128–38.

bound for foreign markets.[16] Mixing it with licit trade moves much of this merchandise.

Irrespective of why drug prices are lower in the Netherlands than elsewhere, the point is that the Netherlands is seen as Europe's distribution hub for soft and hard drugs and that tourists visit the country to stock up on drug merchandise. (In 1999, a gram of heroin fell in price to 60 guilders because of falling demand for and a glut of heroin on the street.)[17] Drug tourism heightened neighboring countries' concern about the whole concept of harm reduction. Young weekend visitors shopping for drugs are an acute embarrassment for countries that are committed to a drug-free society. German and French governments accused the Netherlands of subverting their efforts to ban drugs from society because they established a clear correlation between availability, demand, and use.[18] According to their understanding of the drug issue, supply equals demand. If the supply of drugs can be destroyed, demand for drugs will disappear. Dutch drug policy enables users who cannot find any affordable drugs at home to obtain their quota of intoxicants across the border.

Dutch drug specialists and law enforcement officers hold very different views on the relationship between supply and demand. They contend that demand for intoxicants is more or less independent of supply and is determined by imponderable factors such as global youth fashion, economic and social marginalization, mental situation, and the drug-taking milieu.[19] Authorities cannot stop people from craving mind-altering substances. But government policy can define the setting of drugs and influence demand for drugs and drug-taking rituals or routines through public information campaigns, by providing social services to vulnerable groups of potential drug abusers, and by divorcing the cannabis culture from hard drug use. Prohibition countries do not buy into this theory. For them, drug users, who are routinely described as abusers/misusers, are seen as the antithesis of mainstream culture and of solid bourgeois morality. Widespread drug use, for them, confirms

---

[16] R. Weijenburg, *Drugs en drugsbestrijding in Nederland* (The Hague: VUGA, 1996) 175. All of these figures are of course estimates and are averages of low and high estimates.

[17] Boekhout van Solinge, "Dutch Drug Policy," 514.

[18] Henk Jan van Vliet, "A Symposium on Drug Decriminalization: The Uneasy Decriminalization: A Perspective on Dutch Drug Policy," *Hofstra Law Review*, 18 (1990), 741–45; Erich Wiedemann, "Frau Antje in den Wechseljahren," *Der Spiegel*, 9 (February 28, 1994), 172–84.

[19] C.M. Ottevanger, "Drug Policy and Drug Tourism," in M. den Boer (ed.), *Schengen, Judicial Cooperation and Policy Coordination* (Maastricht: European Institute of Public Administration, 1997), 165–80. The author was acting chief of police of the Rotterdam-Rijnmond police force.

the decay of civil society and addicts are disruptive to the general morality.[20]

No country has been as blunt in its repugnance for Dutch harm reduction as France. President Chirac is a confirmed prohibitionist and has made a big issue out of the Netherlands' unorthodox views on fighting drug dependency and use.[21] The Gaullist party takes a hard line against drug consumption and possession for several reasons. First, some of the rhetoric and language is meant to reassure French voters that France will be French and that international frontiers will be closely guarded. In the spring of 1996, an official report by the French senator Paul Masson (RPR) discussing the implications of the Schengen Treaty bluntly named the Netherlands a "narco-state" and one of the main reasons why France should think twice about dismantling its border controls.[22] France had been dragging its feet for years about the ratification of Schengen because it feared a loss of national security control. The "threat" of Dutch drug permissiveness was a timely pretext to postpone, yet again, French ratification of Schengen and to uphold the sanctity of national borders.[23] In 2000, France again refused to implement the Schengen provisions on borderless travel on the grounds that large quantities of Dutch cannabis and heroin passed through Belgium into France.

But the second reason why France is the Netherlands' most unrelenting and fiercest critic has to do with a sudden wave of heroin use/abuse in northern parts of the country in spite of very repressive and strong anti-drug action by law enforcement agencies. The resurgence of a hard drug epidemic, which is now linked with the spread of AIDS and drug-resistant tuberculosis, is deeply disappointing after years of police action and custom surveillance to stamp out drugs from French society. One easy explanation was that the existence of Dutch harm reduction policy, a couple of hundred miles from Paris, undermined French anti-drug policy and aggravated French heroin troubles.

---

[20] Isabelle Stengers and Olivier Ralet, *Drogues: le défi hollandais* (Paris: Les empêcheurs de penser en rond, 1991).

[21] Apparently, President Chirac has firsthand knowledge of the tragedy of drug addiction. A son-in-law died of a cocaine overdose.

[22] In 1994, France was opposed to the location of Europol in The Hague because of Dutch permissiveness towards soft drugs. Neil Walker, "European Integration and Policing," in Malcolm Anderson and Monica den Boer (eds.), *Policing across National Boundaries* (London: Pinter, 1994), 32. And the French ambassador to the Netherlands portrayed the country as an "airport surrounded by coffee shops." *The Economist*, October 12, 1996, 58. French intelligence also suspects Islamist groups of raising money for fundamentalist causes through drug trafficking.

[23] Cited in John Keeler and Martin Schain, "Mitterrand's Legacy, Chirac's Challenge," in John Keeler and Martin Schain (eds.), *Chirac's Challenge: Liberalization, Europeanization, and Malaise in France* (New York: St. Martin's Press, 1996), 11.

Aside from the manifest political calculations of blaming another country for domestic drug problem, France's approach to drugs is indeed very different, mirroring a different police organization, criminal law system, and convictions. Hard drug addicts are excluded from society and medical or social assistance is unavailable to them. They become drug refugees, go underground, and live a criminal lifestyle. Many of the addicts belong to minorities and to vulnerable social groups, which only reinforces the contempt expressed by law enforcement agencies and the political leadership. The treatment of drug addicts is the opposite of the Dutch system: it stigmatizes them and denies them a role in society. Predictably, the Gaullist bloc is more passionate with respect to the reliance on police action to deal with drug use and trafficking than are the socialists. In the summer of 1999, the cabinet of Lionel Jospin admitted, following a report by the Minister of Health (Bernard Kouchner), that alcohol and tobacco kill more French people than psychotropic drugs, and Jospin, in a major turnaround, put forward money to build 600 treatment centers to tackle substance abuse.[24]

To be sure, the French are not ready to embrace the decriminalization of soft drugs, which remains an anathema. All policy regimes are shaped by cultural mentalities, institutional interests and abilities, and social structures. Dutch drug policy mirrors Dutch sentencing philosophy, which strongly emphasizes rehabilitation and leniency. Dutch judicial authorities adhere to the idea that the existence of a crime need not require punishment. By contrast, the French hold the view that the state ought to punish the offender if a crime is committed. France also has a centralized paramilitary national police force, the Gendarmerie, which is under the aegis of the Ministry of Defense. The purpose of the Gendarmerie is to protect the integrity of the nation-state from internal threats. Generally, the existence of a paramilitary police force is associated with a more repressive approach to fighting crime and is more dismissive of data protection law or privacy rights. The Netherlands constructed a decentralized police force with considerable local autonomy in order to avoid the possible emergence of authoritarianism.[25]

What keeps the attention focused on the Netherlands is an estimate by France's Central Office for the Repression of Illegal Traffic in Drugs that 80 percent of all heroin consumed in Paris comes from the Netherlands.[26] Although most coffee shops have never sold heroin, French

---

[24] "What's a Drug?" *The Economist*, June 26, 1999, 60.
[25] Didier Bigo. "European Internal Security," in Anderson and der Boer (eds.), *Policing across National Boundaries*, 171–72.
[26] Larry Collins, "Holland's Half-Baked Drug Experiment," *Foreign Affairs*, 78 (May/June, 1999), 83.

officials were convinced that the Dutch coffee shops were in some way responsible for the French heroin epidemic. The fixation on coffee shops is at first sight confusing. French imports of *nederwiet* (Dutch-grown marijuana), which is considered among the purest or strongest marijuana on the market with an exceptionally high content of tetrahy-drocannabinol (THC) (the ingredient sought by drug takers) were modest. In 1994, close to 56,000 kilograms of cannabis were confiscated by French customs of which 41 percent came originally from Morocco, 20 percent from Spain, and a minuscule 1.5 percent from the Nether-lands.[27] The closing of Dutch coffee shops seems therefore to be super-fluous if the goal is to address the problem of heroin misuse in France. But it is important to remember that different cultures interpret the nature of the drug crisis differently. French officials see a salient correla-tion between cautious experimentation with soft drugs and actual heroin addiction. They contend that drug-taking starts innocently enough and then moves to more risky substances. French tourists, visiting the Netherlands, fall under the spell of soft drugs and gravitate towards heroin once they are back in France. According to this reasoning, closing all Dutch coffee shops would reduce demand for hard drugs in France. No matter how often Dutch officials tried to enlighten their French counterparts on the logic of harm reduction, President Chirac continued to insist that only the closure of all coffee shops would satisfy French grievances.

The tussle between France and the Netherlands was deeply embarras-sing to Dutch officials with ongoing European contacts. Eventually, the Dutch authorities agreed to implement measures suggested by the French customs service. In 1997, international judicial and custom cooperation was greatly strengthened and institutionalized. Mixed teams of French and Dutch officials were constituted in order to assist with the search for illicit goods. The Dutch agreed, after years of resisting for reasons of cost-effectiveness, to install a huge scanner to detect drugs hidden in shipping containers.[28] Police reports written up against French drug visitors are simultaneously translated into French so that no time is lost by having to wait for the translation. All in all, many steps have been undertaken to tighten judicial and custom cooperation and demonstrate a sincere commitment to root out drug trafficking.

In 1997, the Dutch parliament also reduced the amount of cannabis a

[27] Henri de Bresson and Alain Franco, "Le contentieux franco-neerlandais sur la lutte contre les stupefiants persiste," *Le Monde* (March 12, 1996), 2.

[28] De Bresson and Franco, "Le contentieux franco-neerlandais sur la lutte contre les stupefiants persiste," 2.

person can buy from 30 grams (sufficient for up to a hundred joints and equal to an ounce) to 5 grams. Dutch consumers usually bought around 3 grams for 25 guilders ($11 in 2000) while foreigners were more likely to purchase the maximum allowable. The new ceiling eliminates, in theory, the trade in cannabis because 5 grams are barely sufficient for fifteen joints.[29] It is important to add that most observers believe that the 5 gram limit will make no difference in cross-border trade and that it will increase the aggravation caused by drug tourists who are forced to shop in more than one establishment to get a decent amount of drugs. But the 5 gram limit placates foreign officials who want to see an end to the cross-border trade.[30] Increased inspection of coffee shops ensures compliance with local rules and many unlicensed sale premises have been closed down.

Because of the ongoing "backdoor" dilemma of how to settle the illegal supply of cannabis, the idea of pseudo-legal commercial cultivation of *nederwiet* is still alive. Since it is now widely recognized that coffee shops promote the growth of organized crime, the Dutch judiciary in some cities closes its eyes to the possession of up to a hundred marijuana plants with the provision that the "truck farmer" does not create any trouble, pays taxes regularly, operates inconspicuously, and generally acts like an ordinary businessperson.[31]

Institutional and political ramifications

International developments threaten the stability of the Dutch model of harm reduction. These pressures will not disappear in the near future because new reports from British and French customs depict the Netherlands not only as Europe's gateway for heroin and marijuana but also as the major manufacturer of synthetic drugs (ecstasy and amphetamines). How the Dutch model will deal with mounting external constraints depends on the ability of domestic institutions to withstand adaptational pressures, on political decisions by relevant public agencies, and on public opinion. As indicated earlier, Dutch drug policy reflected more elite preferences than popular desires and domestic criticism of the country's approach to combating drug misuse has steadily increased in the 1990s. Previously, public opinion and diverse

---

[29] Report of Minister van Volksgezondheid, Welzijn, en Sport, Minister van Justitie, Staatssecretaris van Binnenlandse Zaken, "Het Nederlandse drugbeleid; continuïteit en verandering," in T. Blom, H. de Doelder, and D.J. Hessing (eds.), *Naar een consistent drugsbeleid* (Deventer: Gouda Quint, 1996), 288.

[30] A.C.M. Jansen, "De meevallers van het gedoogbeleid voor de cannabisbranche," in Blom et al. (eds.), *Naar een consistent drugsbeleid*, 96–97.

[31] Collins, "Holland's Half-Baked Drug Experiment," 90–91.

groups of observers resigned themselves to the practice of drug toleration because it yielded definite benefits in terms of mortality rates,
deviancy, crime, and social dislocation. But when city councils explored
innovative ways to minimize the risks of hard drug addiction by, among
other things, subsidizing and managing heroin cafés for registered
addicts (Amsterdam municipal government tried this in different ways
between 1979 and 1982), local communities protested furiously.[32] That
is to say, prohibitionists and drug liberals entered a truce after the mid-
1980s to stick with a middle ground. Yet many people continued to hold
negative feelings towards drug use and users.[33] Conveniently, policy
officials did not ask what the Dutch people thought of their country's
drug policy and their lack of opinion could then be interpreted as tacit
consent. When pressed to justify why certain measures were taken, the
authorities referred to scientific studies and to the country's vaunted
attachment to nonabsolutist decision-making. Many contentious issues
(abortion, pornography, prostitution, and euthanasia) were resolved in
the same manner as the drug problem.

In the 1990s, passive consent turned into active opposition. Drug
addicts were seen as a major nuisance in contrast to the sympathetic
views of the 1980s when they were considered sick and in need of
assistance.[34] Perceptions and attitudes have changed as drugs have
become more visible, as drug addicts blend in with homeless people,
and as crime itself is seen to be on the rise. The situation may feel
especially intimidating as many non-ethnic Dutch seem to constitute a
large proportion of hard-core drug users. Heavy drug users, moreover,
are highly conspicuous because of the growth of drug-dealing sites. The
proliferation of public spaces in which drugs are used and traded has
stimulated a new debate on nuisance. The latter refers to gatherings of
homeless people and hard-core drug users, trafficking of drugs in private
residences, noise created by coffee shop visitors, presence of foreign
drug tourists, and the sight of discarded needles and other drug-related
paraphernalia in public spaces. It also is a code word for crime and
many voters see a correlation between the country's drug policies and
lawlessness.[35]

---

[32] Derks et al., "Integrating Care, Cure, and Control: Drug Treatment System in the
Netherlands," 88–89.

[33] Ossebaard and van de Wijngaart, "Purple Haze: The Remaking of Dutch Drug Policy,"
267.

[34] Anton van Kalmthout, "Some Aspects of New Dutch Drug Policies: Continuity and
Change," in Helge Waal (ed.), *Patterns on the European Drug Scene* (Oslo: National
Institute for Alcohol and Drug Research, 1998), 17.

[35] Commission Européenne, *Les Européens et la drogue* (Brussels: European Commission,
1995), 6–7, 10.

The connection between drugs and crime is to some extent puzzling. Crime rates have not surged in the 1990s and it is far from obvious that harm reduction engenders crime.[36] But there is a prevailing sense that crime rates have exploded. Sixty percent of the Dutch public gave crime fighting the highest political priority in 1992 and rated public safety as one of five major social problems since 1993. Politicians began to pass tougher sentencing laws in the mid-1980s yet 90 percent of the Dutch population believed that punishment was too lenient in 1993.[37] Crime is of course a hot topic across Europe. In 1999, 89 percent of EU citizens and 95 percent of the Dutch considered fighting organized crime and drug trafficking a high priority for the EU in contrast with 34 percent of the European population, which fears a further loss of national identity and culture. The unease about crime is further fueled by a report commissioned by the Dutch Parliament to assess the growth of organized crime and the possible involvement of the Dutch police in drug trafficking. The expert report, published in 1998, found no evidence to suggest that the Dutch police have been corrupted by the ubiquity of street drugs, but it did draw attention to scores of other challenges and made references to the European debate on people smuggling, fraud, car theft, illegal weapons trade, and of course, drug trafficking.[38]

Disquiet about crime articulates concerns that go beyond drug-related aggravation and also characterizes other European societies with different approaches to drug use. Alarm about crime discloses an embryonic uneasiness about the new Europe, the inflow of people from inside and outside Europe, and the future consequences of further European integration. In the Netherlands, the focus has been on drug policy and the pervasiveness of drugs generally in society to give substance to this feeling of decreased personal safety and increased public disorder. Certainly, whatever the origins of the crime fear, it has lent credibility to a new discourse that places public order ahead of public health and has propelled new voices to the forefront of the debate on drug policy.

Pioneers in this debate were border towns, where coffee shops regularly sold two-thirds of their turnover during the two weekend

---

[36] Sociaal en Cultureel Planbureau, *Social and Cultural Report 1996* (Rijswijk: Sociaal en Cultureel Planbureau, 1997), 387–89.

[37] Chris Baerveldt, Hans Bunkers, Micha de Winter, and Jan Kooistra, "Assessing a Moral Panic Relating to Crime and Drugs Policy in the Netherlands: Towards a Testable Theory," *Crime, Law and Social Change*, 29 (1998), 31–47; Marcel de Kort and Tom Cramer, "Pragmatism versus Ideology: Dutch Drug Policy Continued," *Journal of Drug Issues*, 29 (1999), 477.

[38] Traa-Commissie, *Inzake opsporing* (The Hague: Sdu, 1996), 421–25; Cyrille Fijnaut, Frank Bovenkerk, Gerben Bruinsma, and Henk van de Bunt, *Organized Crime in the Netherlands* (Boston: Kluwer, 1998).

days.[39] Starting in 1991, five different provincial towns each published their own report on local drug predicaments and all came to the conclusion that the situation was out of control. Local authorities went to the central government to press for new legislation to stem the flow of drug tourism. One of their main gripes, mentioned in each of the reports, was that coffee shop customers urinated in the front yards or doorways of houses of local residents. Although it is difficult to understand why tourists would do such a thing since every coffee shop has public toilets, this flagrant offense against middle-class decency epitomizes more than anything else what is wrong with the current drug policy regime.[40] There is no excuse for young people displaying such a lack of common civility. In 1997, a small town on the Dutch–Belgian border (Hulst) held a referendum on whether the city council should prohibit retail establishments from selling soft drugs. No fewer than 96 percent of the voters indicated that they would like to see all coffee shops closed.[41]

Citizens' revolts against coffee shops and open drug scenes propelled local authorities into action prior to the fracas with France and already reflected growing concern about the apparent increase in socially disruptive lifestyles caused by the greater circulation of people. The clashes with other countries have simply hardened the determination to tackle the situation and reverse the consequences of past decisions. This is what happened in Rotterdam, a city that acquired a European-wide reputation for its cheap heroin. Because the local police had turned a blind eye to street dealing of hard drugs, many public spaces became meeting points for addicts, dealers, prostitutes, homeless people, and others. The sight of foreign and resident drug users, who haunted the main railway station and downtown areas, was frightening for local residents and citizen groups pressured the Rotterdam city council to clamp down on the coffee shops and street dealing. In 1995, the drug situation was becoming chaotic and, at the same time that the quarrel with France took new turns, the Rotterdam regional police in consultation with the mayor and local office of the public prosecutor launched a campaign to rid the city of drug tourists. The operations entailed keeping foreign visitors under close surveillance and arresting them when they approached a drug escort, visited a dealer's address or committed an offense. Local residents joined in and threw stones at cars with French license plates to stop the drug traffic. Surveillance by the

---

[39] Korf, "Drugstoerisme in de grensstreek: mogelijkheden voor beheersing," 228.
[40] Jansen, "De meevallers van het gedoogbeleid voor de cannabisbranche," 96.
[41] Larry Collins, "Reply: Dazed and Confused," *Foreign Affairs*, 78 (November/December, 1999), 136–39.

police and community policing managed to drive off drug tourists and higher administrative penalties for the smallest infraction of local ordinances altered the city's free-wheeling image.[42] The Rotterdam police also closed down establishments that sold soft drugs without a permit and coffee shops that sold alcohol without a license. Tighter control reduced the number of coffee shops in the Rotterdam metropolitan area from 200 to 55.[43]

Municipal governments are more likely to respond to local discontent, especially as public opinion is less acquiescent. The gap between expert views and those of the voters has subsequently widened. In a 1995 survey, 32 percent of the population believed that all drugs should be prohibited while 40 percent felt that drug policy ought to differentiate between different sorts of drugs. Although alcohol kills more people per year than drugs, only 17 percent considered alcohol to be a greater danger. The same survey also examined people's attitudes towards hard drugs and programs dispensing heroin to serious addicts under medical supervision: 46 percent of the people rejected the medical distribution of heroin and only 32 percent endorsed the idea. By contrast, 77 percent of the population agreed with the statement that police repression minimizes the risk of drug addiction.[44]

When a group of professionals attending a conference on drug therapies and policy measures were asked to fill out the same survey, their responses differed radically. First, they did not believe that drugs were fundamentally wrong. Second, they emphatically regarded prohibition as ineffective. Third, they considered alcohol to be a bigger problem than drugs and strongly supported the harm reduction approach based on the coffee shop policy. Fourth, they also rejected compulsory treatment of addiction, and were inclined to favor the medical dispensing of heroin to hard-core addicts. Finally, when asked how the general public would fill out the questionnaire, they were fully cognizant of the fact that the electorate favored harsher police action and more efforts to cure addicts of their drug habit, and that they took a

[42] R.A.F. Gerding, "Aanpak drugsoverlast te Rotterdam: de rol van het Openbaar Ministerie," in 181–91; Ottevanger, "Drug Policy and Drug Tourism," in Blom et al. *Naar een consistent drugsbeleid*, 175–80.

[43] Tim Boekhout van Solinge, "De Frans–Nederlandse drugbetrekkingen," *Amsterdams Drug Tijdschrift*, 2 (1996), 12–14.

[44] D.J. Hessing, H. Elfers, and A. Zeijkovic, "Drugsbeleid: Houding tegenover verstrekking en tegenover dwang en drang," in Blom et al. (eds.), *Naar een consistent drugsbeleid*, 245; T. Blom, H. de Doelder, and D.J. Hessing, "De paarse drugsnota en de aanpak van hard drugsverslaafden," in Blom et al. (eds.), *Naar een consistent drugsbeleid*, 72–81; Erik Ødegård, "Legality and Legitimacy. On Attitudes to Drugs and Social Sanctions," *British Journal of Criminology*, 35 (1995), 525–42

skeptical view of new harm reduction experiments such as the medical dispensing of heroin to hard-core addicts.

To be sure, drug experts and social activists never had public opinion on their side. But what helped move drug policy in a slightly more repressive direction was the installation of a Minister of Justice who personally disliked the coffee shop regime. The Lubbers III coalition (1990–94), composed of socialists and Christian democrats, appointed a conservative Christian democrat to lead the Ministry of Justice (Professor E. Hirsch Ballin).[45] Under his leadership, the department's tone changed and more attention was given to drug trafficking and organized crime than ever before. In addition to Ballin's personal dislike of drug tolerance, liaison officials from the Ministry of Justice were also subject to angry outbursts from other member governments in council meetings on justice and home affairs. Foreign complaints convinced them that some features of the current drug laws had to be reconsidered because the Schengen Convention (now added to the TEC) compels the Netherlands to vigorously combat undesirable international side-effects of its policies. Justice officials bear the brunt of EU hostility towards drug decriminalization and feel considerable pressure to engage in a constructive dialogue with their European counterparts. Most likely, even if a conservative politician had not taken over the leadership of the Ministry of Justice in 1990, its outlook and emphasis would have undergone a shift with its ongoing involvement in the difficult task of deepening European judicial coordination. The Dutch elite is European-minded and wants to promote improved cooperation in policing and home affairs. State officials veto any blatant, obvious attacks on Dutch judicial autonomy but otherwise cannot avoid making small concessions to placate EU criticism.

Whereas the Ministry of Justice has gained new authority in the field of drug control policy thanks to its European contacts and obligations, the Ministry of Public Health has witnessed a gradual loss of influence in the 1990s. Public health officials and social welfare agencies do not participate in intergovernmental discussions on international drug issues. European coordination of public health is negligible.[46] In addition, the Ministry of Public Health suffered years of budget cuts, which spared law enforcement and judicial agencies. Budget cuts of the 1990s were part of a larger reorganization of state structures, which aimed to

---

[45] Incidently, Ballin was forced to resign in the wake of the revelation of police irregularities in the fight against drug trafficking.

[46] Tom Blom and Hans van Mastrigt, "The Future of the Dutch Model in the Context of the War on Drugs," in Ed Leuw and I. Haen Marshall (eds.), *Between Prohibition and Legalization: The Dutch Experiment in Drug Policy* (New York: Kugler, 1995), 270–72.

increase the self-sufficiency of local authorities from general revenue funds. Cost-cutting measures reduced budget allocations to public health and diminished the resources with which it could provide varied packages of assistance programs, medical intervention, and care. Instead, the central government transferred the responsibility for social assistance to the local governing authorities and legislative reforms (1994 and 1997) reduced the discretionary power of central government agencies to create a general fund from which individual municipalities receive their budgetary allotments.[47] On the one hand, municipalities will be able to determine their own policy with regard to the public health aspects of the drug problem and could, if so desired, create innovative treatment modalities to cope with particular addiction problems. On the other, health ministry officials have lost a central instrument with which to guide drug policy and have no access to extra-discretionary funding to launch new initiatives. To complicate matters, the central government also abolished the interdepartmental committee on drugs and alcohol in the early 1990s. This committee eased coordination between the departments of health and justice, which has subsequently suffered and deprives health officials of access to important drug-related deliberations.

A confluence of developments such as the ascendance of the Ministry of Justice in domestic drug debates, the existing anti-drug mood of the electorate, and the decline of status of public health explains why a disproportionate amount of the 1996 joint ministerial report *Change and Continuity* was devoted to crime and criminality. Five of the six points of action centered on buttressing law and order. The report recommended the reduction of the number of coffee shops by half, combating the nuisance and petty criminality caused by drug users, coffee shops, and dealers, intensifying the fight against international drug trafficking, curtailing the large-scale cultivation of marijuana sharply, and expelling illegal drug users expeditiously. The only non-repressive measure was the recommendation to launch a limited experiment in government-supervised distribution of free heroin to hard-core addicts. More so than previous government statements on drug control policy, this report strikes a public security crisis tone.

Social treatment of addicts has also undergone a transformation in that mandatory treatment programs receive priority and money has been set aside to build more detention/correction facilities. Parliamentary deliberations resulted in legislative bills that stress the importance

---

[47] Netherlands Bureau for Economic Policy Analysis, *Challenging Neighbours: Rethinking German and Dutch Economic Institutions* (Berlin: Springer, 1997), 214–16.

of building cordial relations with EU partners by combating drug tourism. New legislation imposed new limits on marijuana production, allowed local authorities to pursue their own coffee shop policies, and raised penalties for various offenses under the Opium Act. In 1999, parliament passed a new law declaring commercial growth of marijuana illegal and setting a maximum penalty of 4 years' imprisonment. Thus, since the mid-1990s, the official debate has been more oriented towards collective concerns with regard to the quality of life and public safety. Hard-core drug users, no longer viewed as either needy or bohemian, are treated more like a public nuisance.

Conclusion

The pursuit of an unconventional drug policy assumes some sort of moral barbed wire that will separate one country from the rest of the world. The quality and availability of drugs have been a consistent draw to foreign users and given rise to a thriving cross-border trade, angering governments in countries with different drug philosophies and upsetting residents who happen to live in areas with a concentration of coffee shops or dealing sites. Dutch drug policy reflects culturally specific values and Dutch officials have always deflected foreign criticism by emphasizing, rightly, the rich history of nonabsolutist problem-solving.[48] Such arguments were persuasive because the Dutch possessed a long record of tolerating unconventional, problematic private activities. The removal of border checks and increased circulation of people forced a re-evaluation of the costs of exceptionalism. At some point, relevant public officials began to wonder whether drug policy was really worth the endless diplomatic squabbles in official EU venues, especially since the Dutch elite is extremely Community-minded. While politicians were seeking to diffuse foreign animosity, domestic opposition to open drug scenes rose and finally tipped the balance in favor of greater coordination with other member states and harsher actions against lifestyles perceived as socially disruptive.

Nevertheless, an important caveat is needed. None of the trends described above suggests a drastic or final break with a long history of state non-interference in controversial private choices. Suspicion of centralized police powers is pervasive, among both voters and politicians, and few organized interests expect assertive state leadership to rid

---

[48] In reply to an extremely critical article in *Foreign Affairs* on Dutch drug policy (see note 26 above), two well-known experts in the Dutch harm reduction method made references to the strong Dutch belief in nonabsolutist problem-solving. Craig Reinarman and Peter Cohen, "Human Nature," *Foreign Affairs*, 78 (1999), 135–37.

society of drug users. But a borderless Europe invites a re-assessment of the domestic and international impact of divergent normative and causal beliefs. The European Union represents a wide range of moralities and drug policies are tailored around a country's collective norms and rules. Outliers such as the Netherlands, however, face severe constraints owing to the heightened circulation of people and to the disappearance of border checks.

7   Irish moral conservatism and European sexual permissiveness

The Irish not only are Catholic in name, belonging to an imaginary religious community, but are also devout practitioners. In 1990, 82 percent of Irish Catholics attended weekly Mass, the highest proportion of any population in the world.[1] The Irish became and remained more Catholic than most other Catholic Europeans if measured by devotion, church attendance, and conviction. The "Irish Devotional Resolution" reflected the loss of language and cultural identity during the nineteenth century and was nourished by the growing resistance to Anglicization. Not until the 1850s, however, did institutional Catholicism plant itself firmly in the Irish mentality. The Great Famine (1845–49) destroyed the livelihood of a rural underclass, whose main religious practices included magic. The famine, which killed nearly one million people and forced another million to seek their fortunes overseas, led to the disappearance of this vast rural underclass and introduced new ideas about land ownership and inheritance rights.[2] The Catholic elite and tenant farmers encouraged the adoption of new rules on ownership with a view to modernizing Ireland and from then on priests, brothers, and nuns became important fixtures in the average Irish household. After the famine disaster, the modernizing state handed over the task of civilizing the Irish population to the Church, which assumed responsibility for fostering discipline, education, and civility.[3] By the time that the Irish Free State was founded in 1922, Catholic ethics were internalized in the minds and hearts of the Irish to the extent that they viewed no conflict between individual autonomy and definition of the

---

[1] Tom Inglis, *Moral Monopoly: The Rise and Fall of the Catholic Church in Modern Ireland* (Dublin: University College Dublin Press, 1987), 209.
[2] Paul Keating and Derry Desmond, *Culture and Capitalism in Contemporary Ireland* (Brookfield, VT: Ashgate, 1993), 7; Emmet J. Larkin, *The Consolidation of the Roman Catholic Church in Ireland, 1860–1870* (Chapel Hill: University of North Carolina Press, 1987).
[3] Jean Baudrillard, "Coming out of Hibernation? The Myth of Modernization in Irish Culture," in Luke Gibbons (ed.), *Transformations in Irish Culture* (Notre Dame: University of Notre Dame Press, 1996), 85.

good life and that of the Church. In fact, it was an important part of Irish identity to have resisted the shallow values of a materialistic global culture. It gave the Irish a sense of self-confidence and mission in a secularizing world.[4]

By the late 1990s, the influence of the Church had dramatically declined. Church attendance had dropped and the number of people joining the Church had abruptly fallen. Educated young professionals are becoming more detached from Catholic practices at the same time as low-income households turn away from religion. Nevertheless, the Irish are still more devoted to the principles of the faith than other European people, if less so than before.[5] Membership in the EC/EU has played a small part in this development. Economic prosperity contributed to the secularization of Irish society and membership in the EC/EU came with sizable financial benefits. Between 1973 and 1999, Ireland received euro 31 billion (US$28 billion) in regional aid, structural funds, and farm subsidies.

The focus of this chapter is mainly on the clash between European sexual permissiveness, as evidenced by the open availability of abortion and contraception, and the greatly more restrictive views on sexual morality held by the Irish. Obviously, none of the institutions of the EU deals directly with private, family issues. In contrast to drug and alcohol control policies, sexual morality does not intersect with any of the existing mandates of the EU nor does it tie in with major intergovernmental programs launched since 1985. None the less, there is a case to be made that European law and treaty obligations, which reflect a quite different ethos, have reshaped the cognitive and normative dimensions of Irish social and political life. That the EC/EU might possibly contaminate Irish values and culture was widely feared by lay Catholic organizations. To affirm Irish adherence to Catholic virtue and chastity, traditionalists used the rule of law to shield Ireland from foreign ideas and trends, and attempted to suppress information on British abortion services while preventing pregnant women from traveling abroad.

The European Court of Justice had little to say about the controversial methods undertaken by the traditionalists to protect Irish sexual purity. Yet at the same time, Ireland's entry into the EU came with the legal

---

[4] John H. Whyte, *Church and State in Modern Ireland, 1923–79* (Dublic: Gill & Macmillan, 1980); Brian Girvin, "Social Change and Moral Politics: The Irish Constitutional Referendum," *Political Studies*, 34 (1986), 63; Richard B. Finnegan and Edward T. McCarron, *Ireland: Historical Echoes, Contemporary Politics* (Boulder: Westview, 2000), 82.

[5] Niamh Hardiman and Chistopher Whelan, "Changing Values," in William Crotty and David E. Schmitt (eds.), *Ireland and the Politics of Change* (New York: Longman, 1998), 66–85.

obligation to defend rights held by Irish citizens as members of the EU. Domestic law could not uphold an absolute moral position incompatible with obligations under Community law and human rights conventions. Since abortion is a lawful medical service in the European Union, the Irish enjoy the right of freedom to travel and to receive information on abortion.

Ireland's abortion case is fundamentally different from Nordic alcohol and Dutch drug control policies. Yet the tortured debate and legal actions surrounding abortion and sexual permissiveness strikingly resemble the developments described in the other three case studies. A shift in values preceded or coincided with growing confusion on how to reconcile a particular standard of behavior at odds with the rest of Europe. Like drugs and alcohol, abortion condenses a specific Irish strategy of action and is embedded in social and state institutions. Nevertheless, multiple developments created an inevitable discordance between a code of conduct acclaimed as ideal and the desire for individual autonomy.

The structure of this chapter follows that of the previous ones. It seeks to establish first the overriding importance of Catholicism in the identity formation of the modern Republic of Ireland. Second, it will show that Catholic doctrine and mores are especially noticeable in the area of sexuality and promoted an image of an idyllic Ireland of large families, no out-of-wedlock children, and no premarital sex. In the second part of the chapter, I document how the Single Market and the veneration of the free movement of people, services, goods, and capital ultimately defeated the strategy of Catholic lay movements to insulate Ireland from new concepts related to sexual freedom and women's rights. EU membership kept alive the "English solution," that is abortions in English clinics, and thus challenged an essential aim of Article 40.3.3 of the Irish Constitution, i.e. the protection of the life of the unborn.

Catholic influence in Irish politics and institutions

Protestant-Christian ethics do not dictate what is good or bad moral behavior. Individuals decide for themselves what is proper behavior. The Calvinist church demanded of its believers a life of good works, which, among other things, included material success and social mobility because hard work and material achievements were in and by themselves sufficient marks of virtue and probity. This differs from Catholicism, which aims to direct all spheres of behavior through its priesthood and discourages individuals from developing their own ethical guidelines. The Church acts as interpreter and explains how to be a good practicing Catholic by adhering to its rules and regulations. The particular history of the Irish nation elevated the Church as legislator and arbiter of morality with the result that a decent person was a devout Catholic. Since the Church shaped the framework for assessing a person's moral standing, Church approval, for being a good Catholic, meant a stamp of approval by society. It was rare, therefore, for a politician to take a public stance against the Church. Important individuals sought to enhance their reputation by contributing to the Church and observing Catholic rules.[6]

In the late twentieth century, the Church possessed large organizational resources and ran schools, hospitals, nursing homes, and charity funds that drew most Irish people into its moral universe. By far the greatest source of institutional power was the Church's control over education. The ecclesiastical hierarchy approved the curriculum and teachers of state schools and local supervisory school boards frequently had half of their members appointed by the local bishop. The Irish state subsidized confessional schools and 3,400 of the 3,500 state schools (in a population of 3.5 million in 1996) were under Catholic management. The Church hierarchy also controlled secondary education. Of 572 secondary schools, 10 percent were officially non-denominational and another 4 percent had another religious affiliation, while the remaining 491 schools were run by either nuns or brothers or lay Catholic management boards and diocesan priests.[7] The Catholic hierarchy exposed young students to, if not indoctrinated them in, the moral and religious teaching of Catholicism.[8]

The symbiotic ties between state and Catholic Church were forged in the nineteenth century. The objectives of Irish nationalism centered on achieving Catholic equality in the face of Protestant hegemony and claims to perpetual ascendancy. Many divisions among the Irish people impeded unity. But the various resentments were channeled into one single issue – the inferior position of Irish Catholics. The Catholic Church supported the organization of Catholic associations to become

---

[6] David Hempton, *Religion and Political Culture in Britain and Ireland.* (New York: Cambridge University Press, 1996), 72–92; Tony Fahey, "Religion and Sexual Culture in Ireland," in Franz X. Eder, Lesley A. Hall, and Gert Hekma (eds.), *Sexual Culture in Europe* (New York: Manchester University Press, 1999), 56–57.

[7] Sheelagh Drudy and Kathleen Lynch, *Schools and Society in Ireland* (Dublin: Gill & Macmillan, 1993), 76–87.

[8] Desmond M. Clarke, *Church and State: Essays in Political Philosophy* (Cork: Cork University Press, 1984), 196–226; Michael P. Hornsby-Smith and Christopher T. Whelan, "Religious and Moral Values," in Christopher T. Whelan (ed.), *Values and Social Change in Ireland* (Dublin: Gill & Macmillan, 1994), 12; Pat O'Connor, *Emerging Voices: Women in Contemporary Irish Society* (Dublin: Institute for Public Administration, 1998), 64–68.

involved in a host of grievances from the administration of justice to the collection of tithes, from the abuses of landlords to the fear of the Orange Order.

The promises of Home Rule – discussed in 1914 to give Ireland autonomy within the British Empire – spurred the growth of political parties. By 1922, Ireland was basically a one-party state, although the Irish party had no provincial branches and no rural presence. It depended on one national institution, which did have a nationwide structure, the Roman Catholic Church. Catholic priests combined the social prestige resulting from their education with the further advantage of not having to seek political office for themselves or their families. Mass was the only regular occasion when large numbers of rural people came together and many political meetings were held on Sundays outside the church.[9]

When Ireland finally gained statehood, the Constitution of the Republic of Ireland (passed in 1937) was confessional in substance and summarized Catholic moral teaching on divorce, contraception, adoption, and the family. The constitution took for granted that Ireland was a Catholic state for a Catholic people. Of the native population 95 percent were Catholic and religion provided the fledgling republic with a strength and symbolic unity that masked the conflict about Northern Ireland. The founding fathers meant to raise Catholic ideology to the status of government principle and the Preamble to the Irish Constitution proclaimed that the people of Ireland acknowledged their obligations to Jesus Christ. A subsection of Article 44 stated: "the State recognizes the special position of the Holy Catholic Apostolic and Roman Catholic Church as the guardian of the faith professed by the great majority of the citizens." Both the Preamble and Article 44 stated the obvious because the Church did hold a special position in Ireland. For example, it is at first blush surprising to discover that this heavily Catholic country never developed a Catholic party in contrast to such countries as the Netherlands or Germany. The simple explanation was that Irish Catholicism was not under siege from workmen's organizations or liberalism so that there was no call for a specific Catholic political organization, popular press, or social associations. Even better, the Irish clergy rarely intervened in politics since in areas of particular interest to the Church – education, family, and health – policy officials stayed with Catholic teaching and values.[10]

References to the special position of the Church were removed from

---

[9] Hempton, *Religion and Political Culture in Britain and Ireland*, 86–89.
[10] Basil Chubb, *The Politics of the Irish Constitution* (Dublin: Institute of Public Administration, 1991), 33–43; Michael A. Poole, "In Search of Ethnicity in Ireland,"

Table 7.1. *Percentage of Catholic population holding traditional religious beliefs, by country, 1990*

	God	Life after death	The devil	% believing in Hell	Sin	Resurrection of the dead	Heaven
Italy	90	60	39	39	72	50	51
Spain	88	45	29	29	61	35	52
Netherlands	91	46	18	12	54	37	46
Ireland	98	80	87	52	86	72	88

Source: Michael P. Hornsby-Smith and Christopher T. Whelan, "Religious and Moral Values," in Christopher T. Whelan (ed.), *Values and Social Change in Ireland* (Dublin: Gill & Macmillan, 1994), 39, Table 2.15.

the Constitution in 1972. Nevertheless, Catholic moral hegemony was still strong in the 1980s and the Irish still held opinions that set them apart from other Catholic European countries.[11] Table 7.1 confirms the widely held observation that Irish Catholics continue to be more closely attached to traditional orthodox beliefs than do Catholics in other countries.

Catholic ethics and sexuality

Most of the Church's pronouncements and declarations on public life centered on sexual moral issues and its teaching was most visible in that part of the curriculum that pertained to sexual morality.[12] Since Catholicism shapes Irish identity, Catholic views on sexuality have also become incorporated in Irish collective self-identity. The mainstream Catholic view disparages the post-1960s lifestyle of sexual liberalization and emancipation and holds up chastity and innocence as "natural" Catholic alternatives. Sexual passions, according to this view, promote the corruption of the health, welfare, and sanity of individuals, and their suppression serves the common good because a society of sexually liberated and selfish individuals produces nothing but moral decay and social chaos.[13] The Church's central message juxtaposed the spirit as the expression of goodness and the flesh as the source of temptation and sin. This obsession with sexual purity is almost unique and unrelated to

in Brian Graham (ed.), *In Search of Ireland: A Cultural Geography* (New York: Routledge, 1997), 128–47.

[11] Hornsby-Smith and Whelan, "Religious and Moral Values," 31–32.

[12] Drudy and Lynch, *Schools and Society in Ireland*, 83; Tom Inglis, *Lessons in Irish Sexuality* (Dublin: University College Dublin Press, 1998).

[13] J.P. O'Carroll, "Bishops, Knights and Pawns? Traditional Thought and the Irish Abortion Referendum Debate of 1983," *Irish Political Studies*, 6 (1991), 64–65.

Catholicism *per se* since it actually grew out of a fusion of British Victorian puritanism and a new post-famine ethos.

After the Great Famine typical Irish views on motherhood, women, and sexuality changed because the disaster resulted in a dramatic transformation of the structure of the Irish farm economy and the family. Until the 1840s, English landlords repeatedly subdivided property in order to increase rental income from Irish tenants. The potato allowed families to subsist on small plots of land because its yield continued to increase despite shrinkage of cultivated acreage. But the Great Famine brought home the danger of tiny plots of land and the risks of a monoculture. After 1850, families tried to keep the land intact, which meant that new patterns of land ownership and inheritance arose. The land went to one son, considered most suitable to continue the farming, whereas one daughter could expect a dowry. The other children had to fend for themselves. Generally, married couples aimed for large families, which was at odds with the new patterns of inheritance rights, the desire for larger farms, and modern agricultural techniques. The Church, therefore, paired the high fertility rate with late marriage, a high rate of celibacy, and emigration. Postponed marriages delayed the pressure to provide a livelihood for new families, celibacy meant that some children joined the priesthood or became lay people, and emigration lifted the pressure to subdivide the farm into ever-smaller plots. Both the Church and the elite extolled service to God and scorned romantic love in order to encourage late marriages and celibacy.

Since extramarital sexual relations were absolutely rejected, sexual puritanism – a necessity – turned into a virtue. Sexual puritanism motivated the young to postpone or abandon marriage and the segregation of the sexes was strictly enforced to hinder romantic involvement. The new arrangements yielded the desired results. On the one hand, Irish households had large families in an era when birth control lowered the number of children per family even in Catholic Europe. On the other, the actual birth rate was below replacement rate and the population steadily declined between 1850 and 1922.[14] In the 1950s, Irish commentators were alarmed as the lack of interest in marriage and sex had contributed to the shrinking of the population (of the counties making up the Republic of Ireland) from 6.5 million in 1841 to 2.9 million in 1951.[15]

Celibacy and late marriage nurtured the myth or image of the asexual Irish. Supposedly, Ireland was filled with virtuous virgins and the Irish

[14] Joe Lee, "State and Nation in Independent Ireland," in Princess Grace Irish Library (ed.), *Irishness in a Changing Society* (Totowa, NJ: Barnes & Noble, 1989), 114.
[15] Mary Kenny, *Goodbye to Catholic Ireland* (London: Sinclair-Stevenson, 1997), 222.

disdain for sex became a source of pride.[16] The Church portrayed marriage as less than ideal, required to produce an heir for the farm and labor for the land. Marriage itself was seen as an inevitable limitation on one's life just as old age is to be accepted as part of life's course. By contrast, celibacy was associated with chastity and the Church held it to be a holier state.[17] Church sermons and teaching stressed the sins of the flesh and priests served as moral police, being intimately familiar with family events and often serving as matchmaker, marriage counselor, and economic and political advisor. The Church's call for chastity and hostility toward romantic love fell on receptive ears because it correlated with people's aspirations for social mobility and improved standards of living. Chastity insured success in the material sphere and many individuals followed the path selected by the Church because it matched their economic interests and, additionally, designated them as good Catholics. Young people in search of a better life either emigrated or remained single if they stayed home. Consequently, Ireland recorded one of the highest numbers of unmarried people in the Western world, and surprisingly, more men than women remained single.[18]

The 1937 Constitution singled out the family as indispensable to the welfare of the nation and the state.[19] Marriage, as an institution, received extensive protection and no provisions for its dissolution were granted (Article 41). Because women organized the family and thus formed the mediating link between the state and the common good, they were prohibited from seeking employment at the expense of their domestic duties. In the 1980s, many of the smaller injunctions and prohibitions were repealed and phased out. But when the Fitzgerald government proposed to replace the old article on the indissoluble marriage with a new one that would allow a court of law to grant a dissolution in certain circumstances, voters said no to the repeal of the ban on divorce, a testimony to the fact that moral conservatism still governed ideas and views on the family and sexuality in 1986.[20]

---

[16] Dympna McLoughlin, "Women and Sexuality in Nineteenth Century Ireland," *Irish Journal of Psychology*, 15 (1994), 266–75.

[17] Richard Stivers, *A Hair of the Dog: Irish Drinking and its American Stereotype* (University Park, PA: Pennsylvania State University Press, 1976), 66.

[18] Inglis, *Lessons in Irish Sexuality*, 34; Fahey, "Religion and Sexual Culture," 53–62.

[19] Anthony Coughlan, "The Constitution and Social Policy," in Frank Litton (ed.), *The Constitution of Ireland, 1937–87* (Dublin: Institute of Public Administration, 1988), 143–61; Finnegan and McCarron, *Ireland: Historical Echoes*, 91–96, 104–07.

[20] Chubb, *The Politics of the Irish Constitution*, 58; Michelle Dillon, *Debating Divorce: Moral Conflict in Ireland* (Lexington, KY: University Press of Kentucky, 1993).

Abortion

Abortion is contrary to the teaching of the Catholic Church and drew out frequent statements by the Catholic hierarchy. The attention to abortion is partly tied up with the Irish conception of being female as codified in the 1937 Constitution. The Irish Constitution defined women mainly as mothers and assigned them to the private home and the domestic sphere.[21] Abortion contradicts basic female existence and of course, after the 1960s, is associated with sexual permissiveness and moral decay. Abortion, according to this worldview, denigrates the status of women as mothers, negates their natural instincts for nurturing, and is evidence of a society composed of self-centered, self-interested individuals whose only concern is their material wellbeing.

Of course, the Catholic Church has taken a strong position against abortion since 1870. In 1869, Pope Pius IX promulgated the papal enactment *Apostolicae Sedis*, which revised the earlier thinking on when animation of the fetus took place by holding that conception itself was the decisive moment in the creation of a human being. The Church did not claim that the human fetus became a person at conception. Rather, church doctrine argued that this question could not be settled and hence abortion could be interpreted as taking the life of an innocent human person. Anti-abortion laws were passed in many European countries after 1870, not only because the Church took a sharper attitude toward this question. As in the case of recreational drugs, the professionalization of the medical field spurred physicians to halt the practice of non-licensed abortionists.[22] In the 1960s, the feminist movement, which employed the discourse of rights to give women control over their sexuality, and the spread of new sexual mores led to the decriminalization of abortion in the first trimester in virtually all EU countries. For Catholic lay organizations and the Church, sexual permissiveness with the corresponding decline in family values was a recipe for social disorder and decay.

Of special worry in the early 1980s was that, even though abortion services had become available in Europe years earlier, it was only recently that Catholic countries introduced new legal provisions for abortion. While there was no reason to suspect that the average Irish person desired to see a change in the legal status of abortion and a

[21] Paul O'Connor, *Key Issues in Irish Family Law* (Dublin: Round Hall Press, 1988); Alpha Connelly (ed.), *Women and the Law in Ireland* (Dublin: Gill & Macmillan, 1993).
[22] Timothy A. Byrnes and Mary C. Segers, "The Politics of Abortion: The Catholic Bishops," in Timothy A. Byrnes and Mary C. Segers (eds.), *The Catholic Church and the Politics of Abortion* (Boulder: Westview, 1992), 2–4.

substantial anti-abortion consensus existed in Ireland in the early 1980s, conservative forces followed the abortion debates abroad with growing unease and decided to take pre-emptive action against the possibility of the Commission issuing a directive decriminalizing abortion, which could then be cited in Irish courts by pro-choice activists.[23] Conservative Catholic lay organizations had witnessed how, through a combination of parliamentary or court action, abortion had been legalized even in Catholic countries.[24] Troubled, conservative interest groups induced the leaders of Fine Gael and Fianna Fáil, in office between 1981 and 1982, to call for an amendment to the constitution that would go beyond the criminalization of abortion, already existent under the Offenses Against the Person Act (1861). The objective was to extend Article 40 of the constitution, which guaranteed the life of the citizen, to include a guarantee of the life of the unborn from conception to birth. Anti-abortion legislation would then be irreversible by any act of parliament or decision by the Supreme Court and could only be overturned after another referendum. Weeks prior to the 1981 general election Fine Gael agreed to schedule a referendum about adding an amendment to Article 40 to protect the life of the unborn and Fianna Fáil followed suit. The political campaign for a pro-life amendment was a pre-emptive strategy because there was really no pro-choice majority in Ireland.[25]

The Pro-Life Amendment Campaign (PLAC) came into existence in early 1981 to lobby for a constitutional ban on abortion. No political party wished to jeopardize votes by antagonizing hundreds of lay Catholic organizations, which fought for the amendment and claimed to represent the majority view of the electorate. The referendum increasingly became a testing ground for the loyalty and respect of the Irish people for the bishops, the Pope, and the teachings of the Church and the referendum was *de facto* a fight about the social and moral future of Ireland.[26]

---

[23] Brian Girvin, "Ireland and the European Union: The Impact of Integration and Social Change on Abortion Policy," in Marianne Githens and Dorothy McBride Stetson (eds.), *Abortion Politics: Public Policy in Cross-Cultural Perspective* (New York: Routledge, 1996), 166; Tom Hesketh, *The Second Partitioning of Ireland? The Abortion Referendum 1983* (Dublin: Brandsma, 1990), 84–88; Vicky Randall, "The Politics of Abortion in Ireland," in Jone Lovenduski and Joyce Outshoorn (eds.), *The New Politics of Abortion* (Newbury Park: Sage, 1986), 69.

[24] Cornelius O'Leary and Tom Hesketh, "The Irish Abortion Referendum Campaigns," *Irish Political Studies*, 3 (1988), 43–62; Chrystel Hug, *The Politics of Sexual Morality in Ireland* (New York: St. Martin's Press, 1999), 144.

[25] Hesketh, *The Second Partitioning of Ireland*, 100.

[26] Inglis, *Moral Monopoly*, 87; Garret Fitzgerald, *All in a Life* (Dublin: Gill & Macmillan, 1991), 416–17, 440–46.

The referendum was held in September 1983 and the question to be decided was whether to amend the constitution by including a statement which acknowledged the right to life of the unborn. Although the campaign was divisive, the actual turnout for the referendum was low – 53 percent.[27] The ratification of the amendment, even with a slim majority, ought to have buried once and for all any further discussions on abortion. The passing of the amendment proved that the Western discourse on individual rights had not yet shaped Irish political debates. Tolerance and freedom of conscience made little impression on elected officials and voters.[28] Individual freedom and the rights of women were regarded as subordinate to the desire to protect a good society.

After its enactment, the Society for the Protection of the Unborn Child (SPUC) used the amendment to prosecute doctors considering therapeutic abortions and the media if it planned to refer to abortion services. The Society went to court to suppress magazines that listed names and addresses of abortion clinics in Britain.[29] In 1985, SPUC tried to close down two clinics in Dublin – Open Door Counselling and Dublin Well Woman Center – which provided non-directive counseling to women. In 1986, the High Court granted an injunction against the two agencies because the constitution outlawed the presentation of any information to women that might lead them to decide to have an abortion. As the judge of the High Court reasoned, "the qualified right to privacy, the rights of association and freedom of expression and the right to disseminate information cannot be invoked to interfere with such a fundamental right as the right to life of the unborn." The effect of that judgment was the end of any pregnancy counseling in case the conversation could be construed as procuring abortions. Live programs in which abortion was discussed were banned from television.

SPUC initiated a second major legal action in October 1988. It asked officers of three students' unions at the University College Dublin not to print abortion information in their welfare manual. When the officers refused, SPUC sought a court injunction. The Supreme Court ruled that SPUC was justified in attempting to suppress the publication of information on abortion. The immediate effects of this legal battle were that the publication of any information about British abortion clinics was now declared illegal and unconstitutional. Libraries removed copies of books that mentioned abortion and British telephone directories because they contained addresses and phone numbers of British

---

[27] Girvin, "Social Change and Moral Politics," 75–76; Chubb, *The Politics of the Irish Constitution*, 55.
[28] Girvin, "Social Change and Moral Politics," 73.
[29] Hug, *The Politics of Sexual Morality*, 158–60.

abortion clinics.[30] Such drastic actions were tolerated by the political leadership, which stayed out of the legal battlefield and refused to clarify questions related to the right to seek information on abortion or the right to travel to obtain an abortion.

European membership and Irish law

When Ireland joined the European Community in 1973, its new partners were rapidly moving away from a traditional moral framework to embrace a very liberal interpretation of lifestyle choices. Access to divorce, contraception, and abortion became easier and religion declined in importance. Irish liberals in the 1970s, an embattled minority, welcomed EC accession in the hope of liberating Irish society from the Catholic ethos. Irish liberals knew that politicians across the political spectrum, afraid of open conflict with the Catholic Church, demonstrated a great resistance to change.[31] Membership in the European Community would presumably compel Irish authorities to address controversial issues that they would have preferred to leave unexplored. In the end, most liberals, in favor of a rights-based legal framework and gender equality, were disappointed by Community law because the EU only influenced aspects of Irish law related to the economic rights of an individual.

The 1937 Constitution gave Irish women political rights but otherwise assigned them the role of full-time wife and mother in an indissoluble marriage and with a natural preference for home duties. Social policies of the postwar period articulated this pre-feminist status of women. The social welfare state, until the Irish parliament had to alter much of its legislation, was founded on the philosophy that women were dependent on men and that society must only support them when this dependence ceased. Abandoned women, single mothers, and wives of prisoners were excluded from social entitlements. Married women were forced to resign from civil service jobs and were not entitled to unemployment benefits because their husbands would look after them. Since women were seen as the property of their husbands, they could not assume inheritance of their spouse's property and could not move to another domicile without losing custody over their children.

In 1970, the Irish feminist movement brought several cases to court to force parliament to address the inferior position of women in society.

---

[30] Ailbhe Smyth, "A Sadistic Farce: Women and Abortion in the Republic of Ireland, 1992," in Ailbhe Smyth (ed.), *Abortion Papers, Ireland* (Dublin: Attic Press, 1992), 16. The phone books were subsequently returned to the public libraries in 1992.
[31] Girvin, "Ireland and the European Union," 129.

They received unexpected assistance from the EC because Community obligations induced parliament to adjust previously discriminatory legislation to give women full economic rights. Slowly but surely, the Irish parliament granted women the right to work after marriage, to equal pay and opportunities, to pregnancy leave and pension rights.[32] Reforms of Irish social policy followed the operationalization of Article 119 of the Treaty of Rome, which gave rise to three different equality directives, covering equal pay for equal work (EC Directive 75/117), equal treatment in the workplace (EC Directive 76/207), and the principle of equal treatment for men and women in social security schemes (EC Directive 79/7).[33]

Nevertheless, the EC was not a genuine ally in the modernization of the Republic's political and cultural attitudes. To the disappointment of feminist groups and liberals, the European Court of Justice did not secularize Ireland because ECJ cases that involved Ireland often brought up questions that were only peripherally related to Community law. The judges of the ECJ, moreover, preferred cordial relations with national courts and did not attempt to broaden the scope of Irish legal cases by handing down rulings at odds with the Irish judiciary. Furthermore, the area of family law or reproductive rights is relatively underdeveloped at the Community level and the Court is on surer ground in areas where ECJ doctrine is highly developed.[34] There was no logical reason to upset the Irish judiciary for the sake of elaborating an issue not of great centrality to the viability of a supranational community.

Abortion does not test fundamental goals of European institution-building in the way that a public monopoly questions the principle of the free movement of goods. Likewise, the Irish abortion question matters little to chiefs of government of other member states and is not a source of friction in intergovernmental arrangements to improve political cooperation. Sexual morality *is* a domestic issue. Europe's impact on the question of reproductive rights in Ireland has been limited and European directives and regulations exerted much greater influence on

---

[32] Yvonne Scannel, "The Constitution and the Role of Women," in Brian Farrell (ed.), *De Valera's Constitution and Ours* (Dublin: Gill & Macmillan, 1988), 123–36.

[33] There were many problems in implementing the directive of equal treatment and the law was not fully operational until 1992. Catherine Hoskyns, *Integrating Gender: Women, Law, and Politics in the European Union* (London: Verso, 1996), 121; Yvonne Galligan, *Women and Politics in Contemporary Ireland* (Washington, DC: Pinter, 1998), 68–89.

[34] Karen Alter, "Who are the Masters of the Treaty? European Governments and the European Court of Justice," *International Organization*, 52 (1998), 121–47; Geoffrey Garrett, Daniel Keleman, and Heiner Schultz, "The European Court of Justice, National Governments and Legal Integration in the European Union," *International Organization*, 52 (1998), 149–76.

the revisions of prewar social policy legislation and the economic rights of women.

Still, the liberal minority counted on the European Court to reverse trends at home. Two cases related to the ban on abortion were submitted to the ECJ. The Court received the first case in late 1989 and the hearing took place in 1991. The case dealt with the publication of information on abortion services abroad. In *The Society of the Unborn Children Ltd. (SPUC) v. Grogan and others* (C-159/90), the attorney general had asked for an injunction against three student unions disseminating information on the medical services of abortion clinics in Britain. The High Court referred the case to the ECJ, pursuant to Article 177 EC (now Article 234 of the TEC), to establish whether the activities of the abortion clinics constituted "services" within the meaning of Article 60 (now Article 50), and if so, whether the Treaty provisions on the freedom to supply services precluded a national rule prohibiting the provision of information concerning abortion services legally performed in another member state.[35]

Two years later, in 1991, another case found its way to the European Court of Human Rights in Strasbourg, which published its decision in the case of *Attorney General (SPUC) v. Open Door Counselling and Dublin Well Woman* in late 1992. That case arose from the 1988 decision of the Irish High Court to prohibit non-directive counseling to pregnant women with respect to abortion. The Irish Supreme Court upheld the lower court decision to forbid counseling on the grounds that the defendants were said to assist in the destruction of the life of the unborn, which was contrary to Article 40.3.3. The two Dublin clinics appealed the decision and claimed that the restrictions violated Articles 8, 10, and 14 of the Convention on the Rights of Man (signed by the twenty-six members of the Council of Europe).

The first case heard was that of *SPUC v. Grogan* (C-159/90) in September 1991. Previously, the ECJ had ruled in *Luisi & Carbone v. Ministero del Tresoro* (Joined Cases 286/82 and 26/83 (1984) ECR 377) that medical treatment constituted a "service" within the meaning of Articles 59 and 60 of the Treaty of Rome (now Articles 49 and 50), so that potential recipients (as well as providers of a service) had a right to travel elsewhere within the Community to receive or provide those services. That implied that the ban on information on abortion services contradicted previous Court rulings with respect to the free movement of services. It also followed that the suppression of information on

---

[35] Gerard Hogan, "Protocol 17," in Patrick Keatinge (ed.), *Maastricht and Ireland: What the Treaty Means* (Dublin: Studies in European Union, 1992), 110–11.

abortion services denoted a restriction of free speech. But the ECJ judges were not willing to provoke the Irish judiciary nor were they ready to engage the Republic of Ireland in an exchange on morality. The final ruling therefore presented a novel argument.

On the one hand, declared the Court, SPUC's contention that the provision of abortion cannot be regarded as a service on the grounds that it is grossly immoral carries no direct bearing on the interpretation of the case. The Court proclaimed that it could not substitute its assessment for that of the legislature in those member states where the activities in question were practiced legally. Consequently, the answer to the High Court's first question must be that medical termination of pregnancy performed in accordance with the law of the state in which it was carried out constituted a service within the meaning of Article 60. On the other hand, the Court reasoned that the link between the students' associations and the clinics operating in another member state was too tenuous for the prohibition on the distribution of information to be regarded as a restriction within the meaning of Article 59. Since the students had not been directly affected by the lack of access to information on abortion, the Irish court had not abused their rights. In short, the students, as third parties, lacked the standing necessary to assert Community rights, which the UK clinics might potentially have had. They were not directly harmed by the fact that they could not advertise services performed by British abortion clinics. In the end, the Court refused to speak out on whether the right to free speech had been compromised and whether the ban on abortion impeded the movement of services.[36]

In its judgment, the European Court of Justice did not make many references to the preliminary report of Advocate General van Gerven. That report mentioned, in passing, that anti-abortion measures had to be proportionate to the desired goal: the safeguarding of the unborn life. Disproportionate measures included subjecting pregnant women to unsolicited examinations, restricting their right to travel, or suppressing information. But the ECJ judges were not ready to challenge a member state on an issue of such enormous moral weight and used a new principle – direct economic interest of the speaker – to void the application of Article 59. In an earlier decision (*GB-INNO-BM v. Confédération du Commerce Luxembourgeois* (C-362/88)), the Court had prevented Luxembourg from disallowing Belgian grocery stores to

---

[36] Caroline Forder, "Abortion: A Constitutional Problem," *Maastricht Journal of European and Comparative Law*, 1 (1994), 56–100; Siofra O'Leary "Resolution by the Court of Justice of Disputes affecting Family Life," in Tamara K. Hervey and David O'Keeffe (eds.), *Sex Equality Law in the European Union* (New York: John Wiley, 1996), 256.

advertise their sales prices in Luxembourg. In *Grogan*, the Court held that the advertising frontier for groceries was distinguishable from the advertising frontier for medical services based on the absence of an economic motivation by the Irish students. The Advocate General argued the opposite and pointed out that the free circulation of consumer information is essential to the Common Market and that abortion services fall under this category.[37]

Although traditionalists and the Irish judiciary scored an important legal victory, disappointment and apprehension dogged the winning party. The sources of this disappointment were twofold. The related case, *Attorney General (SPUC) v. Open Door Counselling and Dublin Well Woman*, was heard in 1991 by the European Court of Human Rights (ECHR), which issued a ruling that potentially contradicted the ECJ interpretation. The judges of the ECHR concluded that national authorities enjoyed a wide margin of discretion with respect to moral issues because they were in a better position to judge what the protection of morals at the national level required. At the same time, the ECHR questioned the link between the provision of information and the destruction of life since many women, after receiving counseling, could have decided to keep the pregnancy. Because the same information could be obtained through other channels and because Irish women none the less found their way to abortion clinics, the practical impact of the Irish court decisions also seemed questionable. In addition, the ECHR drew attention to the health risks of the injunction, which forced women to seek abortion at a later stage and deprived them of follow-up care. In light of all these reasons, the ECHR found the injunction contrary to the freedom of expression.

Conveniently, the European Court of Human Rights primarily recommends or urges action and carries limited weight. But its legal ruling demonstrated that one could be respectful of national ethical norms and still dismiss the suppression of information on abortion services on the grounds that it harmed the health and welfare of women.[38] Although the ECHR cannot compel parties to abide by its rulings, at about the same time the Commission in Brussels issued a report urging the member states to adopt the European Convention on Human Rights, and if chiefs of government decided to do so, then

---

[37] Elizabeth Spalin, "Abortion, Speech, and the European Community," *Journal of Social Welfare and Family Law*, 2 (1992), 19–21; Renaud Dehousse, *The European Court of Justice* (New York: St. Martin's Press, 1998), 65, 132, 165, 170; Dena T. Sacco and Alexia Brown, "Regulation of Abortion in the European Community," *Harvard International Law Journal*, 33 (1992), 291–304.

[38] O'Leary, "Resolution by the Court of Justice of Disputes affecting Family Life," 265–66.

decisions of the ECHR would take precedence over domestic law.[39] Thus, the ECHR interpretation created some doubts about the future protection of the abortion ban.

Second, the ECJ ruling itself left open the possibility that another party, if it could demonstrate direct injury from the ban on abortion information in Ireland, would elicit a different ruling from the Court. The judges noted that the ban on information on abortion services abroad would be in conflict with Community law and Single Market principles of the free circulation of people and provision of services if an economic agent was harmed by Irish policy. Whereas SPUC had argued vigorously that medical termination of pregnancy was "grossly immoral" and should fall outside the scope of Article 60, the ECJ did not accept the absolutist pro-life approach of SPUC and thus opened the door to future cases, which challenged the gender-biased construction of medical services.[40]

Pyrrhic victory

The free movement of people is a fundamental right and the cornerstone of the Treaty of Rome. To create an abortion-free zone, Irish authorities fell back on methods of repression – limiting the right of pregnant women to travel and censoring books, magazines, newspapers, and broadcasts that contained information about abortion – incompatible with the preservation of a functioning democracy. The ECJ did not come to the defense of the civil rights of EU citizens in Ireland, however. An event took place in early 1992 that led the ECJ decision to be seen in a new light.

In early 1992, the parents of a 14-year-old girl were on their way to England to procure an abortion for their daughter who had recently been a victim of rape. Just prior to their departure, they went to the police to check whether they could use the results of DNA tests on fetal tissue to apprehend the man guilty of the rape. The police reported the parents (not the rapist) to the office of the district attorney on the grounds that a crime was about to be committed – namely an abortion outside Irish territory. On February 6, 1992, the attorney general (principal law officer of the state) obtained an interim court injunction restraining the girl from having an abortion in England. The High Court granted the injunction with the argument that Article 40.3.3 required the courts to grant an injunction to restrain the right to travel abroad as otherwise the guarantee with regard to the unborn might be

---

[39] Hug, *The Politics of Sexual Morality*, 172.
[40] Spalin, "Abortion, Speech, and the European Community," 20.

rendered worthless. Recognizing that, under Community law, there was a right to travel, the Court held that Ireland can derogate this right on grounds of public policy, public security, or public health. The presiding judge Costello (of the High Court) did not think that stopping a woman from going abroad to prevent the termination of life of the unborn was disproportionate to the aim which the eighth amendment sought to achieve.[41] On February 17, 1992, the High Court confirmed the injunction and ruled that the girl and her parents were prohibited from leaving the Irish Republic for the next nine months. The High Court reasoned that the fetus demanded the absolute protection of the law while the girl's suicidal tendencies (she told the police and her parents that she felt like throwing herself under a train) could be handled by the loving care of her family "during the difficult months ahead."

The X-case, as it became known, more than any other anti-abortion battle generated intense attention and debate. After all, the logical extension of the Court ruling would be that all pregnant women must be confined to Ireland in case they could or might seek an abortion abroad. To intercept pregnant women, the Irish authorities would have to set up pregnancy testing facilities at border crossings. Political leaders saw a major crisis looming and applied intense pressure on the girl and her parents to appeal to the Supreme Court. The government of Albert Reynolds paid the expenses of the appeal, which was heard on February 24–26, 1992. The Supreme Court's first step was to lift the injunction and permit the victim to travel to England. It released its judgment on March 5. To everybody's surprise, the Supreme Court put a new interpretation on Article 40.3.3. Four of the five judges concluded that the Constitution did not forbid abortion when there was "a real and substantial risk to the life, as distinct from the health, of the mother." Catholic interpretation of this concept is that abortion is legitimate in cases of ectopic pregnancy or cancer of the uterus, both of which are indisputable unintended acts.[42] The 14-year-old girl did not qualify under these conditions. But she had threatened and even tried to commit suicide. The judges ruled that a real danger existed that she would take her own life if she had to continue with the pregnancy. They therefore decided that the life of the mother (who was suicidal) must take precedence over the right to life of the unborn child. Such a termination of the pregnancy, the Supreme Court reasoned, would have been lawful if performed in Ireland. The travel ban could not be

[41] Hogan, "Protocol 17," 112.
[42] Kathy Rudy, *Beyond Pro-Life and Pro-Choice: Moral Diversity in the Abortion Debate* (Boston: Beacon Press, 1996), 24–26; Tom Hesketh, "The Irish Abortion Referendum Campaigns," *Irish Political Studies*, 3 (1988), 43–62.

sustained for this particular case, as there could be no objection to traveling abroad to perform an act that would have been lawful in Ireland.[43]

At the same time, three of the five judges maintained that the state was entitled to prevent women from going abroad for an abortion if that act was inconsistent with the constitution. Thus, X could obtain an abortion because her procedure was lawful according to the Irish Constitution. Other women, whose situation was different, i.e. they were not suicidal, could be barred from traveling abroad for an abortion.

The decision left great confusion. The Supreme Court ruled that for all intents and purposes the eighth amendment permitted abortion if a woman could demonstrate that her life was in danger. Such an interpretation defeated the entire aim of the amendment, which was to rule out once and for all any prospect of a legal abortion on Irish soil. But it also couched its decision in such a fashion that the right to travel was subordinate to the right to life of the unborn so that pregnant women were not entitled to seek an abortion abroad unless their life was at risk. In one stroke, the Supreme Court ruling contradicted the constitutional amendment on the right of the unborn and negated the right to free movement for citizens of the EC.

As attention focused on the dilemma of reconciling the Supreme Court judgment with the eighth amendment and with the free movement of people encoded by Community law, another predicament came to light. Two months before the X-case, a couple of "anti-abortion veterans" had pressured the Prime Minister and Minister of Foreign Affairs (Gerry Collins) to insert a special protocol in the Treaty on European Union to pre-empt any future EC challenge against Article 40.3.3. Collins called it an "insurance policy" against abortion legalization.[44] They were spurred into action because the earlier court decision in the Grogan case was only a partial victory owing to its narrowly technical (and problematic) reasoning. Lay Catholic organizations begged the government to add a protocol in the Maastricht Treaty, effectively voiding any future ECJ judgments in favor of abortion advertisement or services in Ireland. Protocol 17 ensured that Community law and future EC treaties would not violate the blanket ban on abortion. Nobody paid much attention to the demands of Reynolds and Collins (Fianna Fáil) for a separate protocol until the Irish Supreme Court ruling on the X-case. Suddenly, Protocol 17 contradicted Irish

---

[43] O'Leary and Hesketh, "The Irish Abortion Referendum Campaigns."
[44] A first draft of a possible protocol included a section on divorce. Some cabinet members found that too much and torpedoed this plan to protect the ban on divorce from European interference. Hug, *The Politics of Sexual Morality*, 172.

law since its meaning had been altered. In addition, Protocol 17 seemed to confirm the Irish authorities' right to restrict travel by Irish women, which is in absolute defiance of a cornerstone of Community law.[45] This situation needed clarification and the government could either organize another referendum to add a clause to Article 40.3.3 to reflect new directions in Irish legal thinking or it could negotiate an addendum to the protocol. A referendum would have been terribly divisive so the best option was to alter the protocol. But the legal experts in Brussels balked at adding an addendum to a protocol in a European treaty to guarantee an amendment to the Irish Constitution. In addition neither the Commission nor the Council was in a mood to redraft the protocol, afraid of opening a Pandora's box of requests for revisions from other member states. The Council was willing only to issue a "Solemn Declaration" (paragraph 1.31 of the TEU) in relation to the protocol, pledging to desist from laying down Community law in conflict with Article 40.3.3 of the Irish Constitution.

The Solemn Declaration probably had little legal bearing and its relationship to the pro-life amendment and Irish court decision continued to sow discord and confusion. The cabinet was therefore forced to agree to call for a referendum to seek the opinion of the voters on three separate questions.[46] The referendum was to be held after the ratification of the TEU.

In November 1992, the abortion referendum took place and listed three questions related to the free travel from one member state to another, the freedom to obtain information on legally available services in other member states, and abortion if the life of the mother is at risk. The last question was worded in such a way that neither liberals nor conservatives were happy with the formulation. It stated that abortion was unlawful unless the life of the mother was at risk, but not at risk of self-destruction.

Not surprisingly, the questions related to the freedom to travel and freedom of information passed easily and demonstrated that voters never intended to restrict the right to information and travel. But no less than 65 percent of the voters turned down the third question on abortion, while approximately 60 percent approved of the first two

---

[45] Anna Eggert and Bill Rolston, "Ireland," in Anna Eggert and Bill Rolston (eds.), *Abortion in the New Europe: A Comparative Handbook* (Westport, CT: Greenwood Press, 1994), 166; Smyth, "A Sadistic Farce," 19. There are other examples of protocols annexed to Community law which offer forms of derogation. Denmark received special protection on the acquisition of second homes and the UK received special rights with regard to the Social Charter.

[46] Eggert and Rolston, "Ireland," 168; Brian Girvin, "Ireland," *Parliamentary Affairs*, 47 (1994), 209.

Table 7.2. *Circumstances under which abortion is approved, 1990*

	% approving Ireland	Europe
Where the mother's health is at risk because of the pregnancy	65	92
Where it is likely that the child would be physically handicapped	32	79
Where the mother is not married	8	27
Where a married couple do not want to have any more children	8	34

Source: Michael P. Hornsby-Smith and Christopher T. Whelan, "Religious and Moral Values," in Christopher T. Whelan (ed.), *Values and Social Change in Ireland* (Dublin: Gill & Macmillan, 1994), 36, Table 2.13.

questions.[47] In other words, the electorate rejected the substantive clause, which would have permitted abortion when there was an illness or disorder of the mother that gave rise to a real and substantial risk to her life.

Value change and encounters with the EU

Although the referendum failed to overturn the absolute proscription on abortion, opinions on sexuality have undergone a sea change and devotion to Catholicism has declined in the 1990s. Sunday Mass attendance has dropped from 91 percent in 1971 to 82 percent in 1989 and 58 percent in 1998.[48] Although the Irish are still more religious than many other Catholic nations, compared with the past it is decidedly less so. One symptom of the growing detachment from Catholic teaching is the gradual softening of views on abortion. In 1973, 74 percent of Irish people thought that abortion was always evil and only 5 percent accepted abortion in cases of rape or illegitimacy.[49] In 1981, 55 percent of the surveyed population totally rejected abortion and 45 percent approved of abortion if the mother's life was at risk because of the pregnancy. In 1990, these percentages shifted again, as table 7.2 demonstrates.

This softening trend has continued and in 1994 71 percent of the population agreed that abortion should be possible if the life of the mother is at risk and 41 percent felt that extreme mental anguish (suicidal tendencies) should be included as one of the reasons.[50] A

[47] Richard Sinnott, *Irish Voters Decide: Voting Behavior in Elections and Referendums since 1918* (New York: Manchester University Press, 1995), 229.
[48] Finnegan and McCarron, *Ireland: Historical Echoes*, 139; O'Connor, *Emerging Voices: Women in Contemporary Irish Society*, 3.
[49] Hug, *The Politics of Sexual Morality*, 150.
[50] Girvin, "Ireland and the European Union," 176.

breakdown of the survey data also revealed that younger cohort groups were most likely to favor abortion. In 1981, 60 percent of those between the ages of 18 and 35 approved of abortion if the mother's life was at risk and that proportion increased to 80 percent of those between the ages of 18 and 35 in 1990.[51] Liberalization of sexual norms is also evident from opinions on premarital sex. In 1973, 71 percent of the Irish population agreed that premarital sex was always wrong. In 1994, the percentage dropped to 32 percent. Young adults (18 to 30), moreover, were strikingly more liberal and only 8 percent disapproved of premarital sex in 1994.[52]

The easing of moral strictures against premarital sex has led to a larger number of unwanted pregnancies and a growing number of women who decide to terminate their pregnancy. In 1967, England decriminalized abortion and approximately 64 Irish women traveled to England for an abortion the following year. Since that date, the number of Irish women has increased every year. In the late 1980s, around 4,000 women went to England. In 1997, the number rose to 5,325 – an increase of nearly 9 percent on the previous year.[53] The 1998 figures from the UK Office for National Statistics show the number of Irish women having abortions in England to be 5,892, which represents a remarkable increase of more than 10 percent since 1997, and the numbers went up another 3.5 percent in 1999.[54] Around 100,000 Irish women have had an abortion in the UK since 1970. This translates into an abortion rate of 6 per thousand women aged between 14 and 44 on average over those thirty years. Compared with the British rate of 14.8 per thousand in 1994, the Irish rate is low. It should be noted, however, that some Irish women may not give an Irish address because they use the address of their friends or relatives living in Britain, which could mean that the real number of Irish women who opt for an abortion may be double this.[55]

Abortion tourism is problematic for three reasons. It questions the efficacy and end goal of the abortion ban, which is to protect the life of the unborn. That life is clearly at risk so long as women terminate unwanted pregnancies in England. Since the life of the unborn is ultimately not protected by the constitution, an auxiliary question is whether it makes sense to use the constitution to legislate morality and whether it is fair to force women to travel to England for this medical

---

[51] Hornsby-Smith and Whelan, "Religious and Moral Values," 71.
[52] Fahey, "Religion and Sexual Culture in Ireland," 62.
[53] Inglis, *Lessons in Irish Sexuality*, 169.
[54] "Abortion has Increased by 10.4 Percent," *Irish Times* (June 8, 1999), 4.
[55] Kenny, *Goodbye to Catholic Ireland*, 243; Hardiman and Whelan, "Changing Values," 78.

procedure, thereby denying them follow-up care. The second predicament is that abortion tourism disputes the conventional view that the Irish have not succumbed to sexual permissiveness and that they embrace a pro-natalist Catholic ethos in contrast to the rest of Europe. Apparently, middle-class, educated married women in their mid- to late twenties are much more likely to obtain an abortion than are young girls and unmarried women. Abortion is thus partly a birth control device, used by married women to determine the size of their families. In that case, abortion tourism questions the Irish commitment to large families, traditional values, and the centrality of motherhood. Third, the abortion ban produces at regular intervals major public policy crises that compel the political establishment to act in haste and without foresight. For example, in late 1997, another case (called C-case) was brought to the attention of the voter when a 13-year-old girl was pregnant as a result of rape. The girl's case was brought to the court because she was in the care of a public agency (Eastern Health Board) and social workers requested permission to arrange for an abortion in Britain. The court gave permission in spite of intervention by pro-life activists.

Of course, the steady growth in the number of women who travel to England points to a gap between official standards of behavior and the everyday experiences of the average Irish man and woman and is indicative of larger structural changes in Irish society. These developments have given Irish citizens growing confidence in their ability to differentiate between institutions of the family and that of the Church. Compared with twenty years ago, more Irish people are cognizant of the fact that not all values are shared universally or to the same degree. Younger generations of voters espouse a new theology in which the needs of the individual and society are separate and in which a good Catholic can none the less reject Catholic teaching as inappropriate or impractical in certain areas of life.

The Church promoted a vision of a society living a simple life, united in its piety and devotion to Catholicism. But Irish society has changed irrevocably. Traces of that change were already visible in the early 1980s although the traditionalists could still claim to represent the majority. In the late 1990s, evidence of this structural change is found everywhere. For example, in 1960, fewer than 3 percent of all births were outside marriage. In 1996, 25 percent of births took place outside marriage.[56] The fertility rate was 6.0 per 1,000 population in 1951 and fell to 1.8

[56] Tony Fahey, "Progress or Decline? Demographic Change in Political Context," in William Crotty and David E. Schmitt (eds.), *Ireland and the Politics of Change* (New York: Longman, 1998), 59; O'Connor, *Emerging Voices: Women in Contemporary Irish Society*, 119–22.

per 1,000 in 1994.[57] Married women as a percentage of women in the labor force rose from 6.8 percent in 1951 to over 50 percent in 1996.[58] Thus, it is no surprise that there is a marked distance between people's public religious observances and their personal decisions. The Irish are becoming increasingly self-directed and critically reflective and no longer accept without questioning the rules and regulations of the Church.

The legal and cultural clashes with Europe did not usher in major shifts in opinion, but they did underscore the gap between a Catholic ethos idealized by public leaders and actual cultural norms embraced by voters who apparently adopt European-type views. Moreover, the encounters with Europe accentuated the futility of creating an abortion-free zone in an era of a tightening web of financial, economic, and cultural interdependencies. Constitutional referenda and amendments are blunt tools to preserve standards of sexual behavior and presuppose a huge impenetrable wall between Ireland and the rest of Europe.

Nevertheless, it is important to note that Ireland is not like other Catholic, let alone non-Catholic, countries. The Church remains a strong institutional presence in a variety of areas of Irish life and in particular in education and health services. The electorate, too, even if it is moving closer to the European mainstream, exhibits passions and traits different from those of Continental Europe. For example, in 1995 a second referendum on divorce was held. This time it passed, but with the smallest margin imaginable of 9,114 votes or 50.3 percent of the vote in total.[59] Irish voters are not totally reconciled to the secular self-centered values pervasive in the rest of the EU and feel decidedly torn between what is good for society (adherence to Catholic ethos) and individual self-fulfillment. Very few groups advocate an openly pro-choice viewpoint because great ambivalence continues to mark Irish thinking on this moral dilemma. A situation of "pick and mix" has emerged which blends a variety of traditional and modern value positions. On moral values, Irish people tend to be more conservative, expressing reservations with regards to abortion, but on gender roles and marriage they tend to be in line with the rest of Europe. They subscribe to equal rights in the workplace, partnership in marriage, and independence for women.[60]

---

[57] Galligan, *Women and Politics in Contemporary Ireland*, 27.
[58] Galligan, *Women and Politics in Contemporary Ireland*, 32.
[59] Brian Girvin, "The Irish Divorce Referendum, November 1995," *Irish Political Studies*, 2 (1996), 174–81.
[60] Hardiman and Whelan, "Changing Values," 77–78; John Coakley, "Society and Political Culture," in John Coakley and Michael Gallagher (eds.), *Politics in the Republic of Ireland* (New York: Routledge, 1999), 32–63.

Although the Irish legislature recognizes the dramatic transformation of Ireland into a post-industrial society, it has been stymied in its efforts to solve the inconsistencies associated with a total ban on abortion.[61] Abortion was an issue during the June 1999 European Parliamentary elections in the wake of the publication of a report by the European Parliament in March 1999. This report, chaired by a Finnish member of the European Parliament, Heidi Hautala, called on member states to legalize abortion in certain circumstances (i.e. in cases of rape and where the life or health of a mother is endangered). The March report stirred outrage in Ireland especially when it was discovered that all four female Irish members of the European Parliament had voted in favor of it. The subsequent debate finally prompted the Fianna Fáil government of Bertie Ahern to fulfill an earlier promise, made during the 1997 election, to organize a referendum on whether to outlaw abortion, to legislate for abortion in situations similar to those in the X-case, or make abortion freely available.[62]

In September 1999, the government (a coalition of Fianna Fáil and the Progressive Democrats) finally published a long-awaited Green Paper on abortion. The 172–page document makes it clear that it is very difficult to arrive at an acceptable wording to provide for a constitutional prohibition on abortion. To be sure, abortion is available only 60 miles away and most European countries set few, if any, restrictions on what is now characterized as a service in European law. The Green Paper quietly acknowledges that constitutional amendments and virtual blanket legislative prohibitions have not reduced – nor can they reduce – the level of terminations among Irish women when abortion is readily available just a short plane or boat journey away.[63]

In May 2000, parliament held hearings to gather ideas on whether a referendum should be held or whether legislative action by parliament would be sufficient to tackle the dilemmas of a future X-case, and, if necessary, how to design a valid referendum. The deliberations demonstrated that emotions still ran high and that abortion continued to be divisive. In contrast to 1983, however, the liberal bloc has the upper hand and is able to steer the direction of the debate.

In October 2000, it became clear that the All-Party Committee on the Constitution could not reach a consensus on the abortion issue. The political parties advocated different solutions ranging from leaving the

---

[61] Girvin, "Ireland and the European Union," 180–82.
[62] Alison O'Connor, "Irish MEPs Split by Gender over Vote on Report's Abortion Clause," *The Irish Times*, (March 10, 1999), 8; Carol Coulter "Meeting Hears Call for Referendum on Abortion This Year," *The Irish Times* (March 8, 1999), 7.
[63] Miriam Donohoe, "Backbenchers Anxious for Referendum," *The Irish Times* (September 11, 1999), 8.

law unchanged to launching a special state agency to reduce the number of crisis pregnancies. The Labour Party, in turn, proposed to provide for abortion where there is a real and substantial threat to the life of the mother, including suicide, representing the most liberal position. However, 77 percent of Irish voters polled in September 2000 favored a referendum and only 6 percent approved of parliament passing new legislation without consulting the electorate. Half the voters, moreover, supported an amendment prohibiting all abortion but allowing for medical intervention to save the mother's life (in case of an ectopic pregnancy or cancer).[64]

Conclusion

Religion, the Catholic Church, and the Irish Republic formed a trinity and defined the main character of the Irish nation. The 1937 Constitution, which was an anti-liberal, anti-modern document, was uncontroversial so long as the Irish remained devoted to Catholicism. Until very recently, Irish voters or citizens did not seek a liberal pluralist society in which the rights and interests of minorities were defended and did not object to Catholic teaching on family and sexual morality. This situation lasted throughout the 1970s after most European societies had cast off traditional Christian views on women, gender relations, and sexual relations in and outside marriage.

The erosion of the Catholic monopoly on morality came from different directions – urbanization, improved education, exposure to Western ideas via the global media industry, the decline of orders of religious sisters and brothers to manage and staff the Catholic-run institutions, and increased prosperity. New ideas endorsed by the Church itself also reformulated views and attitudes on family matters. Following Vatican II, the Irish Catholic Church adopted more liberal attitudes. While abortion remained an anathema, single motherhood was quietly countenanced as the lesser of two evils. The legal fight against the dissemination of abortion information was led by Catholic lay organizations while the religious hierarchy kept silent. As single motherhood no longer received harsh treatment by the Church, premarital sex was also quietly condoned. To some extent, the Church itself contributed to the destigmatization of sexual promiscuity and dissipated much of the traditional Catholic obsession with sexual purity as a key feature of high moral principles.

Against this background, the efforts to create an abortion-free zone

---

[64] Maria O'Halloran, "77 Percent Favour Abortion Referendum," *Irish Times* (September 27, 2000), 4.

faced incredible hurdles and could only be achieved by extreme methods – limiting the right of pregnant women to travel and censoring books, magazines, newspapers, and broadcasts that contain information about abortion – incompatible with the preservation of a functioning democracy and at odds with basic European principles. Although the EC/EU kept silent on the Irish proceedings, many Irish people relied on their consciences to make life choices and embraced the ethical individualism commonly found in the rest of the EU. Therefore, irrespective of how restrictively the Irish judiciary acted, women took the exit option and went to England, a country separated from Ireland only by a narrow body of water, for an abortion. Over time, the number of Irish women who availed themselves of the English option increased and made a mockery of the whole concept of protecting the life of the unborn.

The Irish people are still different in terms of their views on abortion (and sexual morality) from voters in other EU member states because of the association between Catholicism and Irish nation-building. Yet debates on abortion have taken on a more European hue and the EU has played a minor yet significant role in the liberalization (and thus indirectly Europeanization) of Irish sexual morality. The gap between typical Irish views on a difficult issue such as individual self-determination and those of the British or other Europeans has narrowed. Still, although the Irish are now comparatively less likely to follow the principles of the faith, they are still more attached to Catholicism than are Catholics of other countries. The collective self-identity of the Irish is still colored by the long and painful struggle against Protestant rule. A more accurate conclusion is that the Irish straddle two different spheres of discourse and action, namely an Irish-Catholic sphere and a liberal-European one, and have reached a point in their history where they pick and choose which course of conduct fits their own personal circumstances.

8   The emergence of a European morality?

In the past fifteen years or so, the scope and density of European Union activities have increased immensely. This study seeks to understand how these developments affect the normative and causal beliefs of the member states. The research design I employed examined singular or deviant morality frameworks, which endured in spite of the ascendance of very different models of behavior in the rest of the European Union. I argued that these morality standards survived new styles of thought and practices because of their centrality to the definition of collective self-identity. Collective ideas on controversial matters, such as drinking alcohol, drug use, or abortion, which deviate from mainstream thinking, foster a sense of national belonging.

Institutional action and political decisions in the spheres of abortion, alcohol, and drugs disclose deeply held beliefs on the self, personhood, and state governance. In the Western world, the self is considered subjective and aspires to autonomy and personal fulfillment. We find our identity through acts of choice and we are not dependent on the authority of religion or traditional morality. Notions of personhood vary greatly from culture to culture and variations reflect different social, political, and economic arrangements as well as different legal, religious, and philosophical legacies. I have argued in this book that Nordic alcohol control policy and the Irish proscription on abortion deviate from the European or Western conceptualization of the self in that they continue to subordinate the freedom to choose to the right of a higher authority to make decisions. I have also shown that the Netherlands diverges from the European center by taking the cult of the self to its logical conclusion and granting the individual the freedom to try out psychotropic drugs, substances that evoke much anxiety and apprehension in the rest of the EU.

Nordic countries designate alcohol as a dangerous intoxicant, which threatens the wellbeing of the individual as well as society. A key causal belief is that the nationalization of the production, distribution, and retail of alcoholic beverages or state intervention is required to control people's bad drinking habits. Drinking belongs to the field of public health, which has acquired the status of a moral crusade, laying down how we should conduct our lives individually and collectively. All of us are constantly urged to "stop smoking," "lose weight," "avoid fat," and, above all, to take responsibility for the care of our bodies and to limit the potential to harm others through taking preventive actions.[1] Yet European governments are also of the opinion that the state should not directly interfere in personal consumer choices and individual development. Primacy is granted to the principle of the autonomous individual and most European governments respect individual self-governance. Therefore, in the new public health debate, citizens have both rights and duties, with the latter referring to our personal responsibilities and social obligations. The Nordic countries differ from this shared Europe-wide understanding. They dismiss the notion that drinking is a private affair and that people are able to make the right decision for themselves.

The Irish Republic maintains that the good life encompasses a life guided by a higher moral authority. Irish normative beliefs question the Western idealization of the free, autonomous, choosing self and have retained an older nineteenth-century concept of a community strengthened by religious faith. Abortion contradicts central religious axioms. Mass opinion rejected abortion on the grounds that it encouraged a disregard for higher spiritual goals. A constitutional ban on abortion preserved the natural order.

The Netherlands conforms to the Western disposition that privileges ethical individualism and personal fulfillment. But it applies this principle to an area of private behavior that generates much concern and apprehension in other societies, namely the drug-taking rituals of young adults. The Dutch interpretation of this pervasive phenomenon is to accept the appeal of chemical substances among certain social groups and the country's normative stance is, therefore, that the total suppression of drug use, like that of alcohol consumption, is plainly impossible. One way or the other, people will always crave this sort of activity. Therefore, effective government intervention involves the decriminalization of personal consumption of drugs in order to prevent users (not abusers) from falling into a criminalized lifestyle and from forming a marginalized, angry group of individuals who stand outside the boundaries of society. Prohibitionist, repressive drug control regimes are counter-productive, according to this line of reasoning, because coercive law enforcement measures will never succeed in banning drug use, but will instead breed organized crime, social corruption, and lawlessness.

[1] Alan Petersen and Deborah Lepton, *The New Public Health: Health and Self in the Age of Risk* (Thousand Oaks, CA: Sage, 1996).

The key finding of this study is that European integration since the 1990s puts enormous strain on cultural divergences in spite of the efforts made by government leaders to shelter central beliefs, institutions, and policies from outside interference. In this chapter, I will draw out some of the broader implications of this study by discussing the resistance to adopting postwar European practice and the endurance of particular sets of national beliefs and policy instruments. I then explore why, after a considerable lag, morality norms are none the less being revised and taking on a more European hue. Next, I will bring up the degree of convergence or divergence in the European Union. Finally, these case studies also serve as a window on the future of post-Maastricht Europe.

Endurance of national norms

Norms and beliefs must be reproduced and adapted to new circumstances. State agencies and expert communities in each of the four countries implemented policies, rules, and regulations drawn from the normative and causal beliefs of society and thus constantly revalidated the national belief system and intellectualized its utility and effectiveness. In Finland and Sweden, social welfare agencies, ministries of finance, state alcohol monopoly companies, and local treatment centers supported drinking restrictions and relied on scientific studies to explore the cause and effect relationships between drinking and scores of social and physical pathologies. In the Netherlands, various state ministries, social welfare agencies, local governments, and law enforcement bodies stood behind drug decriminalization and employed science to illustrate the superiority of this approach. In Ireland, the Church, lay Catholic movements, and professional associations in fields dominated by Catholic-financed or administered organizations (e.g. medical doctors) lent support to the absolute ban on abortion. In all countries, knowledge-bearing elites – occupational groups whose livelihoods and status depend on their use of specialized or expert knowledge – operated within the normative parameters set by society and actively advocated either alcohol restrictions, abortion ban, or drug decriminalization.[2] Since political decision-makers turn to institutions and organizations whose ideas align with their own, technical specialists, if they seek to influence policy deliberations, must work within the operating premises

---

[2] This definition of knowledge-bearing elites comes from Nicholas Ziegler, *Governing Ideas: Strategies for Innovation in France and Germany* (Ithaca: Cornell University Press, 1997).

or assumptions of the national framework of reference.[3] Over time, they flesh out existing ideas and reinforce the "logic of appropriateness," which dictates how things are done at home.

The question I examined in the empirical chapters of this book is why these morality standards withstood the emergence of new concepts of personhood while others, presumably, disappeared. In other words, why did these practices endure when other national idiosyncrasies adapted to new developments and trends? Part of the answer to this question is that the policy regimes contained beliefs, opinions, or concepts that speak to the "national character" of each country. The term "national character" should be used with great care and sensitivity because it lends itself to cheesy stereotyping. Nevertheless, abortion, alcohol, and drugs provide insight into what it means to be Irish, Finnish or Swedish, and Dutch.

Stereotypical descriptions of Finnish and Swedish national character routinely refer to their social awkwardness. They lack, by their own account, the gift for small talk and drink excessively during social occasions. At the same time, Sweden and Finland were, until relatively recently, prototypical agrarian societies where the dominant alcoholic beverage was vodka or spirits. In spirit-drinking cultures, binge drinking, that is the consumption of excessive amounts of alcohol in one sitting, was common. Thus, binge drinking was an ingrained ritual, not only because Swedes and Finns were shy and awkward in social situations, but also because spirits were associated with agrarian rituals that entailed irregular spurts of heaving drinking. Alcohol became a target for state intervention when urbanization and industrialization transformed social relations and gave rise to new demands with regards to discipline, self-control, and the work ethic. State alcohol control policies have endured until now because Swedes and Finns believed themselves to be incapable of handling intoxicants and assigned negative meaning to intoxication. Drunkenness was indicative of sloth, idleness, and irresponsibility while sobriety or abstinence was equated with trustworthiness, diligence, and honesty.

A similar analysis explains the special Irish devotion to the Catholic faith. A good Irish citizen was a practicing Catholic. Irish public figures, to prove their credentials, openly demonstrated their attachment to the faith. The elevation of Catholic doctrine to represent the moral standards of society was due to the special role played by the nuns, priests, and lay brothers and sisters in the formation of the independent Republic of Ireland. The Church was the only institution that succeeded in bringing the Irish together to rescue them from claims of perpetual

---

[3] Bruno Latour, *Science in Action* (Cambridge, MA: Harvard University Press, 1987).

dominance by the British. The modern constitution of Ireland reflected the special contribution made by the Catholic Church and contained many references to Catholic principles. Legal discourse, political thinking, and cultural values incorporated Catholic teaching and thereby sustained the moral hegemony of Catholicism.

Permissive is an adjective often used in reference to the Netherlands. Toleration was a strategy, adopted at the time of the formation of the Dutch republic, to survive internal religious divisions and the hostility of neighboring countries. Socio-cultural organizations exercised moral leadership over their followers and relegated central state agencies to the margins of the moral sphere. When this system of segmentation and control suddenly fell apart in the 1960s, state agencies opted for toleration by avoiding the persecution of private activities still considered punishable by the law. State agencies closed their eyes to troubling private activities because policy action in this arena provoked divisive emotions while an older tradition already existed that allowed individuals or social groups to find their own moral center.

Ireland and the Nordic countries failed to embrace the postwar ideal of the self as free and autonomous while the Netherlands refused to make an exception for drug-taking. New concepts in vogue in the European Union and the West went against their core beliefs of who they were, and why they were different in the first place. Expert, technical, academic, or professional communities were the loudest defenders against any encroachment of foreign ideas or practices on national arrangements.

Why change in the 1990s?

It makes sense that sensitive social policies, whose antecedents date from the formation of the modern nation-state and are incorporated in the interventionist welfare state, are immune to new practices, beliefs, and opinions coming from outside the national polity. The European Union and its member governments fully acknowledge the right of national communities to map out life choice strategies for members of their own society and did not expect conformity or uniformity.

Why change then after so many decades of stability? Analyses drawn from the constructivist approach, found in sociology and international relations, are not very helpful. First, constructivist interpretations would have predicted a diffusion of norms and be unable to account for the survival of nineteenth-century temperance ideals in Finland and Sweden or illiberal constitutional laws in Ireland. Second, constructivist accounts attribute adaptation to European concepts in part to the learning process of professional elites or politicians whose interaction with European counterparts helps diffuse new ideas. In reality, in all four cases, decision-makers whether they are politicians or specialists are the least likely to be seduced by extant European standards.

Institutionalist analyses provide a better answer. In retrospect, inter-governmental bargains or agreements to protect national values and norms failed to reckon with the cumulative consequences of the earlier agreement to promote the free circulation of people. No amount of political wriggling can undo the implications of the free movement of people, goods, and services. Supranational or intergovernmental agreements interfere with the strategic intentions of governments to retain tight control over the course of integration.[4] Because governments are at a disadvantage in forecasting the complex interdependence of many different issues resolved at the European level, gaps in member state control are likely to emerge that cannot be repaired.[5] Governments also tend to overlook details and miscalculate the agility of domestic actors to exploit the openings or opportunities created by the new agreements or measures to expand their reach and to forge a (tacit) alliance with supranational institutions.[6]

Something of this sort happened in the 1990s. The agents of change, ironically, are the people or national citizens themselves. Consumers steer the process of change once ongoing exposure to European-oriented values has altered their perceptions and expectations. To be sure, learning matters, as constructivists like to argue, except that, rather than the establishment, the disciples are regular Irish, Finnish, or Swedish citizens who increasingly gravitate towards an ethics of the self. Assimilation of European ideals alters thinking on alcohol and abortion, which is why the free movement of people becomes an issue that those governments cannot solve. Individuals had already adopted new views on alcohol, abortion, or drugs. The removal of borders created a golden

4 Paul Pierson, "The Path to European Integration: A Historical Institutionalist Analysis," *Comparative Political Studies*, 29 (1996), 123–63; Alec Stone Sweet and Wayne Sandholtz, "Integration, Supranational Governance, and the Institutionalization of the European Polity," in Wayne Sandholtz and Alec Stone Sweet (eds.), *European Integration and Supranational Governance* (New York: Oxford University Press, 1998), 14–20.
5 Simon Bulmer, "New Institutionalism and the Governance of the EU," *Journal of European Public Policy*, 5 (1998), 365–86.
6 Barry Jones and Michael Keating (eds.), *The European Union and the Regions* (Oxford: Clarendon Press, 1995); Liesbet Hooghe (ed.), *Cohesion Policy and European Integration: Building Multi-Level Governance* (New York: Oxford University Press, 1996); Beate Kohler-Koch, "The Strength of Weakness: The Transformation of Governance in the EU," in Sverker Gustavsson and Leif Lewin (eds.), *The Future of the Nation State* (New York: Routledge, 1996), 169–97; Gary Marks, "Structural Policy and Multilevel Governance in the European Community," in Alan Cafruny and Glenda Rosenthal (eds.), *The State of the European Community* (Boulder: Lynne Rienner, 1993).

opportunity for people who already identified closely with Europe. They had been Europeanized in the cultural-consumption sense prior to the momentous decision to move forward with the Single Market. The following examples help illustrate this dynamic.

Compared with thirty years ago, alcohol consumption figures as well as the mix of alcoholic beverages have converged in Europe despite little direct government attention to volumes and patterns of alcohol consumption outside the Nordic countries. Since the late 1970s, consumption has steadily dropped in wine-drinking countries and increased in low-consumption countries.[7] Political action cannot take credit for new lifestyles because governments in wine-producing countries are notorious for their strong dislike of any restrictions on drinking. Rather, less wine is consumed in these countries because the population has abandoned a typical Mediterranean lifestyle of long lunches, followed by long siestas, and late dinners. In Northern Europe, urbanization and the decline of temperance organizations lifted the moral stigma against drinking at the same time as people switched from hard liquor to light alcoholic beverages.[8]

While the young and educated in France and Italy have lowered their alcohol consumption and reject the casual heavy drinking of their elders, the same cohort groups in Sweden and Finland enjoy a glass of wine during mealtimes and have increased their alcohol intake. Eventually, changed consumption patterns affect cognitive constructions on drinking alcohol. At some point, Swedes and Finns began to realize that their drinking habits did not differ dramatically from those of other Europeans and that binge drinking, although still prevalent, no longer described their relationship with alcohol. Nordic alcohol experts reacted to this "Europeanization" or normalization of drinking attitudes by turning a previously moralistic discourse into a scientific theory, thereby unwittingly authenticating new ideas on enlightened drinking habits. Once new ideas settled in and became common knowledge, middle-class consumers dismissed state intervention in the alcoholic beverage market as patronizing and unnecessary.

[7] Antoni Gual and Joan Colom, "Why Has Alcohol Consumption Declined in Countries of Southern Europe?" *Addiction*, 92 (1997), 24; Pekka Sulkunen, "Drinking in France 1965–79. An Analysis of Household Consumption Data," *British Journal of Addiction*, 84 (1989), 61–72.

[8] Klaus Mäkelä, "Mediterranean Mysteries: Mechanism of Declining Alcohol Consumption," *Addiction*, 93 (1998), 1301–04; Véronique Nahoum-Grappe, "France," in Dwight B. Heath (ed.), *International Handbook on Alcohol and Culture* (Westport, CT: Greenwood Press, 1995), 75–87. There are still real differences in the consumption of beverages across Europe. Some countries are huge coffee drinkers, others consume large quantities of milk, while beer is definitely more popular in non-wine-growing countries than in Southern Europe, etc.

Drugs are also a consumer commodity and their pattern of consumption is also influenced by factors mostly unrelated to government policy. Critics of Dutch harm reduction blame a surge in marijuana smoking on the proliferation of coffee shops. But many studies show that consumption of particular categories of drugs goes through cycles and that the popularity of marijuana peaked in 1980, then declined, and surged again in the 1990s.[9] Germany, Sweden, and the Netherlands have very different regulatory systems to deal with drug use. Yet the same kinds of drugs and prevalence rates are found in all three countries.

As marijuana became popular again in the 1990s, more and more foreign tourists visited Dutch drug-selling coffee shops, in response to which entrepreneurs opened more establishments to sell cannabis to tourists arriving in small border towns. After a while, many local residents began to complain that the situation was out of control and that the Netherlands had become a drug haven for junkies and other undesirable people from neighboring countries. In their opinion, the gentle approach to drug-taking was really a breeding ground for crime, vandalism, dirt and noise, and other nuisances, which seemed to thrive in post-Cold War Europe. Voters accepted the harm reduction model promulgated by the experts, but felt that harm was done to them because drug toleration brought along many annoying consequences. They in fact repeated arguments typically heard in prohibitionist countries, which attribute to drugs all kinds of security risks and associate drugs with the infiltration of foreign elements into the national polity.

In Ireland, a decline in religion meant that young people began to be more assertive as to which principles of the faith applied to their lives. One of the most notable breaks with the past was in the incidence of premarital sex, which the Church quietly condoned as inevitable and which led to an increase in out-of-wedlock births. In response, the Church did not condemn single motherhood because it regarded this situation as the lesser of two evils with abortion being far worse. Europeanization of the sexual code of conduct diminished the typical Irish Catholic obsession with sexual purity and paved the way for a reconsideration of the blanket ban on abortion.

Until the completion of the Single Market, which stimulated physical arbitrage between states with different legal codes and tax systems, authorities could ignore the emergence of new desires and habits among

---

[9] The figures are cited in Ministerie van Volksgezondheid, Welzijn, en Sport, *Drugbeleid: Voortgangsrapportage* (The Hague: VWS, 1997); Ethan Nadelmann, "Commonsense Drug Policy," *Foreign Affairs*, 77 (January-February, 1998), 123. See also, Marja Abraham, Peter Cohen, Roelf-Jan van Til, and Marieke Langemeijer, *Licit and Illicit Drug Use in Amsterdam III: Developments in Drug Use 1987–1997* (Amsterdam: CEDRO, 1998), 24, Table 3.1. (*www.frw.uva.nl/cedro/library/prvasd97.pdf*).

the population. But the flow of people or "sin tourism" draws renewed attention to national rules to shape collective norms. It punctures the veil of silence surrounding the national morality regimes. For long periods of time, it was not politically or socially legitimate to question alcohol, drug, or abortion arrangements. Relatively little in the way of politics surrounded these value-oriented or cultural issues because they were taken for granted and were seen as superior solutions to universal predicaments. Just as asset holders gain new freedoms and are able to restructure their relationship with state agencies so do individuals accumulate new powers to escape domestic restrictions (Ireland and the Nordic countries) or overwhelm the more liberal, tolerant regime of another country (the Netherlands). The increased circulation of people accentuates the tensions and contradictions in the national system of morality standards.

Voters, however, are incapable of framing an alternative repertoire of knowledge to justify new standards of governance. A key mediating variable is the emergence of organized interests, opposed to the existing situation, and able to "empower" or translate new patterns of desires and beliefs. Thus, domestic actors whose interests were positively affected by Europeanization and who commanded the capacity and the resources to act within a domestic context, exploited the growing tensions related to value shifts, market integration, and sin tourism.[10]

Critics appropriated the European rhetoric of an efficient world of free markets and deregulation to construct a new framework for policy deliberation and action. In Finland and Sweden, discourse and language concepts taken from the EU helped a diverse coalition of liquor producers, the food retail sector, conservatives, urban young professionals, and mass media to reverse the classic trade-off between the individual inconveniences of restrictive drinking rules and the general welfare of all. Inspired by the language of neo-liberalism, anti-alcohol policy advocates blamed excessive state control for the nefarious habit of binge drinking because, they claimed, high prices spur clandestine consumption of illicit (smuggled or home-made) alcohol and therefore interfere with the learning of integrated drinking routines and prudent alcohol use. Rather than protecting the population from alcohol misuse, critics accused the authorities of causing bad drinking habits because of misguided policy measures.

---

[10] This is also the conclusion of Maria Green Cowles, Thomas Risse, and James Caporaso, "Europeanisation and Domestic Change," in Thomas Risse, Maria Green Cowles, and James Caporaso (eds.), *Transforming Europe: Europeanization and Domestic Change* (Ithaca: Cornell University Press, 2001), 1–20.

Tentative efforts in the 1970s to exploit Article 119 of the Treaty of Rome to eliminate gender discrimination and inequality eventually generated scores of EU directives, incorporated in Irish social legislation, to bring about equality for women in the labor market, in training programs, and in the social security system. Legislative changes, accompanied by new policy debates, initially mobilized the Catholic right to "copperfast" the criminalization of abortion. But the focus on women's issues and gender-based rights also encouraged embattled feminists and liberals to expect further changes and to look to Community law to roll back the moral hegemony of Catholicism. The European Parliament report on abortion in early 1999, a report which took a relatively restrictive view of abortion, was seized by liberals to pressure the leaders into a frank exchange on the difficulties of dictating a particular sexual morality when everybody else in Europe seems to hold a diametrically different view. The debate itself desensitizes Irish voters and removes the stigma of supporting a qualified "pro-choice" position.

In the Netherlands, the media fed a moral panic about rising crime rates, which were supposedly linked to the proliferation of drug-dealing sites. Since the implosion of the Soviet Union, official EU venues agonize about the rising threat coming from illegal immigration, organized crime, drug trafficking, infectious diseases, and information warfare.[11] Dutch conservatives and the media, mirroring public sentiment, simply latched onto this debate and gave credibility to the idea that "permissiveness" equals a deterioration of public safety. They pounced on the fact that harm reduction came with externalities that perpetrated a different sort of harm on society.

In every case, opponents engaged in smokescreen tactics by hiding behind lofty European ideals to push for a narrow domestic agenda. The literature on domestic adjustments in the wake of supranational institution-building and market integration is filled with examples of how elites hide behind a European smokescreen to ease the implementation of difficult domestic reforms.[12] Policy executives enlarge their

[11] Ronald D. Crelingsten, "The Discourse and Practice of Counter-Terrorism in Liberal Democracies," *Australian Journal of Politics and History*, 44 (1998), 389–413; Martha Crenshaw (ed.), *Terrorism in Context* (Philadelphia: University of Philadelphia Press, 1995); Laurence Lustgarten and Ian Leigh, *In from the Cold: National Security and Parliamentary Democracy* (Oxford: Clarendon Press, 1994).

[12] For example, Alistair Cole and Helen Drake, "The Europeanization of the French Polity: Continuity, Change, and Adaptation," *Journal of European Public Policy*, 7 (2000), 26–43; Kenneth Dyson and Mike Featherstone, *The Road to Maastricht: Negotiating Economic and Monetary Union* (New York: Oxford University Press, 1999); Claudio Radalli, "How Does Europeanization Produce Policy Change?" *Comparative Political Studies*, 30 (1997), 553–75; Wayne Sandholtz, "Membership Matters: Limits of the Functional Approach to European Institutions," *Journal of Common Market*

autonomy in relation to other domestic actors by binding themselves to European agreements. Interestingly, the EU is also an ally for public opinion, which picks and chooses different elements of a European dialogue to fault national decision-makers for being behind the times and out of tune with the rest of the EU. This seems to suggest that "Europe" is taken for granted as a normal part of political life and that national citizens already articulate some degree of collective identification with the EU. They look at the European Union to advance an alternative agenda contrary to the preferences of the national leadership.

Institutionalist accounts of European integration emphasize the unexpected ways in which marginalized interests are able to seize the upper hand and check the powers of state officials. This study is another example of how regional integration creates incentive structures, forms a new language, and offers real opportunities to groups of people who otherwise do not have much of a voice.

Convergence and divergence

Of course, domestic critics of national morality standards could employ Europe in support of their arguments because different branches of the EU did expect some progress towards adaptation to European conventions. The Commission disapproved of alcohol control policies. Aside from the philosophical clash, the Commission is hostile to all kinds of public monopolies, including a retail monopoly on alcoholic beverages. The Netherlands was caught in endless diplomatic skirmishes with strong prohibitionist countries that routinely accused the Dutch of thwarting the formation of a genuine common Europe-wide judicial space. The European Court of Justice refused to condemn abortion as immoral and proceeded to define it as a lawful medical service, which came as a shock to Catholic traditionalists.

Nevertheless, the European Union does not offer a real alternative by positively prescribing an institutional model to which domestic arrangements related to drinking, drug use, or abortion must conform. Either its influence is confined to altering domestic opportunity structures and the distribution of power and resources between domestic actors or it affects the beliefs and expectation of domestic actors. Mostly, morality norms are a classic example of negative integration. Neither the

Studies, 34 (1996), 403–29; Alberta Sbragia, "Italy Pays for Europe: Political Leadership, Political Choice, and Institutional Adaptation," in Risse et al. (eds.), *Transforming Europe,* 79–96; Vivien Schmidt, "Democracy and Discourse in an Integrating Europe and a Globalizing World," in Steven Weber (ed.), *Regionalization and Globalization* (New York: Columbia University Press, 2000), 229–309.

Commission nor the Council spells out how Sweden and Finland should cope with alcohol misuse beyond the broad expectation that they remove barriers to free trade and free mobility. Implementation of new rules creates new opportunity structures for actors in that the private sector is finally a player in the field of alcohol legislation. Otherwise, the European Union mainly encouraged a re-examination of unstated assumptions, namely that alcohol control policy is sacred and beyond discussion, but, aside from bringing forward a fresh examination of existing norms, did not displace old arrangements with new structures and institutions.

Drugs and abortion do not fall under the remit of the European Union and are not expected to obtain a particular outcome. There is no question of institutional fit or misfit since there are no explicit institutional guidelines to accept. Political constraints emerge once the combat against international drug trafficking is placed at the top of the inter-governmental agenda of the EU. Diplomatic spats become embarrassing for Dutch liaison officials who are persuaded to meet the complaints of their EU partners at least halfway. Abortion is even further removed from developments in the EU. To some extent, nobody cares whether Ireland recognizes women's reproductive rights or not. The constitutional proscription on abortion has no consequences for intergovernmental cooperation or supranational institution-building.

Therefore, the depth of the "misfit" between European and national structures does not dictate the pace of change. What matters is not how strong the misfit is between domestic and European institutions, but rather whether the EU cares about the divergence in rules and regulations and collective understandings. In other words, the objective gap between each country and the EU varies but this variation does not determine whether the morality standards will survive or not. Rather, of greater importance is whether the EU itself possesses transparent guidelines on how member states ought to think about abortion, alcohol, or drugs. Once actual guidelines, templates, and expectations are in place at the European level, then the institutions of the EU are on surer ground to demand adaptation and conformity while the resulting changes in domestic political opportunities enable dissenting domestic groups to call for domestic adjustments.

Of the three situations examined in this book, only alcohol control policy clashes directly with existing Community legislation because it is built on a public monopoly and rests on personal import quotas to protect the domestic market against lower foreign retail prices. It follows that Sweden and Finland experience the greatest adaptational pressures to conform to a liberal EU regime that mainly relies on informal control mechanisms and imposes low alcohol taxes. Because Nordic drinking restrictions intersect with Single Market rules, they face the greatest risk of losing their distinct character.

Generally, the debate on economic and institutional convergence highlights two broad mechanisms through which exceptionalisms are reduced and homogenization is increased.[13] The first explanation is competitive selection. The main premise here is that increasingly competitive global markets reduce the room for variation in performance. Competition favors the most efficient institutions or arrangements, although the speed and magnitude of change are determined by the ability of institutions to withstand outside pressure. But many observers see isomorphism – increasing similarity of institutions across different national contexts – as the result of competitive selection.

Mimesis is the second general mechanism. As global markets are increasingly competitive, there remains considerable variation in performance and ways of doing things. Decision-makers really do not know in advance what will and will not work in any given setting, much less be "efficient." Mimesis comes about as institutions respond to a confusing array of signals and copy templates that seem to work. Actors will mimic characteristics of other actors who appear to be doing well. Frequent interaction among different levels of institutions – e.g. among European and domestic structures – prompts a learning process and decision-makers, unsure of where they are going, look at others for inspiration.[14]

Both mechanisms engender institutional convergence. They prioritize best practices, a term which has no bearing on the actual outcome or efficiency. Rather, governments, institutions, or agents gravitate towards a model that is socially sanctioned and considered sensible or appropriate. Obviously, when seeking an alternative model that works better in integrating markets, Swedish and Finnish authorities look at neighboring countries or at the EU itself. If some form of adaptation is considered, the most attractive model is what exists in other member states. Competitive selection applies pressure to minimize the divergence from the center; mimesis occurs when authorities consider modifications and adjustments along the lines of existing arrangements in the EU. Thus, adjustment is most likely to occur in congruence with an

---

[13] This is a huge topic. Not everybody agrees that markets produce convergence. For a range of views, see Suzanne Berger and Ronald Dore (eds.), *National Diversity and Global Capitalism* (Ithaca: Cornell University Press, 1996); Herbert Kitschelt, Peter Lange, Gary Marks, and John D. Stephens (eds.), *Continuity and Change in Contemporary Capitalism* (New York: Cambridge University Press, 1999).

[14] Steven Weber, "Globalization and European Political Economy," in Steven Weber (ed.), *Regionalization and Globalization* (New York: Columbia University Press, 2000).

existing European model or standard since national leaders need to avoid future friction.

European integration and cultural distinctiveness

All in all, it must be noted that the actual pace of change described in this study is quite modest. It would be premature to conclude that the Finns and Swedes now view drinking like the Danes or Italians or that the Dutch have come to favor a coercive anti-drug campaign. Many Irish experience disquiet over using abortion as a simple birth control device. In a fundamental way, each of these countries still embraces a style of thinking and a repertoire of action that sets it apart from the rest of the EU.

The explanation for the gradual, piecemeal adaptation of EU models is that the preferences and ideas of each country are internalized and deeply embedded in the institutional structures. Collective self-identities are sticky by definition and are unlikely to change quickly.[15] At the same time, external pressures are diffused and refracted through existing institutional arrangements, norms, and rules. Institutions not only constrain and enable actors' specific choices and strategies, but also influence the way they conceive of their ultimate interests in the first place.[16] The ways in which the pressures from outside are evaluated, debated, and distilled lead to policy reforms that fit with existing institutional capabilities and policy options.

For example, Finnish drinking attitudes have advanced furthest in adopting a Continental outlook and Finnish state agencies seem relatively at ease with the idea of liberalization. Finland, more so than Sweden, has distanced itself from its temperance history. Yet any institutional and policy reforms to be considered will not bridge the gap between Finland and, say, Southern Europe. First, the organization of the alcoholic beverage market will continue to display features distinct from those of wine-drinking countries in that the public monopoly (Alko) will stay in operation. Public opinion, despite its European outlook, still expresses misgivings with regards to spirits, which are associated with binge drinking and thus provoke considerable anxiety. The monopoly company should, therefore, in the opinion of the overwhelming majority of Finns continue to exist, if only to control the sale

---

[15] Jeffrey T. Checkel, "International Norms and Domestic Politics: Bridging the Rationalist–Constructivist Divide," *European Journal of International Relations*, 3 (1997), 473–95; Risse, Cowles, and Caporaso (eds.), *Europeanization and Domestic Change*.

[16] Peter Hall and Rosemary Taylor, "Political Science and the Three New Institutionalisms," *Political Studies*, 44 (1996), 946.

of spirits. Second, there are still a sizable number of alcohol researchers, funded by taxpayers' money, who pose questions and publicize research findings that tint policy deliberations and public discourse. Finnish alcohol researchers ask different questions and seek different answers than academic communities in France or Italy, assuming for the moment that these two countries have a community of dedicated social scientists and medical experts who examine the impact of drinking on society. (France and Italy do not consider drinking to be problematic so why research an unproblematic topic?) Finally, state agencies themselves prefer to preserve various elements of alcohol control policy, and in particular, the Finnish Ministry of Finance, which is otherwise extremely Europe-minded, wants to continue to restrict access to alcohol. The reason is instrumental. Restrictions mostly involve extremely high excise taxes, which in turn yield state revenues that are difficult to replace at this point. If, as many experts foresee, liberalization results in increased alcohol consumption, the incidence of alcohol-related accidents, fatalities, diseases, or injuries will also rise, and the state will have to lay out more public funds to look after victims of alcohol misuse. For practical reasons, finance ministry officials hope to keep prices (and excise taxes) high. Thus even in Finland, where support for the nineteenth-century temperance ideas has dramatically shrunk, policy reforms will not erase all vestiges of decades of restrictive drinking measures.

Likewise, abortion is being liberalized in Ireland but the debate itself, considering the presence of powerful Catholic lay organizations, precludes certain outcomes. Irish voters are not asked to consider the reproductive rights of women. Rather, the public debate is on how to arrive at an acceptable compromise that takes into consideration exceptional circumstances in which an early pregnancy termination could save the life of a woman. The background against which public deliberations unfold is the knowledge that abortion is readily available just a short plane or boat journey away. Extensive support programs and local agencies involved in the management of drug problems, in addition to a real aversion to coercive state measures to govern private behavior, lead to policy outcomes that will continue to differentiate the Netherlands from France or Sweden.

The findings of this study do not point to an end to Europe's famous mélange of cultural diversity and lend support to the contention that not much will fundamentally change in the foreseeable future. Changes are taking place and the direction of adaptation is towards mainstream EU thinking, but the pace is slow and change is piecemeal. Whether this is good or bad depends on one's vision for Europe and one's hope for the future. One thing is sure, however. Genuine political union will take a long time to emerge. For the reasons sketched out in this study, on morality norms and national culture member governments face a loss of national sovereignty and are required to make adjustments that they do not necessarily desire. But national institutions package reforms in such a fashion that adjustments are ultimately modest and perhaps inconsistent with what prevails in the rest of Europe. Furthermore, the main pressure for change comes from the abolition of borders and the desire of consumers to enjoy goods and services not easily available at home. These same consumers, however, do not automatically support political union! They want to exercise their rights as European consumers and to have the conveniences enjoyed by other European citizens. Yet these same people expect their governments to act in congruence with national sensibilities, protocols, history, and rules, and thus call on national leaders to protect national institutions from Europeanization. The really interesting question, of course, and one I cannot answer here, is whether the Europeanization of consumer behavior and the search for choice and individual freedom will result in a further lessening of cultural divergences. This is the sort of riddle where only time will tell.

Bibliography

Abraham, Marja, "Illicit Drug Use, Urbanization, and Lifestyle in the Netherlands," *Journal of Drug Issues*, 29 (1999), 565–86.

Abraham, Marja, Peter Cohen, Roelf-Jan van Til, and Marieke Langemeijer, *Licit and Illicit Drug Use in Amsterdam III: Developments in Drug Use 1987–1997*, Amsterdam: CEDRO, 1998 (*www.frw.uva.nl/cedro/library/prvasd97.pdf*).

Adler, Emanuel, "Seizing the Middle Ground. Constructivism in World Politics," *European Journal of International Relations*, 3 (1997), 319–63.

Adler, Emanuel and Michael Barnett (eds.), *Security Communities*, New York: Cambridge University Press, 1998.

Ahlström, Salme and Esa Österberg, "Changes in Climate of Opinion Concerning Alcohol Policy in Finland in the 1980s," *Contemporary Drug Problems*, 22 (1992), 431–57.

Ahlström-Laakso, Salme, "European Drinking Habits: A Review of Research and Some Suggestions for Conceptual Integration of Findings," in Michael W. Everett, Jack O. Waddell, and Dwight B. Heath (eds.), *Cross-Cultural Approaches to the Study of Alcohol*, The Hague: Mouton, 1973.

Alapuro, Risto, *State and Revolution in Finland*, Berkeley: University of California Press, 1988.

Alasuutari, Pertti, *Desire and Craving: A Cultural Theory of Alcoholism*, Albany: State University of New York Press, 1992.

Allardt, Erik, "Drinking Norms and Drinking Habits," in E. Allardt, T. Markannen, and M. Takala (eds.), *Drinking and Drinkers*, Stockholm: Almquist & Wiksell, 1958.

Alter, Karen, "Who Are the Masters of the Treaty? European Governments and the European Court of Justice," *International Organization*, 52 (1998), 121–47.

The Amsterdam Group, "The Socio-Economic Impact of the European Alcoholic Drinks Industry," *Alcoholic Beverages and European Society*, The Amsterdam Group, 1993.

Arter, David, *Politics and Policy-Making in Finland*, New York: St. Martin's Press, 1987.

Baerveldt, Chris, Hans Bunkers, Micha de Winter, and Jan Kooistra, "Assessing a Moral Panic Relating to Crime and Drugs Policy in the Netherlands: Towards a Testable Theory," *Crime, Law and Social Change*, 29 (1998), 31–47.

186

Baldwin-Edwards, Martin and Bill Hebenton, "Will SIS be Europe's 'Big Brother'?" in Malcolm Anderson and Monica den Boer (eds.), *Policing across National Boundaries*, London: Pinter, 1994.

Barrett, Deborah and David John Frank, "Population Control for National Development: From World Discourse to National Policies," in John Boli and George M. Thomas (eds.), *Constructing World Culture: International Nongovernmental Organizations since 1875*, Stanford: Stanford University Press, 1999.

Barrows, Susanna, and Robin Room (eds.), *Drinking: Behavior and Belief in Modern History*, Berkeley: University of California Press, 1991.

Baudrillard, Jean, "Coming out of Hibernation? The Myth of Modernization in Irish Culture," in Luke Gibbons (ed.), *Transformations in Irish Culture*, Notre Dame: University of Notre Dame Press, 1996.

Baumgartl, Bernd and Adrian Favell (eds.), *New Xenophobia in Europe*, Boston: Kluwer Law International, 1995.

Berger, Susan and Ronald Dore (eds.), *National Diversity and Global Capitalism*, Ithaca: Cornell University Press, 1996.

Berger, Thomas, "Norms, Identity, and National Security in Germany and Japan," in Peter Katzenstein (ed.), *The Culture of National Security: Norms and Identity in World Politics*, New York: Columbia University Press, 1996.

Bergesen, Albert (ed.), *Studies of the Modern World-System*, New York: Academic Press, 1980.

Bergmark, Anders and Lars Oscarsson, "Swedish Alcohol Treatment in Transition," *Nordic Alcohol Studies*, 11 (1994), 43–54.

Bigo, Didier, "European Internal Security," in Malcolm Anderson and Monica den Boer (eds.), *Policing across National Boundaries*, London: Pinter, 1994.

Bless, R., D.J. Korf, and M. Freeman, "Open Drug Scenes: A Cross-National Comparison of Concepts and Urban Strategies," *European Addiction Research*, 1 (1995), 128–38.

Blom, Tom and Hans van Mastrigt, "The Future of the Dutch Model in the Context of the War on Drugs," in Ed Leuw and I. Haen Marshall (eds.), *Between Prohibition and Legalization: The Dutch Experiment in Drug Policy*, New York: Kugler, 1995.

Blom, Tom, Hans de Doelder, and D.J. Hessing, "De paarse drugsnota en de aanpak van hard drugsverslaafden," in T. Blom, H. de Doelder, and D.J. Hessing (eds.), *Naar een consistent drugsbeleid*, Deventer: Gouda Quint, 1996.

Blomqvist, Jan, "The 'Swedish Model' of Dealing with Alcohol Problems: Historical Trends and Future Challenges," *Contemporary Drug Problems*, 25 (1998), 253–321.

Boekhout van Solinge, Tim, "Dutch Drug Policy in a European Context," *Journal of Drug Issues*, 29 (1999), 511–29.

  "De Frans–Nederlandse drugbetrekkingen," *Amsterdams Drug Tijdschrift*, 2 (1996), 12–14.

Boli, John and George M. Thomas, "INGOs and the Organization of World Culture," in John Boli and George M. Thomas (eds.), *Constructing World Culture: International Nongovernmental Organizations since 1875*, Stanford: Stanford University Press, 1999.

Boli, John and George M. Thomas (eds.), *Constructing World Culture: International Nongovernmental Organizations since 1875*, Stanford: Stanford University Press, 1999.

Bruun, Kettil, and Lennart Nilsson, "Folkets protester," in Kettil Bruun and Per Frånberg (eds.), *Den svenska supen: en historia om brännvin, bratt, och byrkrati*, Stockholm: Prisma, 1985.

Bruun, Kettil, *Alcohol Control Policies in Public Health Perspective*, Helsinki: Finnish Foundation for Alcohol Studies, 1975 .

Buchmann, Marlis, *The Script of Life in Modern Society*, Chicago: University of Chicago Press, 1989.

Bull, Hedley, *The Anarchical Society: A Study of Order in World Politics*, New York: Columbia University Press, 1977.

Bull, Hedley and Adam Watson (eds.), *Expansion of International Society*, Oxford: Clarendon Press, 1984.

Bulmer, Simon, "New Institutionalism and the Governance of the EU," *Journal of European Public Policy*, 5 (1998), 365–86.

Buzan, Barry, "From International System to International Society: Structural Realism and Regime Theory meet the English School," *International Organization*, 47 (1993), 327–52.

Bygvra, Susanne, "Border Shopping Between Denmark and West Germany," *Contemporary Drug Problems* 17 (1990), 595–611.

Byrnes, Timothy A. and Mary C. Segers, "The Politics of Abortion: The Catholic Bishops," in Timothy A. Byrnes and Mary C. Segers (eds.), *The Catholic Church and the Politics of Abortion*, Boulder: Westview, 1992.

Checkel, Jeffrey T., "The Constructivist Turn in International Relations Theory," *World Politics*, 50 (1998), 324–48.

  "International Norms and Domestic Politics: Bridging the Rationalist–Constructivist Divide," *European Journal of International Relations*, 3 (1997), 473–95.

  "Norms, Institutions, and National Identity in Contemporary Europe," *International Studies Quarterly*, 43 (1999), 83–114.

Childs, Marquis, *Sweden: The Middle Way*, New Haven, NJ: Yale University Press, 1939.

Christiansen, Thomas, Knud Erik Jørgensen, and Antje Wiener (eds.), "The Social Construction of Europe," *Journal of European Public Policy*, 6 (1999), 528–719.

Chubb, Basil, *The Politics of the Irish Constitution*, Dublin: Institute of Public Administration, 1991.

Claes, Monica and Bruno de Witte, "Report of the Netherlands," in A.-M. Slaughter, A. Stone Sweet, and J. Weiler (eds.) *The European Court and National Courts*, Oxford: Hart Publishing, 1998.

Clarke, Desmond M., *Church and State: Essays in Political Philosophy*, Cork: Cork University Press, 1984.

Coakley, John, "Society and Political Culture," in John Coakley and Michael Gallagher (eds.), *Politics in the Republic of Ireland*, New York: Routledge, 1999.

Cole, Alistair and Helen Drake, "The Europeanization of the French Polity: Continuity, Change, and Adaptation," *Journal of European Public Policy*, 7 (2000), 26–43.

Collins, Larry, "Holland's Half-Baked Drug Experiment," *Foreign Affairs*, 78 (May/June, 1999), 82–99.

"Reply: Dazed and Confused," *Foreign Affairs*, 78 (November/December, 1999), 136–39.

Connelly, Alpha (ed.), *Women and the Law in Ireland*, Dublin: Gill & Macmillan, 1993.

Coughlan, Anthony, "The Constitution and Social Policy," in Frank Litton (ed.), *The Constitution of Ireland 1937–87*, Dublin: Institute of Public Administration, 1988.

Cowles, Maria Green and Thomas Risse, "Transforming Europe: Conclusions," in Thomas Risse, Maria Green Cowles, and James Caporaso (eds.), *Transforming Europe: Europeanization and Domestic Change*, Ithaca: Cornell University Press, 2001.

Cowles, Maria Green, Thomas Risse, and James Caporaso, "Europeanization and Domestic Change," in Thomas Risse, Maria Green Cowles, and James Caporaso (eds.), *Transforming Europe: Europeanization and Domestic Change*, Ithaca: Cornell University Press, 2001.

Crane, Diane "Introduction," in Diane Crane (ed.), *Sociology of Culture*, New York: Routledge, 1994.

Crelingsten, Ronald D., "The Discourse and Practice of Counter-Terrorism in Liberal Democracies," *Australian Journal of Politics and History*, 44 (1998), 389–413.

Crenshaw, Martha (ed.), *Terrorism in Context*, Philadelphia: University of Philadelphia Press, 1995.

Cuskey, Walter R., Arnold Klein, and William Krasner, *Drug-trip Abroad. American Drug Refugees in Amsterdam and London*, Philadelphia: University of Pennsylvania Press, 1972.

Daun, Åke, *Swedish Mentality*, University Park, PA: Pennsylvania State University Press, 1996.

Davies, Phil and Dermot Walsh, *Alcohol Problems and Alcohol Control in Europe*, New York: Gardner Press, 1983.

De Kort, Marcel, "A Short History of Drugs in the Netherlands," in Ed Leuw and I. Haen Marshall (eds.), *Between Prohibition and Legalization: The Dutch Experiment in Drug Policy*, New York: Kugler, 1995.

Tussen patiënt en delinquent: Geschiedenis van het Nederlandse drugsbeleid, Hilversum: Verloren, 1995.

De Kort, Marcel and Ton Cramer, "Pragmatism versus Ideology: Dutch Drug Policy Continued," *Journal of Drug Issues*, 29 (1999), 473–93.

De Kort, Marcel and Dirk J. Korf, "The Development of Drug Trade and Drug Control in the Netherlands: A Historical Perspective," *Crime, Law, and Social Change*, 17 (1992), 123–44.

De Lint, Jan, "Anti-Drink Propaganda and Alcohol Control Measures: A Report on the Dutch Experience," in Eric Single, Patricia Morgan, and Jan de Lint (eds.), *Alcohol, Society, and the State*, vol. II, Toronto: Addiction Research Foundation, 1981.

Dehousse, Renaud, *The European Court of Justice*, New York: St. Martin's Press, 1998.

Derks, Jack, T.M. Marten, J. Hoekstra, and Charles D. Kaplan, "Integrating

Care, Cure, and Control: Drug Treatment System in the Netherlands," in Harald Klingemann and Geoffrey Hunt (eds.), *Treatment Systems in an International Perspective: Drugs, Demons, and Delinquents,* Thousand Oaks, CA: Sage, 1998.

Dillon, Michelle, *Debating Divorce: Moral Conflict in Ireland,* Lexington, KY: University Press of Kentucky, 1993.

DiMaggio, Paul, "Culture and Economy," in Neil J. Smelser and Richard Swedberg (eds.), *The Handbook of Economic Sociology,* Princeton: Princeton University Press, 1994.

Dinan, Desmond, *Ever Closer Union,* Boulder: Lynne Rienner, 1999.

Dobbin, Frank, *Forging Industrial Policy,* New York: Cambridge University Press, 1994.

Douglas, Mary, *How Institutions Think,* Syracuse: Syracuse University Press, 1986.

Downes, David, *Contrasts in Tolerance: Postwar Penal Policy in the Netherlands, and England and Wales,* New York: Oxford University Press, 1988.

Drudy, Sheelagh and Kathleen Lynch, *Schools and Society in Ireland,* Dublin: Gill & Macmillan, 1993.

Duster, Troy, *The Legislation of Morality: Law, Drugs, and Moral Judgment,* New York: The Free Press, 1970.

Dyson, Kenneth and Mike Featherstone, *The Road to Maastricht: Negotiating Economic and Monetary Union,* New York: Oxford University Press, 1999.

Edwards, Griffith, *Alcohol Policy and the Public Good,* New York: Oxford University Press, 1994.

Eggert, Anna and Bill Rolston, "Ireland," in Anna Eggert and Bill Rolston (eds.), *Abortion in the New Europe: A Comparative Handbook,* Westport, CT: Greenwood Press, 1994.

Eriksen, Sidsel, "Drunken Danes and Sober Swedes? Religious Revivalism and the Temperance Movements as Keys to Danish and Swedish Folk Cultures," in Bo Stråth (ed.), *Language and the Construction of Class Identities. The Struggle for Discursive Power in Social Organization,* Gothenburg: University of Gothenburg Press, 1990.

"The Making of the Danish Liberal Drinking Style: The Construction of a 'Wet' Alcohol Discourse in Denmark," *Contemporary Drug Problems,* 20 (1993), 1–30.

Ester, Peter, Loek Halman, and Ruud de Moor (eds.), *The Individualizing Society: Value Change in Europe and North America,* Tilburg: Tilburg University Press, 1993.

Estievenaert, Georges (ed.), *Policies and Strategies to Combat Drugs in Europe: The Treaty on European Union: Framework for a New European Strategy to Combat Drugs?* Boston: Martinus Nijhoff, 1995 .

European Policy Advisory Service/Euro Pas, *State Alcohol Monopolies and the Accession of the Nordic Countries to the EC,* Brussels: Euro Pas, 1993.

Eyre, Dana P. and Mark C. Suchman, "Status, Norms, and the Proliferation of Conventional Weapons: An Institutional Theory Approach," in Peter Katzenstein (ed.), *The Culture of National Security: Norms and Identity in World Politics,* New York: Columbia University Press, 1996.

Fahey, Tony, "Progress or Decline? Demographic Change in Political Context," in William Crotty and David E. Schmitt (eds.), *Ireland and the Politics of Change*, New York: Longman, 1998.

Fahey, Tony, "Religion and Sexual Culture in Ireland," in Franz X. Eder, Lesley A. Hall, and Gert Hekma (eds.), *Sexual Culture in Europe*, New York: Manchester University Press, 1999.

Fahrenkrug, Hermann, "Alcohol Control Policy in the EC Member States," *Contemporary Drug Problems*, 17 (1990), 497–524.

Featherstone, Mike, *Undoing Culture: Globalization, Postmodernism, and Identity*, Thousand Oaks, CA: Sage, 1995.

Fijnaut, Cyrille, Frank Bovenkerk, Gerben Bruinsma, and Henk van de Bunt, *Organized Crime in the Netherlands*, Boston: Kluwer, 1998.

Finnegan, Richard B. and Edward T. McCarron, *Ireland: Historical Echoes, Contemporary Politics*, Boulder: Westview Press, 2000.

Finnemore, Martha, *National Interests in International Society*, Ithaca: Cornell University Press, 1996.

"Norms, Culture and World Politics: Insights from Sociology's Institutionalism," *International Organization*, 50 (1996), 325–48.

Fitzgerald, Garret, *All in a Life*, Dublin: Gill & Macmillan, 1991.

Fligstein, Neil, *The Transformation of Corporate Control*, Cambridge, MA: Harvard University Press, 1990.

Florini, Ann, "The Evolution of International Norms," *International Studies Quarterly*, 40 (1996), 363–90.

Forder, Caroline, "Abortion: A Constitutional Problem," *Maastricht Journal of European and Comparative Law*, 1 (1994), 56–100.

Frånberg, Per, "The Social and Political Significance of Two Swedish Restrictive Systems," *Contemporary Drug Problems*, 12 (1985), 53–67.

"Den svenska supen," in Kettil Bruun and Per Frånberg (eds.), *Den svenska supen: en historia om brännvin, bratt, och byrkrati*, Stockholm: Prisma, 1985.

Frånberg, Per and Ilpo Koskikallio, "Regionala och lokala varianter," in Kettil Bruun and Per Frånberg (eds.), *Den svenska supen: en historia om brännvin, bratt, och byrkrati*, Stockholm: Prisma, 1985.

Friman, H. Richard, *NarcoDiplomacy: Exporting the US War on Drugs*, Ithaca: Cornell University Press, 1996.

Galligan, Yvonne, *Women and Politics in Contemporary Ireland*, Washington, DC: Pinter, 1998.

Garretsen, Henk F.L. and Ien van de Goor, "The Netherlands," in Dwight B. Heath (ed.), *International Handbook on Alcohol and Culture*, Westport, CT: Greenwood Press, 1995.

Garrett, Geoffrey, Daniel Keleman, and Heiner Schultz, "The European Court of Justice, National Governments and Legal Integration in the European Union," *International Organization*, 52 (1998), 149–76.

Gaster, Saskia, "Drugdebat in Tweede Kamer," *Amsterdams Drug Tijdschrift*, 1 (1996), 3–7.

Gellner, Ernest, *Culture, Identity, and Politics*, New York: Cambridge University Press, 1987.

Gerding, R.A.F., "Aanpak drugsoverlast te Rotterdam: de rol van het Openbaar Ministerie," in T. Blom, H. de Doelder, and D.J. Hessing (eds.), *Naar een consistent drugsbeleid*, Deventer: Gouda Quint, 1996.

Germer, Peter, "Alcohol and the Single Market: Juridical Aspects," *Contemporary Drugs Problems*, 17 (1990), 481–96.

Gerritsen, Jan-Willem, *De politieke economie van de roes: De ontwikkeling van reguleringsregimes voor alcohol en opiaten*, Amsterdam: Amsterdam University Press, 1993.

Giddens, Anthony, *The Consequences of Modernity*, New York: Cambridge University Press, 1990.

Girvin, Brian, "Ireland," *Parliamentary Affairs*, 47 (1994), 203–20.

"Ireland and the European Union: The Impact of Integration and Social Change on Abortion Policy," in Marianne Githens and Dorothy McBride Stetson (eds.), *Abortion Politics: Public Policy in Cross-Cultural Perspective*, New York: Routledge, 1996.

"The Irish Divorce Referendum, November 1995," *Irish Political Studies*, 2 (1996), 174–81.

"Social Change and Moral Politics: The Irish Constitutional Referendum," *Political Studies*, 34 (1986), 61–81.

Gladdish, Ken, *Governing from the Center. Politics and Policy-Making in the Netherlands*, London: Hurst, 1991 .

Gong, Gerrit, *The Standard of "Civilisation" in International Society*, Oxford: Clarendon Press, 1984.

Goode, Erich and Nachman Ben-Yehuda, *Moral Panics: The Social Construction of Deviance*, Cambridge: Blackwell, 1994.

Gould, Arthur, "Pollution Rituals in Sweden," *Scandinavian Journal of Social Welfare*, 3 (1994), 85–93.

Granell, Francisco, "The European Union's Enlargement Negotiations with Austria, Finland, Norway, and Sweden," *Journal of Common Market Studies*, 33 (1995), 117–41.

Gstöhl, Sieglinde, "The Nordic Countries and the EEA," in Lee Miles (ed.), *The European Union and the Nordic Countries*, New York: Routledge, 1996.

Gual, Antoni and Joan Colom, "Why Has Alcohol Consumption Declined in Countries of Southern Europe?" *Addiction*, 92 (1997), 21–31.

Gundelach, Peter, "National Value Differences: Modernization or Institutionalization?" *International Journal of Comparative Sociology*, 35 (1994), 37–59.

Gurowitz, Amy, "Mobilizing International Norms: Domestic Actors, Immigrants, and the Japanese State," *World Politics*, 51 (1999), 413–45.

Gusfield, Joseph R., *Contested Meanings: The Construction of Alcohol Problems*, Madison: University of Wisconsin Press, 1996.

Haas, Peter (ed.), *Knowledge, Power, and International Policy Coordination*, Columbia, SC: University of South Carolina Press, 1996.

Haije, Marcel Dela, "Drugsrunners en drugtoeristen: criminaliteit, overlast en onveiligheidsgevoelens in de grote stad," unpublished MA thesis, Erasmus University, 1995.

Häikiö, Martti, *A Brief History of Modern Finland*, Helsinki: University of Helsinki Press, 1992.

Hall, Peter, "Policy Paradigms, Social Learning, and the State: The Case of Economic Policy-Making in Britain," *Comparative Politics*, 25 (1993), 275–96.

Hall, Peter and Rosemary Taylor, "Political Science and the Three New Institutionalisms," *Political Studies*, 44 (1996), 936–57.

Halman, Loek and Ruud de Moor, "Religion, Churches, and Moral Values," in Peter Ester, Loek Halman, and Ruud de Moor (eds.), *The Individualizing Society: Value Change in Europe and North America*, Tilburg: Tilburg University Press, 1993.

Hardiman, Niamh, and Chistopher Whelan, "Changing Values," in William Crotty and David E. Schmitt (eds.), *Ireland and the Politics of Change*, New York: Longman, 1998.

Harding, Stephen, David Phillips, and Michael Fogarty, *Contrasting Values in Western Europe: Unity, Diversity, and Change*, London: Macmillan, 1986.

't Hart, A.C., "Criminal Law Policy in the Netherlands," in Jan van Dijk (ed.), *Criminal Law in Action*, Arnhem: Gouda Quint, 1986.

Heath, Dwight B. (ed.), *International Handbook on Alcohol and Culture*, Westport, CT: Greenwood Press, 1995.

Hebenton, Bill and Terry Thomas, *Policing Europe: Cooperation, Conflict, and Control*, New York: St. Martin's Press, 1995.

Heclo, Hugh and Henrik Madsen, *Policy and Politics in Sweden: Principled Pragmatism*, Philadelphia: Temple University Press, 1987.

Heelas, Paul, Scott Lash, and Paul Morris (eds.), *Detraditionalization: Critical Reflections on Authority and Identity*, Cambridge, MA: Blackwell, 1996.

Hempton, David, *Religion and Political Culture in Britain and Ireland*, New York: Cambridge University Press, 1996.

Hesketh, Tom, "The Irish Abortion Referendum Campaigns," *Irish Political Studies*, 3 (1988), 43–62.

The Second Partitioning of Ireland? The Abortion Referendum 1983, Dublin: Brandsma, 1990.

Hessing, D.J., H. Elfers, and A. Zeijkovic, "Drugsbeleid: Houding tegenover verstrekking en tegenover dwang en drang," in T. Blom, H. de Doelder, and D.J. Hessing (eds.), *Naar een consistent drugsbeleid*, Deventer: Gouda Quint, 1996.

Himmelstein, Jerome, *The Strange Career of Marihuana*, Westport, CT: Greenwood Press, 1983.

Hobsbawn, Eric, *Nations and Nationalism since 1780*, New York: Cambridge University Press, 1990.

Hogan, Gerard, "Protocol 17," in Patrick Keatinge (ed.), *Maastricht and Ireland: What the Treaty Means*, Dublin: Studies in European Union, 1992.

Holder, Harold, *Alcohol and the Community. A Systems Approach to Prevention*, New York: Cambridge University Press, 1998.

Holder, Harold, Eckart Kühlhorn, Sturla Nordlund, Esa Österberg, Anders Romelsjö, and Trygve Ugland, *European Integration and Nordic Alcohol Policies: Changes in Alcohol Controls and Consequences in Finland, Norway, and Sweden*, Brookfield, VT: Ashgate, 1998.

Holder, Harold, Eckart Kühlhorn, Sturla Nordlund, Esa Österberg, Anders Romelsjö, and Trygve Ugland, "Potential Consequences from Possible Changes to Nordic Retail Alcohol Monopolies Resulting from EU Membership," *Addiction*, 90 (1995), 1603–18.

Hooghe, Liesbet (ed.), *Cohesion Policy and European Integration: Building Multi-Level Governance*, New York: Oxford University Press, 1996.

Hornsby-Smith, Michael P. and Christopher T. Whelan, "Religious and Moral Values," in Christopher T. Whelan (ed.), *Values and Social Change in Ireland*, Dublin: Gill & Macmillan, 1994.

Hoskyns, Catherine, *Integrating Gender: Women, Law, and Politics in the European Union*, London: Verso, 1996.

Hug, Chrystel, *The Politics of Sexual Morality in Ireland*, New York: St. Martin's Press, 1999.

Hurst Cherrington, Ernest, *Standard Encyclopedia of the Alcohol Problem*, 6 vols., Westerville, OH: American Issue Publishing, 1925–30.

Immergut, Ellen, *Health Politics: Interests and Institutions in Western Europe*, New York: Cambridge University Press, 1992.

Ingebritsen, Christine, *The Nordic States and European Unity*, Ithaca: Cornell University Press, 1998.

"The Politics of Whaling in Norway and Iceland," *Scandinavian Review* (Winter 1997/98), 9–15.

Inglis, Tom, *Lessons in Irish Sexuality*, Dublin: University College Dublin Press, 1998.

Moral Monopoly: The Rise and Fall of the Catholic Church in Modern Ireland, Dublin: University College Dublin Press, 1987.

Jansen, A.C.M., *Cannabis in Amsterdam: een geografie van hashish en marijuana*, Muiderberg: Coutinho, 1989.

"The Development of a 'Legal' Consumers' Market for Cannabis: The 'Coffee Shop' Phenomenon," in Ed Leuw and I. Haen Marshall (eds.), *Between Prohibition and Legalization: The Dutch Experiment in Drug Policy*, New York: Kugler Publications, 1994.

"De meevallers van het gedoogbeleid voor de cannabisbranche," in T. Blom, H. de Doelder, and D.J. Hessing (eds.), *Naar een consistent drugsbeleid*, Deventer: Gouda Quint, 1996.

Jepperson, Ron, Alex Wendt, and Peter Katzenstein, "Norms, Identity, and Culture in National Security," in Peter Katzenstein (ed.), *The Culture of National Security: Norms and Identity in World Politics*, New York: Columbia University Press, 1996.

Johansson, Lennart, *Systemet lagom. Rusdrycker, intresseorganisationer och politisk kultur under förbudsdebattends tidevarv, 1900–1922*, Lund: Lund University Press, 1995 .

Jones, Barry and Michael Keating (eds.), *The European Union and the Regions*, Oxford: Clarendon Press, 1995.

Jones, Trevor, *Policing and Democracy in the Netherlands*, London: Policy Studies Institute, 1995.

Kallenautio, Jorma, "Finnish Prohibition as an Economic Policy Issue," *Scandinavian Economic History Review*, 29 (1981), 203–28.

Kaminski, Dan, "The Transformation of Social Control in Europe: The Case of Drug Addiction and its Socio-Penal Management," *European Journal of Crime, Criminal Law, and Criminal Justice*, 5 (1997), 123–33.

Katzenstein, Peter (ed.), *The Culture of National Security: Norms and Identity in World Politics*, New York: Columbia University Press, 1996.

Keating, Paul and Derry Desmond, *Culture and Capitalism in Contemporary Ireland*, Brookfield, VT: Ashgate, 1993.

Keck, Margaret and Kathryn Sikkink, *Activists beyond Borders: Transnational Advocacy Networks in International Politics*, Ithaca: Cornell University Press, 1998.

Keeler, John and Martin Schain, "Mitterrand's Legacy, Chirac's Challenge," in John Keeler and Martin Schain (eds.), *Chirac's Challenge: Liberalization, Europeanization, and Malaise in France*, New York: St. Martin's Press, 1996.

Kelk, Constantijn, Laurence Koffman, and Jos Silvis, "Sentencing Practices, Policy, and Discretion," in Phil Fennell, Christopher Harding, Nico Jörg, and Bert Swart (eds.), *Criminal Justice in Europe: A Comparative Study*, Oxford: Clarendon Press, 1995.

Kenny, Mary, *Goodbye to Catholic Ireland*, London: Sinclair-Stevenson, 1997.

Kier, Elizabeth, "Culture and French Military Doctrine Before World War I," in Peter Katzenstein (ed.), *The Culture of National Security: Norms and Identity in World Politics*, New York: Columbia University Press, 1996.

Kirby, D.G., *Finland in the Twentieth Century*, London: C. Hurt, 1979.

Kitschelt, Herbert, Peter Lange, Gary Marks, and John D. Stephens (eds.), *Continuity and Change in Contemporary Capitalism*, New York: Cambridge University Press, 1999.

Klotz, Audie, *Norms in International Relations: The Struggle against Apartheid*, Ithaca: Cornell University Press, 1995.

Kohler-Koch, Beate, "The Strength of Weakness: The Transformation of Governance in the EU," in Sverker Gustavsson and Leif Lewin (eds.), *The Future of the Nation State*, New York: Routledge, 1996.

Kohler-Koch Beate and Rainer Eising (eds.), *The Transformation of Governance in the European Union*, New York: Routledge, 1999.

Korf, Dirk J., "Drugstoerisme in de grensstreek: mogelijkheden voor beheersing," in T. Blom, H. de Doelder, and D.J. Hessing (eds.), *Naar een consistent drugsbeleid*, Deventer: Gouda Quint, 1996.

Korf, Dirk J., Heleen Riper, and Bruce Bullington, "Windmills in their Minds? Drug Policy and Drug Research in the Netherlands," *Journal of Drug Issues*, 29 (1999), 451–72.

Koski, Heikki and Esa Österberg, "From Large Projects to Case Consultation-Interaction of Alcohol Research and Policy in Finland," *Addiction*, 88, Supplement (1993), 143–50.

Koskikallo, Ilpo, "The Social History of Restaurants in Sweden and Finland: A Comparative Study," *Contemporary Drug Problems*, 12 (1985), 11–30.

Kreitman, Norman, "Alcohol Consumption and the Preventive Paradox," *British Journal of Addiction*, 81 (1986), 353–63.

Kuusi, Pekka, *Alcohol Sales Experiment in Rural Finland*, trans. Alfred Westphalen, Helsinki: Finnish Foundation for Alcohol Studies, 1957.

Social Policy for the Sixties: A Plan for Finland, trans. Jaakko Railo, Helsinki: Finnish Social Policy Association, 1964.

Laffan, Briggid, "The Politics of Identity and Political Order in Europe," *Journal of Common Market Studies*, 34 (1996), 81–102.

Larkin, Emmet J., *The Consolidation of the Roman Catholic Church in Ireland, 1860–1870*, Chapel Hill: University of North Carolina Press, 1987.

Latour, Bruno, *Science in Action*, Cambridge, MA: Harvard University Press, 1987.

Ledermann, Sully, *Alcool, Alcoolisme, Alcoolisation. Données scientifiques de caractère physiologique, économique et social*, Paris: Presses Universitaires de France, 1956.

Lee, Joe, *Ireland 1912–1985: Politics and Society*, New York: Cambridge University Press, 1985.

"State and Nation in Independent Ireland," in Princess Grace Irish Library (ed.), *Irishness in a Changing Society*, Totowa, NJ: Barnes & Noble, 1989.

Leifman, Håkan, *Perspectives on Alcohol Prevention*, Stockholm: Almqvist & Wiksell, 1996.

Lemmens, Paul H.H.M. and Henk F.L. Garretsen, "Unstable Pragmatism: Dutch Drug Policy under National and International Pressure," *Addiction*, 93 (1998), 157–63.

Leuw, Ed and I. Haen Marshall (eds.), *Between Prohibition and Legalisation: the Dutch Experiment in Drug Policy*, New York: Kugler Publications, 1994.

Levine, Harry G., "Alcohol Problems in Nordic and English-speaking Cultures," in Malcolm Lader, Griffith Edwards, and D. Colin Drummond (eds.), *The Nature of Alcohol and Drug Related Problems*, New York: Oxford University Press, 1992.

Lijphart, Arend, "From Politics of Accommodation to Adversarial Politics in the Netherlands: A Reassessment," in Hans Daalder and Galen Irwin (eds.), *Politics in the Netherlands: How Much Change?* London: Frank Cass, 1989.

The Politics of Accommodation: Pluralism and Democracy in the Netherlands, Berkeley: University of California Press, 1975.

Lindblad, Hans and Sven Lundkvist, *Tusen nyktra: 100 år med riksdagens nykterhetsgrupper*, Stockholm: Sober, 1996 .

Loya, Thomas A. and John Boli, "Standardization in the World Polity: Technical Rationality over Power," in John Boli and George M. Thomas (eds.), *Constructing World Culture: International Nongovernmental Organizations since 1875*, Stanford: Stanford University Press, 1999.

Lucassen, J. and Rinus Penninx, *Nieuwkomers, nakomelingen, Nederlanders. Immigranten in Nederland 1550–1994*, Amsterdam: Het Spinhuis, 1994.

Lundkvist, Sven, "Popular Movements and Reforms," in Steven Koblik (ed.), *Sweden's Development from Poverty to Affluence 1750–1970*, Minneapolis: University of Minnesota Press, 1975.

"The Popular Movements in Swedish Society, 1850–1920," *Scandinavian Journal of History*, 5 (1980), 219–38.

Lustgarten, Laurence and Ian Leigh, *In from the Cold: National Security and Parliamentary Democracy*, Oxford: Clarendon Press, 1994.

Macdonald, Sharon (ed.), *Inside European Identities: Ethnography in Western Europe*, Providence, RI: Berg, 1993.

Madely, John T.S., "Politics and the Pulpit: The Case of Protestant Europe," *West European Politics*, 5 (1982), 149–71.

Mäkelä, Klaus, "Mediterranean Mysteries: Mechanism of Declining Alcohol Consumption," *Addiction*, 93 (1998), 1301–04.

Mäkelä, Klaus and Matti Viikari, "Notes on Alcohol and the State," *Acta Sociologica*, 20 (1977), 155–80.

Mäkelä, Klaus, Esa Österberg, and Pekka Sulkunen, "Drink in Finland: Increasing Alcohol Availability in a Monopoly State," in Patricia Morgan, Jan de Lint and Eric Single (eds.), *Alcohol, Society, and the State: The Social History of Control Policy in Seven Countries*, Toronto: Addiction Research Foundation, 1981.

March, James G. and Johan P. Olsen, *Rediscovering Institutions: The Organizational Basis of Politics*, New York: The Free Press, 1989.

Maris, C.W., "Dutch Weed and Logic: Part I," *International Journal of Drug Policy*, 7 (1996), 80–87.

"Dutch Weed and Logic: Part II: The Logic of the Harm Principle," *International Journal of Drug Policy*, 7 (1996), 142–52.

Marks, Gary, "Structural Policy and Multilevel Governance in the European Community," in Alan Cafruny and Glenda Rosenthal (eds.), *The State of the European Community*, Boulder: Lynne Rienner, 1993.

Martin, William, C. and Karen Hopkins, "Cleavage Crystallization and Party Linkages in Finland, 1900–1918," in Kay Lawson (ed.), *Political Parties and Linkage: A Comparative Perspective*, New Haven, NJ: Yale University Press, 1980.

McCourt, Frank, *Angela's Ashes. A Memoir*, New York: Scribner, 1996.

McLoughlin, Dympna, "Women and Sexuality in Nineteenth Century Ireland," *Irish Journal of Psychology*, 15 (1994), 266–75.

Meyer, John W., "Rationalized Environments," in Richard W. Scott and John W. Meyer (eds.), *Institutional Environments and Organizations: Structural Complexity and Individualism*, Thousand Oaks, CA: Sage, 1994.

Meyer, John W., "The World Polity and the Authority of the Nation-State," in George M. Thomas, John W. Meyer, Francisco O. Ramirez, and John Boli (eds.), *Institutional Structure: Constituting State, Society, and the Individual*, Beverly Hills: Sage, 1987.

Meyer, John W., John Boli, and George M. Thomas, "Ontology and Rationalization in the Western Cultural Account," in Richard W. Scott and John W. Meyer (eds.), *Institutional Environments and Organizations: Structural Complexity and Individualism*, Thousand Oaks, CA: Sage, 1994.

Meyer, John, John Boli, and George M. Thomas, "World Society and the Nation-State," *American Journal of Sociology*, 103 (1997), 144–81.

Micheletti, Michele, *Civil Society and State Relations in Sweden*, Brookfield, VT: Avebury, 1995.

Miles, Lee, *The Nordic Countries and the 1995 EU Enlargement*, New York: Routledge, 1996.

Milhøj, Anders, "Structural Changes in the Danish Alcohol Market," *Nordic Alcohol Studies*, 13 (1996), 33–42.

Ministerie van Volksgezondheid, Welzijn, en Sport, *Drugbeleid: Voortgangsrapportage*, The Hague: VWS, 1997.

Ministry of Health and Social Affairs, *The Swedish Alcohol Policy: Caring about People's Health*, Stockholm: Ministry of Health and Social Affairs, 1993.

Moravcsik, Andrew, "A New Statecraft? Supranational Enterpreneurs and International Cooperation," *International Organization*, 53 (1999), 267–306.

Musto, David F., *The American Disease: Origins of Narcotic Control*, New Haven, NJ: Yale University Press, 1973.

Nadelmann, Ethan, "Commonsense Drug Policy," *Foreign Affairs*, 77 (January/ February, 1998), 111–26.

"Global Prohibition Regimes: The Evolution of Norms in International Society," *International Organization*, 44 (1990), 479–526.

Nahoum-Grappe, Véronique, "France," in Dwight B. Heath (ed.), *International Handbook on Alcohol and Culture*, Westport, CT: Greenwood Press, 1995.

Netherlands Bureau for Economic Policy Analysis, *Challenging Neighbours: Rethinking German and Dutch Economic Institutions*, Berlin: Springer, 1997.

Nilsson, Tom, "Alcohol in Sweden – A Country Profile," in Timo Kortteinen (ed.), *State Monopolies and Alcohol Prevention*, Helsinki: Social Research Institute of Alcohol Studies, 1989.

Nordlund, Sturla, "Holdningsendringer og Vinmonopolets framtid," *Nordisk alkohol- & narkotikatidskrift*, 15 (1998), 223–33.

Nyberg, Karin, and Peter Allebeck, "Sweden," in Dwight B. Heath (ed.), *International Handbook on Alcohol and Culture*, Westport, CT: Greenwood Press, 1995.

Nycander, Svante, "Ivan Bratt: The Man who Saved Sweden from Prohibition," *Addiction*, 93 (1998), 17–26.

Svenskarna och spriten: Alkoholpolitik 1855–1995, Malmö: Sober, 1996.

O'Carroll, J.P., "Bishops, Knights and Pawns? Traditional Thought and the Irish Abortion Referendum Debate of 1983," *Irish Political Studies*, 6 (1991), 53–71.

O'Connor, Pat, *Emerging Voices: Women in Contemporary Irish Society*, Dublin: Institute for Public Administration, 1998.

O'Connor, Paul, *Key Issues in Irish Family Law*, Dublin: Round Hall Press, 1988.

Ødegård, Erik, "Legality and Legitimacy. On Attitudes to Drugs and Social Sanctions," *British Journal of Criminology*, 35 (1995), 525–42.

O'Faolain, Nuala, *Are You Somebody? The Life and Times of Nuala O'Faolain*, Dublin: New Island Books, 1997.

Ohlsson, Sven, "Alkoholsmuggling till Sverige," Stockholm: Generaltullstyrelsen/Kontrolbyrn, 1997.

O'Leary, Cornelius and Tom Hesketh, "The Irish Abortion Referendum Campaigns," *Irish Political Studies*, 3 (1988), 43–62.

O'Leary, Siofra, "Resolution by the Court of Justice of Disputes affecting Family Life," in Tamara K. Hervey and David O'Keeffe (eds.), *Sex Equality Law in the European Union*, New York: John Wiley, 1996.

Olsen, Johan P., "Europeanization and Nation-State Dynamics," in Sverker Gustavsson and Leif Lewin (eds.), *The Future of the Nation State*, New York: Routledge, 1996.

Ossebaard, H.C. and G.F. van de Wijngaart, "Purple Haze: The Remaking of Dutch Drug Policy," *International Journal of Drug Policy*, 9 (1998), 263–71.

Österberg, Esa, "Changes in Public Attitudes towards Alcohol Control in Finland," paper presented at the 38th International Congress on Alcohol, Drugs, and Other Dependencies, Vienna, August 16–20, 1999.

"Do Alcohol Prices Affect Consumption and Related Problems?" in Harold D. Holder and Griffith Edwards (eds.), *Alcohol and Public Policy: Evidence and Issues*, New York: Oxford University Press, 1995.

"Finnish Social Alcohol Research and Alcohol Policy," *Nordic Alcohol Studies*, 11 (1994), 60–67.

"Finland," in Timo Kortteinen (ed.), *State Monopolies and Alcohol Prevention*, Helsinki: Social Research Institute of Alcohol Studies, 1989.

"From Home Distillation to the State Alcohol Monopoly," *Contemporary Drug Problems*, 12 (1985), 31–52.

"The Relationship between Alcohol Consumption Patterns and the Harmful Consequences of Drinking," in Martin Plant, Cees Goos, Wolfram Kemp, and Esa Österberg (eds.), *Alcohol and Drugs*, Edinburgh: Edinburgh University Press, 1990.

Österberg, Esa, Sami Kajalo, Kalervo Leppänen, Kari Niilola, Timo Rauhanen, Jukka Salomaa, and Iikko B. Voipo, "Alkoholkonsumtion och – priser i Finland till å 2004. Fyra scenarier," *Nordisk alkohol- & narkotikatidskrift*, 15 (1998), 212–22.

Österberg, Esa and Juhani Pekhonen, "Travellers' Imports of Alcohol into Finland: Changes caused by Finnish EU membership," *Nordic Alcohol Studies*, 13 (1996), 22–32.

Österberg, Esa, Kari Haavisto, Raija Ahtola, and Maija Kaivomurmi, "The Booze Rally on the Eastern Border, Alcohol Consumption and Problems Caused by Alcohol." Originally published as "Itärajan viinaralli, alkoholin kulutus ja alkoholihaitat," *Alkoholipolitiikka*, 61 (1996), 325–35.

Ottevanger, C.M., "Drug Policy and Drug Tourism," in M. den Boer (ed.), *Schengen, Judicial Cooperation and Policy Coordination*, Maastricht: European Institute of Public Administration, 1997.

Outrive, L. and Cyrille Fijnhout, "Police and the Organization of Prevention," in Maurice Punch (ed.), *Control in the Police Organization*, Cambridge, MA: MIT Press, 1983 .

Outshoorn, Joyce, *De politieke strijd rondom de Abortuswetgeving in Nederland 1964–84*, The Hague: VUGA, 1986.

Pantel, Melissa, "Unity-in-Diversity: Cultural Policy and EU Legitimacy," in Thomas Banchoff and Mitchell P. Smith (eds.), *Legitimacy and the European Union*, New York: Routledge, 1999.

Parssinen, Terry M., *Secret Passions, Secret Remedies. Narcotic Drugs in British Society*, Philadelphia: Institute for the Study of Human Issues, 1983.

Pedersen, Thomas, *European Union and the EFTA Countries*, New York: Pinter, 1994.

Peltonen, Matti, "A Bourgeois Bureaucracy," in Matti Peltonen (ed.), *State, Culture, and the Bourgeoisie: Aspects of the Peculiarity of the Finnish*, Jyväskylä: University of Jyväskylä Press, 1989.

"The Problem of Being a Finn," in Marjatta Rahikainen (ed.), *Austerity and Prosperity: Perspective of Finnish Society*, Helsinki: University of Helsinki Press, 1993.

Talolliset ja Torpparit: Vuosisadan vaihteen maatakouskysymys Suomessa, Helsinki: SHS, 1992.

"Vekande, makt, sociologi: Debatten 1948 mellan Veli Verkko och Pekka Kuusi om 'det finska ölsinnet,' " *Nordisk Alkoholtidskrift*, 8 (1991), 221–37.

Petersen, Alan and Deborah Lupton, *The New Public Health: Health and Self in the Age of Risk*, Thousand Oaks, CA.: Sage, 1996.

Petersen, Nikolaj, "The Nordic Trio and the Future of the EU," in Geoffrey Edwards and Alfred Pijpers (eds.), *The Politics of European Treaty Reform*, Washington, DC: Pinter, 1997.

Petite, Michel, *The Treaty of Amsterdam*, Cambridge, MA: Jean Monnet Working Papers 2/1998 (*www.law.harvard.edu/programs/JeanMonnet/papers/98/98-2-.html*).

Phillips-Martinsson, Jean, *Swedes, As Others See Them*, Stockholm: Affärsförlaget, 1981.

Pierson, Paul, "The Path to European Integration: A Historical Institutionalist Analysis," *Comparative Political Studies*, 29 (1996), 123–63.

Poole, Michael A., "In Search of Ethnicity in Ireland," in Brian Graham (ed.), *In Search of Ireland: A Cultural Geography*, New York: Routledge, 1997.

Powell, Walter W., "Expanding the Scope of Institutional Analysis," in Walter W. Powell and Paul J. DiMaggio (eds.), *The New Institutionalism in Organizational Analysis*, Chicago: University of Chicago, 1991.

Powell, Walter and Paul DiMaggio, "The Iron Cage Revisited: Institutional Isomorphism and Collective Rationality," in Walter W. Powell and Paul DiMaggio (eds.), *The New Institutionalism in Organizational Analysis*, Chicago: University of Chicago Press, 1991.

Powell, Walter W. and Paul J. DiMaggio (eds.), *The New Institutionalism in Organizational Analysis*, Chicago: University of Chicago Press, 1991.

Prestwich, Patricia E., *Drink and the Politics of Social Reform: Antialcoholism in France since 1870*, Palo Alto: The Society for the Promotion of Science and Scholarship, 1988.

Radalli, Claudio, "How Does Europeanization Produce Policy Change?" *Comparative Political Studies*, 30 (1997), 553–75.

Ramsteat, Mats, "Liver Cirrhosis Mortality in 15 EU Countries," *Nordic Studies on Alcohol and Drugs*, 16 (1999), 57.

Randall, Vicky, "The Politics of Abortion in Ireland," in Jone Lovenduski and Joyce Outshoorn (eds.), *The New Politics of Abortion*, Newbury Park: Sage, 1986.

Rehm, Jürgen, "Draining the Ocean to Prevent Shark Attacks?" *Nordic Studies on Alcohol and Drugs*, 16 (1999), 46–54.

Reinarman, Craig and Peter Cohen, "Human Nature," *Foreign Affairs*, 78 (1999), 135–37.

Reinarman, Craig and Harry Levine (eds.), *Crack in America*, Berkeley: University of California Press, 1997.

Report of Minister van Volksgezondheid, Welzijn, en Sport, Minister van Justitie, Staatssecretaris van Binnenlandse Zaken, "Het Nederlandse drugbeleid; continuïteit en verandering," in T. Blom, H. de Doelder, and D.J. Hessing (eds.), *Naar een consistent drugsbeleid*, Deventer: Gouda Quint, 1996.

Risse-Kappen, Thomas, "Collective Identity in a Democratic Community," in Peter Katzenstein (ed.), *The Culture of National Security: Norms and Identity in World Politics*, New York: Columbia University Press, 1996.

Rochon, Thomas R., *Culture Moves: Ideas, Activism, and Changing Values*, Princeton: Princeton University Press, 1998.

The Netherlands: Negotiating Sovereignty in an Independent World, Boulder, CO: Westview Press, 1999.

Roe, Emery, *Narrative Policy Analysis: Theory and Practice*, Durham, NC: Duke University Press, 1994.

Roizen, Ron, "How Does the Nation's 'Alcohol Problem' Change from Era to Era?" in Sarah Tracy and Caroline Acker (eds.), *Altering the American Consciousness: Essays on the History of Alcohol and Drug Use in the United States, 1800–1997*, Amherst: University of Massachusetts Press, 2000.

Rose, Nikolas, *Inventing Our Selves: Psychology, Power, and Personhood*, New York: Cambridge University Press, 1996.

Rosenqvist, Pia, "Nykterhetsnämnderna," in Kettil Bruun and Per Frånberg (eds.), *Den svenska supen: en historia om brännvin, bratt, och byrkrati*, Stockholm: Prisma, 1985.

"The Physicians and the Swedish Alcohol Question in the Early Twentieth Century," *Contemporary Drug Problems*, 13 (1986), 503–25.

Rosenqvist, Pia and Jukka-Pekka Takala, "Two Experiments with Lay Boards: The Emergence of Compulsory Treatment of Alcoholics in Sweden and Finland," *Contemporary Drug Problems*, 14 (1987), 15–38.

Rothstein, Bo, *Just Institutions Matter: The Moral and Political Logic of the Universal Welfare State*, New York: Cambridge University Press, 1998.

The Social Democratic State, Pittsburgh: University of Pittsburgh Press, 1996.

Rudy, Kathy, *Beyond Pro-Life and Pro-Choice: Moral Diversity in the Abortion Debate*, Boston: Beacon Press, 1996.

Ruggie, John Gerard, "What Makes the World Hang Together? Neo-Utilitarianism and the Social Constructivist Challenge," *International Organization*, 52 (1998), 855–85.

Rüter, C.F., "De grote verdwijntruc," in T. Blom, H. de Doelder, and D.J. Hessing (eds.), *Naar een consistent drugsbeleid*, Deventer; Gouda Quint, 1996.

Sacco, Dena T. and Alexia Brown, "Regulation of Abortion in the European Community," *Harvard International Law Journal*, 33 (1992), 291–304.

Saglie, Jo, "Attitude Change and Policy Decisions: The Case of Norwegian Alcohol Policy," *Scandinavian Political Studies*, 19 (1996), 309–27.

Sandholtz, Wayne, "Membership Matters: Limits of the Functional Approach to European Institutions," *Journal of Common Market Studies*, 34 (1996), 403–29.

Sbragia, Alberta, "Italy Pays for Europe: Political Leadership, Political Choice, and Institutional Adaptation," in Thomas Risse, Maria Green Cowles, and James Caporaso (eds.), *Europeanization and Domestic Change*, Ithaca: Cornell University Press, 2000.

Scannel, Yvonne, "The Constitution and the Role of Women," in Brian Farrell (ed.), *De Valera's Constitution and Ours*, Dublin: Gill & Macmillan, 1988.

Scheerer, Sebastian, "The New Dutch and German Drug Laws: Social and Political Conditions for Criminalization and Decriminalization," *Law and Society*, 12 (1978), 585–604.

Schiøler, Peter, "Denmark," in Dwight B. Heath, (ed.), *International Handbook on Alcohol and Culture*, Westport, CT: Greenwood Press, 1995.

Schmidt, Vivien, "Democracy and Discourse in an Integrating Europe and a Globalizing World," in Steven Weber (ed.), *Regionalization and Globalization*, New York: Columbia University Press, 2000.

"Politics, Values, and the Power of Discourse in the Reform of the Welfare State," in Fritz Scharpf and Vivien Schmidt (eds.), *From Vulnerability to Competitiveness: Welfare and Work in the Open Economy*, New York: Oxford University Press, 2000.

Schofer, Evan, "Science Associations in the International Sphere, 1875–1990," in John Boli and George M. Thomas (eds.), *Constructing World Culture: International Nongovernmental Organizations since 1875*, Stanford: Stanford University Press, 1999.

Scott, W. Richard and John W. Meyer (eds.), *Institutional Environments and Organizations: Structural Complexity and Individualism*, Thousand Oaks, CA: Sage, 1994.

Senghaas, Dieter, *The European Experience: A Historical Critique of Development Theory*, Dover, NH: Berg, 1985 .

Shklar, Judith N., *Ordinary Vices*, Cambridge, MA: Harvard University Press, 1984.

Simpura, Jussi, "Alcohol and European Transformation," *Addiction*, 92 (1997), 33–41.

Simpura, Jussi, Herman Fahrenkrug, Marita Hyttinen, and Thorkil Thorsen, "Drinking, Everyday Life Situations and Cultural Norms in Denmark, Finland, and West Germany," *Journal of Drug Issues*, 20 (1990), 403–16.

Simpura, Jussi and Pirjo Paakkanen, "New Beverages, New Drinking Contexts? Signs of Modernization in Finnish Drinking Habits from 1984 to 1992, Compared with Trends in the European Community," *Addiction*, 90 (1995), 673–84.

Singer, Brian C.J., "Cultural vs. Contractual Nations: Rethinking their Opposition," *History and Theory*, 35 (1996), 309–37.

Singleton, Frederick Bernard, *A Short History of Finland*, New York: Cambridge University Press, 1989.

Sinnott, Richard, *Irish Voters Decide: Voting Behavior in Elections and Referendums since 1918*, New York: Manchester University Press, 1995.

Skog, Ole-Jørgen, "The Collectivity of Drinking Cultures: A Theory of the Distribution of Alcohol Consumption," *British Journal of Addiction*, 80 (1985), 83–99.

"Drinking and the Distribution of Alcohol Consumption," in David J. Pittman and Helene Raskin White (eds.), *Society, Culture, and Drinking Patterns Reexamined*, New Brunswick, NJ: Rutgers Center of Alcohol Studies, 1991.

"Implications of the Distribution Theory for Drinking and Alcoholism," in David J. Pittman and Helene Raskin White (eds.), *Society, Culture, and Drinking Patterns Reexamined*, New Brunswick, NJ: Rutgers Center of Alcohol Studies, 1991.

"Social Interaction and the Distribution of Alcohol Consumption," *Journal of Drug Issues*, 10 (1980), 71–92.

Smith, Anthony D., "A Europe of Nations – or the Nation of Europe?" *Journal of Peace Research*, 30 (1993), 129–35.

"National Identity and the Idea of European Unity," *International Affairs*, 68 (1992), 55–76.

Smyth, Ailbhe, "A Sadistic Farce: Women and Abortion in the Republic of

Ireland, 1992," in Ailbhe Smyth (ed.), *Abortion Papers, Ireland*, Dublin: Attic Press, 1992.

Sociaal en Cultureel Planbureau, *Social and Cultural Report 1992*, Rijswijk: Sociaal en Cultureel Planbureau, 1993.

Social and Cultural Report 1996, Rijswijk: Sociaal en Cultureel Planbureau, 1997.

SOU, *Svensk alkoholpolitik bakgrund och nuläge*, Stockholm: SOU/Socialdepartementet, 1994.

Sournia, Jean-Charles, *A History of Alcoholism*, trans. Nick Handley and Gareth Stanton, Cambridge, MA: Basil Blackwell, 1990.

Soysal, Yasemin Nohuglu, *The Limits of Citizenship: Migrants and Postnational Membership in Europe*, Chicago: University of Chicago Press, 1994.

Spalin, Elizabeth, "Abortion, Speech, and the European Community," *Journal of Social Welfare and Family Law*, 2 (1992), 17–32.

Stengers, Isabelle and Olivier Ralet, *Drogues: le défi hollandais*, Paris: Les empêcheurs de penser en rond, 1991.

Stenius, Henrik, "The Breakthrough of the Principle of Mass Organization in Finland," *Scandinavian Journal of History*, 5 (1980), 197–217.

Stenius, Kerstin, "Lugnet efter stormen inom Alko. Intervju med Reijo Salmi," *Nordisk alkohol- & narkotikatidskrift*, 16 (1999), 385–87.

Stichting Toekomstscenario's Gezondheidzorg, *Verkenning Drugsbeleid in Nederland*, Zoetermeer: STG, 1998.

Stivers, Richard, *A Hair of the Dog: Irish Drinking and its American Stereotype*, University Park, PA: Pennsylvania State University Press, 1976.

Strang, David and John W. Meyer, "Institutional Conditions for Diffusion," in Richard W. Scott and John W. Meyer (eds.), *Institutional Environments and Organizations*, Thousand Oaks, CA, Sage, 1994.

Sulkunen, Irma, *History of the Finnish Temperance Movement: Temperance as a Civic Religion*, trans. Martin Hall, Lewiston, NY: Edwin Mellen, 1990.

"Temperance as a Civic Religion: The Cultural Foundation of the Finnish Working-Class Temperance Ideology," *Contemporary Drug Problems*, 12 (1985), 267–86.

Sulkunen, Pekka, "Alcohol Policies fin de siècle," *Health Policy*, 7 (1987), 325–38.

"The Conservative Mind. Why does the New Middle Class Hate Alcohol Control?" *Addiction Research*, 1 (1994), 295–308.

"Drinking in France 1965–79. An Analysis of Household Consumption Data," *British Journal of Addiction*, 84 (1989), 61–72.

"Ethics of Alcohol Policy in a Saturated Society," *Addiction*, 92 (1997), 1117–23.

Sutton, Caroline, *Swedish Alcohol Discourse: Construction of a Social Problem*, Uppsala: Studia Sociologica Upsaliensia 45, 1998.

The Swedish Alcohol Discourse: From Inappropriate Behavior to "Our Greatest Public Health Threat," Stockholm: Stockholm International Studies, 2, 1996.

Swedish National Institute of Public Health, *Swedish Alcohol Policy*, Stockholm, 1995.

Sweet, Alec Stone and Wayne Sandholtz, "Integration, Supranational

Governance, and the Institutionalization of the European Polity," in Wayne Sandholtz and Alec Stone Sweet (eds.), *European Integration and Supranational Governance*, New York: Oxford University Press, 1998.

Swidler, Ann, "Culture in Action: Symbols and Strategies," *American Sociological Review*, 51 (1986), 273–86.

Tannenwald, Nina, "The Taboo on Nuclear Weapons," *International Organization*, 53 (1999), 433–69.

Thom, Betsy, *Dealing with Drink: Alcohol and Social Policy: From Treatment to Management*, New York: Free Association, 1999.

Tigerstedt, Christoffer, "The European Community and Alcohol Policy," *Contemporary Drug Problems*, 17 (1990), 461–79.

"Det finns inte längre någon alkoholpolitik," *Nordisk alkohol- & narkotikatidskrift*, 16 (1999), 79–91.

Tigerstedt, Christoffer and Pia Rosenqvist, "The Fall of a Scandinavian Tradition? Recent Changes in Scandinavian and Finnish Alcohol Policy," *Nordic Alcohol Studies*, 12 (1995), 89–96.

Tomasson, Richard F., "Alcohol and Alcohol Control in Sweden," *Scandinavian Studies*, 70 (1998), 477–509.

Traa-Commissie, *Inzake opsporing*, The Hague: Sdu, 1996.

Ugland, Trygve, "European Integration and the Corrupting Gaps in the Systems," in Pekka Sulkunen, Caroline Sutton, Christoffer Tigerstadt, and Katariina Warpenius (eds.), *Broking/en Spirits: Power and Ideas in Nordic Alcohol Control*, Helsinki: NAD, 2000.

"Europeanization of the Nordic Alcohol Monopoly Systems: Collisions between Ideologies and Political Cultures," *Nordic Studies on Alcohol and Drugs*, 14 (1997), 7–15.

Valverde, Mariana, *Diseases of the Will: Alcohol and the Dilemmas of Freedom*, New York: Cambridge University Press, 1998.

Van den Brink, Wim, Vincent Hendriks, and Jam M. van Ree, "Medical Co-Prescription of Heroin to Chronic, Treatment-Resistant Methadone Patients in the Netherlands," *Journal of Drug Issues*, 29 (1999), 587–608.

Van Heerikhuizen, Bart, "What is Typically Dutch? Sociologists in the 1930s and 1940s on the Dutch National Character," *Netherlands' Journal of Sociology*, 18 (1982), 103–25.

Van Kalmthout, Anton, "Some Aspects of New Dutch Drug Policies: Continuity and Change," in Helge Waal (ed.), *Patterns on the European Drug Scene*, Oslo: National Institute for Alcohol and Drug Research, 1998.

Van Kersbergen, Kees, *Social Capitalism: A Study of Christian Democracy and the Welfare State*, New York: Routledge, 1995.

Van Vliet, Henk Jan, "A Symposium on Drug Decriminalization: The Uneasy Decriminalization: A Perspective on Dutch Drug Policy," *Hofstra Law Review*, 18 (1990), 717–50.

Vanvugt, Ewald, *Wettig Opium*, Haarlem: In de Knipscheer, 1985.

Voorhoeve, J.C.C., *Peace, Profits and Principles: A Study of Dutch Foreign Policy*, The Hague: Martinus Nijhoff, 1979 .

Wæver, Ole, Barry Buzan, Morten Kelstrup, and Pierre Lemaitre, *Identity, Migrant and the New Security Agenda in Europe*, London: Pinter, 1993.

Walker, Neil, "European Integration and Policing," in Malcolm Anderson and

Monica den Boer (eds.), *Policing across National Boundaries*, London: Pinter, 1994.

Watkins, Susan Cotts, *From Provinces into Nations: Demographic Integration in Western Europe*, Princeton: Princeton University Press, 1991.

Weber, Steven, "Globalization and European Political Economy," in Steven Weber (ed.), *Regionalization and Globalization*, New York: Columbia University Press, 2000.

Weijenburg, R., *Drugs en drugsbestrijding in Nederland*, The Hague: VUGA, 1996.

Wendt, Alexander, "Anarchy is What States Make of It: The Social Construction of Power Politics," *International Organization*, 46 (1992), 391–425.

"Collective Identity Formation and the International State," *American Political Science Review*, 88 (1994), 384–96.

White, Stephen, *Russia Goes Dry: Alcohol, State and Society*, New York: Cambridge University Press, 1996.

Whyte, John H., *Church and State in Modern Ireland, 1923–79*, Dublin: Gill & Macmillan, 1980.

Wood, Stephen, *Germany, Europe, and the Persistence of Nations: Transformation, Interests, and Identity 1989–1996*, Brookfield, VT: Ashgate, 1998.

Ziegler, J. Nicholas, *Governing Ideas: Strategies for Innovation in France and Germany*, Ithaca: Cornell University Press, 1997.

Index